New Horizons for a Data-Driven Economy

José María Cavanillas • Edward Curry •
Wolfgang Wahlster

Editors

New Horizons for a Data-Driven Economy

A Roadmap for Usage and Exploitation of
Big Data in Europe

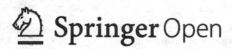 Springer Open

Editors
José María Cavanillas
Atos Spain, S.A.
Madrid, Spain

Edward Curry
National University of Ireland Galway
Galway, Ireland

Wolfgang Wahlster
German Research Centre for
  Artificial Intelligence (DFKI)
Saarbrücken, Germany

ISBN 978-3-319-79353-5   ISBN 978-3-319-21569-3   (eBook)
DOI 10.1007/978-3-319-21569-3

Foreword[1]

This book reports on preparatory work toward an important policy objective of the European Commission: turning Europe into a safe and privacy-respecting society that thrives by extracting maximum value from the data it produces and reuses, be it in support of important societal goals or as fuel for innovation in productive activities.

Our plans for Europe are described in our July 2014 Communication on a data-driven economy, where we spell out a three-pronged approach addressing regulatory issues (such as personal data protection and data ownership), framework conditions (such as data standards and infrastructures), and community building.

The first visible step of our community building efforts is a massive commitment (534 million Euros by 2020), which we signed in October 2014, to enter in a Public Private Partnership with the Big Data Value Association (BDVA): with the help from industrial parties and groups that represent relevant societal concerns (such as privacy), we intend to identify and solve technical problems and framework conditions (such as skill development) that stand in the way of European companies increasing their productivity and innovativeness by making efficient use of data technologies. By shouldering some of the financial risk of these activities, we plan to leverage even more massive European investment: for every public Euro invested by the Commission, our industry partners have committed to investing four private Euros.

Naturally, this requires some well-informed and clear thinking on which domains of data-related activities hold the greatest promise for a safe and prosperous Europe and on how we can avoid wasteful duplication in the development of data infrastructures, formats, and technologies. The book you are holding in your hands gives you a first lay of the land: it results from more than two years of work

---

[1] The views expressed in the article are the sole responsibility of the author and in no way represent the view of the European Commission and its services.

(also funded by the European Union) aimed at identifying issues and opportunities that are specifically European in character.

We fully expect that many of these results will be included and further elaborated over the years in the strategic planning of the BDVA, and we are happy to share them in this book with the broader public.

We hope that you will find them informative and that they will help you shape your own thinking on what your expectations and active role might be in a better Europe that has taught itself to run on data.

Luxembourg City, Luxembourg   Giuseppe Abbamonte
October 2015   Directorate G Media & Data
                                              European Commission DG CONNECT

Foreword

Data has become a factor just as important to production as labor, capital, and land. For the new value creators in today's technology start-ups, little capital and office space is required. Both can be almost free when a firm is growing 1 % per day, on any metric. But without talent, and without the right kind of data, such a takeoff is highly improbable.

We see the same forces at play in SAP's Innovation Center Network. Attracting the right talent was critical to establish the first Innovation Center in Potsdam. And having large, real-world datasets from customers and co-innovation partners is critical to many of our innovations. To make a difference in cancer treatment and research with our Medical Research Insights app, we critically depended on data-driven collaboration with the National Center for Tumor Diseases. The same holds for incubating SAP's new sports line of business by co-innovating with the German national soccer team based on real-time sensor feeds from their players. And it holds true for SAP's many initiatives in the Internet of Things, like the predictive maintenance apps with John Deere and Kaeser.

The Big Data Value Association (BDVA) is poised to make a difference both for data availability and for talent. By bringing together businesses with leading researchers, software and hardware partners, and enabling co-innovation around large, real-world datasets, BDVA can help lower the data barrier. And helping educate the next generation of thought leaders, especially in data science, computer science, and related fields, BDVA can help increase the supply of talent. Both are critical so Europe can begin to lead, not follow, in creating value from big data.

By clearly defining the opportunity in big data, by examining the big data value chain, and by deep-diving into industry sector applications, this book charts a way forward to new value creation and new opportunities from big data. Decision makers, policy advisors, researchers, and practitioners on all levels can benefit from this.

Jürgen Müller

Berlin, Germany

Vice President, SAP Innovation Center Network

Brussels, Belgium

President, Big Data Value Association

Preface

Welcome to our humble contribution to the huge universe of big data literature. We could ironically say there are almost as many books, leaflets, conferences, and essays about the possibilities of big data as data itself to be collected, curated, stored, and analyzed, yet a single zettabyte of useful data is an amount of information we are currently incapable of writing, and as described in this book, 16 zettabytes of data are waiting for us in 2020.

However, according to many research and industrial organisations, this contribution is actually not that humble and is even unique in many senses.

First of all, this book is not just another approach made by a single player looking down from a corner of the world. It is the compendium of more than 2 years of work performed by a set of major European research centers and industries. It is the compilation and processed synthesis of what we all have done, prepared, foreseen, and anticipated in many aspects of this challenging technological context that is becoming the major axis of the new digitally transformed business environment.

But the most important part of the book is you, the reader. It is commonly said that "a map is useless for the one who does not know where to go." This book is a map. An immediate goal of this book is to become a "User's Manual" for those who want to blaze their own trail in the big data jungle. But it can also be used as a reference book for those experts who are sailing their own big data ship and want to clarify specific aspects on their journey.

You reader, either trailblazer or old sailor, have to make your own way through the book. In this map, you will not only find answers and discussions about legal aspects of big data but also about social impact and education needs and requirements. You will also find business perspectives, discussions, and estimations of big data actuations in the different sectors of the economy, ranging from the public sector to the retailing actors. And you will also find technological discussions about the different stages of data and how to address these emerging technologies.

We worked on all these matters within the context of a European Commission project called BIG (Big Data Public Private Forum), which was an enormous challenge and one that we reckon has been successfully achieved and accomplished.

The book is divided into four parts: Part I "The Big Data Opportunity" explores the value potential of big data with a particular focus on the European context. Chapter 1 sets the scene for the value potential of big data and examines the legal, business, and social dimensions that need to be addressed to deliver on its promise. Next, Chap. 2 briefly introduces the European Commission's BIG project and its remit to establish a big data research roadmap for Horizon 2020 to support and foster research and innovation in the European Research Area.

Part II "The Big Data Value Chain" details the complete big data lifecycle from a technical point of view, ranging from data acquisition, analysis, curation, and storage to data usage and exploitation. Chapter 3 introduces the core concepts of the big data value chain. The next five chapters detail each stage of the data value chain, including a state-of-the-art summary, emerging use cases, and key open research questions. Chapter 4 provides comprehensive coverage of big data acquisition, which is the process of gathering, filtering, and cleaning data before it is put in a data warehouse or any other storage solution for further processing. Chapter 5 discusses big data analysis that focuses on transforming raw acquired data into a coherent, usable resource suitable for analysis to support decision-making and domain-specific usage scenarios. Chapter 6 investigates how the emerging big data landscape is defining new requirements for data curation infrastructures and how big data curation infrastructures are evolving to meet these challenges. Chapter 7 provides a concise overview of big data storage systems that are capable of dealing with high velocity, high volumes, and high varieties of data. Finally, Chap. 8 examines the business goals that need access to data and their analyses and integration into business decision-making in different sectors.

Part III "Usage and Exploitation of Big Data" illustrates the value creation possibilities of big data applications in various sectors, including industry, healthcare, finance, energy, media, and public services. Chapter 9 provides the conceptual background and overview of big data-driven innovation in society, highlighting factors and challenges associated with the adequate diffusion, uptake, and sustainability of big data-driven initiatives. The remaining chapters describe the state of the art of big data in different sectors, examining enabling factors, industrial needs, and application scenarios and distilling the analysis into a comprehensive set of requirements across the entire big data value chain. Chapter 10 details the wide variety of opportunities for big data technologies to improve overall healthcare delivery. Chapter 11 investigates the potential value to be gained from big data by government organizations by boosting productivity in an environment with signif-icant budgetary constraints. Chapter 12 explores the numerous advantages of big data for financial institutions. Chapter 13 examines the domain-specific big data technologies needed for cyber-physical energy and transport systems, where the focus needs to move beyond big data to smart data technologies. Chapter 14 discusses the media and entertainment sectors which are in many respects an early adopter of big data technologies because it enables them to drive digital transformation, exploiting more fully not only data which was already available but also new sources of data from both inside and outside the organization.

Finally, Part IV "A Roadmap for Big Data Research" identifies and prioritizes the cross-sectorial requirements for big data research and outlines the most urgent and challenging technological, economic, political, and societal issues for big data in Europe. Chapter 15 details the process used to consolidate the big data requirements from different sectors into a single prioritized set of cross-sector requirements that were used to define the technology policy, business, and society roadmaps together with action recommendations. Chapter 16 describes the roadmaps in the areas of technology, business, policy, and society. The chapter introduces the Big Data Value Association (BDVA) and the Big Data Value contractual Public Private Partnership (BDV cPPP) which provide a framework for industrial leadership, investment, and commitment of both the private and public sides to build a data-driven economy across Europe.

We invite you to read this book at your convenience, and we wish that you will enjoy it as much as we have whilst preparing its contents.

Ciudad Real, Spain   José María Cavanillas
Galway, Ireland   Edward Curry
Saarbrücken, Germany   Wolfgang Wahlster
October 2015

Book Acknowledgements

The authors would like to acknowledge the support, openness, and good humor of all their colleagues who contributed to the BIG project and to this book in ways both big and small. The editors would like to thank Meggan Gregory for her support in the preparation of the final manuscript. Thanks also go to Ralf Gerstner, Viktoria Meyer, and all at Springer for their professionalism and assistance throughout the journey of this book.

Project Acknowledgements

The first person I would like to acknowledge is Edward Curry, the real alma mater of this book. He and his team at the National University of Ireland Galway have been working hard for the BIG project and fueling strongly this compilation from their rainy, green, and blue beautiful hometown where we met, under the sunshine, on that very first day. That day he promised us all that it was the only sunny day in Galway that year. He brought slides of the Galway streets under the rain to show he was telling the truth, and I was even accused of having brought the sun from Spain.

Many people have collaborated for this success as well in our company Atos. Our Atos colleagues, Alicia García, Blanca Jordán, Nuria de Lama, Felicia Lobillo, Josep Martrat, Ricard Munné, Tomás Pariente, Ana María Piñuela, Pedro Soria, and too many others to be mentioned, have worked hard and participated in this success. Let me mention as well the initial leadership of Diana Pottecher, who spun off to carry out her own data business in the wilderness of the Internet.

In the case of the Deutsche Forschungszentrum für Künstliche Intelligenz, DFKI, the impulse coming from its CEO, Wolfgang Wahlster, was a leveraging factor for receiving the work of researchers such as Tilman Becker, Sabrina Hoppe, and Denise Paradowski as well as many others.

The participation of Siemens has been especially welcome, namely from researchers Stephan Guido, Yi Huang, Johannes Riedl, Sebnem Rusitschka, and Sonja Zillner, as well as from the large team at Siemens Research.

The French company Exalead has been one of the main fuellers of the project and its contents, mainly from a great professional, Amar-Djalil Mezaour.

The German company AGT has as well contributed strongly, namely, from researchers Herman Ravkin, Martin Strohbach, and Panayotis Kikiras.

The Anglo-Austrian team, consisting of John Domingue, Dieter Fensel, Nelia Lasierra, Sabrina Neurerer, Serge Tymaniuk, Iker Larizgoitia, Michael Rogger, Ioannis Stavrakantonakis, Amy Strub, and Ioan Toma from STI International and University of Innsbruck, also performed really memorable work in the project.

Thanks as well to Helen Lippell from Press Association; to Axel Ngonga, Sebastian Hellman, and Sandra Praetor from the University of Leipzig; as well as to Daniel Dietrich, Pablo Mendes, and Walter Palmetshofer from Open Knowledge Foundation.

Others within the National University of Ireland Galway who helped immensely are Andre Freitas, Umair ul Hassan, Aftab Iqbal, Nur Aini Rakhmawati, and Stefan Decker. The BIG project has received funding from the European Union's Seventh Framework Programme for research, technological development and demonstration under grant agreement no 318062. The work has been supported in part by Science Foundation Ireland under grant SFI/12/RC/2289.

Finally, the Technical Working Groups and Sectorial Forums gratefully acknowledge the debt we owe to all our interviewees and subject matter experts who gave up their valuable time and provided extremely useful input for us. In particular, we would like to thank the following people for participating in public interviews: Matt Asay, Kevin Ashley, Sören Auer, Ricardo Baeza-Yates, François Bancilhon, Richard Benjamins, Helen Berman, Lukas Biewald, James Cheney, Hjalmar Gislason, Carole Goble, Paul Groth, Alon Halvey, Usman Haque, Steve Harris, Jim Hendler, Alek Kołcz, Prasanna Lal Das, Helen Lippell, Nick Lynch, Peter Mika, Andy Palmer, Andreas Ribbrock, Joe Sewash, John Sheridan, Kelly Stirman, Jeni Tennison, Bill Thompson, Andraž Tori, Frank van Harmelen, Marco Viceconti, Jim Webber, and Antony Williams. We would also like to thank the many CEOs, CTOs, VPs, Directors, Founders, Professors, Researchers, and Technical Experts who provided inputs to the project from organizations including AGT International, Associated Press, Atos, BBC, CGIA, Chemspider/Royal Society of Chemistry, Cosm (Pachube), CrowdFlower, Data Publica, Data Tamer, DataMarket Inc., Digital Curation Centre, European Commission, Exalead, Experian, Fraunhofer, Garlik, Geomapp, German Research Centre for Artificial Intelligence, Google, Insight, Legislation.gov.uk, MapR, MongoDB, National University of Ireland Galway, Neo, Open Data Institute, Open Knowledge Foundation, Pistoia Alliance, Press Association, Rensselaer Polytechnic Institute, Rutgers University (Protein Data Bank), SAP, Siemens, Software AG, STI International, Telefoncica, Teradata GmbH, Twitter, University of Amsterdam, University of Edinburgh, University of Innsbruck, University of Leipzig, University of Manchester, University of Sheffield, VPH Institute, VU University Amsterdam, World Bank, Yahoo!, and Zemanta. Without your support this work would not have been possible.

Ciudad Real, Spain   José María Cavanillas
October 2015

Contents

List of Contributors

Tilman Becker German Research Centre for Artificial Intelligence (DFKI), Saarbrücken, Germany

José María Cavanillas Atos Spain, S.A., Madrid, Spain

Edward Curry Insight Centre for Data Analytics, National University of Ireland Galway, Lower Dangan, Galway, Ireland

Jörg Daubert AGT International, Darmstadt, Germany

Nuria De Lama Atos Spain, S.A., Madrid, Spain

John Domingue STI International, Vienna, Austria; and Knowledge Media Institute, The Open University, Walton Hall, Milton Keynes, UK

Anna Fensel University of Innsbruck, Innsbruck, Austria

André Freitas Insight Centre for Data Analytics, National University of Ireland Galway, Lower Dangan, Galway, Ireland

Kazim Hussain Atos Spain, S.A., Madrid, Spain

Anja Jentzsch Open Knowledge Foundation (OKF), Berlin, Germany

Nelia Lasierra University of Innsbruck, Innsbruck, Austria

Helen Lippell Press Association, London, UK

Mario Lischka acentrix GmbH, Munich, Germany

Klaus Lyko University of Leipzig, Leipzig, Germany

Ricard Munné Atos Spain, S.A., Barcelona, Spain

Sabrina Neururer Department of Medical Statistics, Informatics and Health Economics, Innsbruck Medical University, Innsbruck, Austria; and Semantic Technology Institute Innsbruck, University of Innsbruck, Innsbruck, Austria

Marcus Nitzschke University of Leipzig, Leipzig, Germany

Axel-Cyrille Ngonga Ngomo University of Leipzig, Leipzig, Germany

Adegboyega Ojo Insight Centre for Data Analytics, National University of Ireland Galway, Lower Dangan, Galway, Ireland

Walter Palmetshofer Open Knowledge Foundation (OKF), Berlin, Germany

Elsa Prieto Atos Spain, S.A., Madrid, Spain

Herman Ravkin Department of Industrial Engineering, Tel-Aviv University, Ramat-Aviv, Tel-Aviv, Israel

Sebnem Rusitschka Corporate Technology, Siemens AG, Munich, Germany

Martin Strohbach AGT International, Darmstadt, Germany

Andreas Thalhammer Institute for Applied Informatics and Formal Description Methods, Karlsruhe Institute of Technology, Karlsruhe, Germany

Tim van Kasteren AGT International, Darmstadt, Germany

Wolfgang Wahlster German Research Centre for Artificial Intelligence (DFKI), Saarbrücken, Germany

Sonja Zillner Corporate Technology, Siemens AG, Munich, Germany; and School of International Business and Entrepreneurship, Steinbeis University, Berlin, Germany

Chapter 1
The Big Data Value Opportunity

José María Cavanillas, Edward Curry, and Wolfgang Wahlster

1.1 Introduction

The volume of data is growing exponentially, and it is expected that by 2020 there will be more than 16 zettabytes (16 Trillion GB) of useful data (Turner et al. 2014). We are on the verge of an era where every device is online, where sensors are ubiquitous in our world generating continuous streams of data, where the sheer volume of data offered and consumed on the Internet will increase by orders of magnitude, where the Internet of Things will produce a digital fingerprint of our world.

Big data is the emerging field where innovative technology offers new ways of extracting value from the tsunami of new information. The ability to effectively manage information and extract knowledge is now seen as a key competitive advantage. Many organizations are building their core business on their ability to collect and analyse information to extract business knowledge and insight. Big data technology adoption within industrial sectors is not a luxury but an imperative need for most organizations to survive and gain competitive advantage.

This chapter explores the value potential of big data with a particular focus on the European context and identifies the positive transformational potential of big

J.M. Cavanillas
Atos Spain, S.A., Albarracín, 25, 28037 Madrid, Spain
e-mail: jose-maria.cavanillas@atos.net

E. Curry (✉)
Insight Centre for Data Analytics, National University of Ireland Galway, Lower Dangan, Galway, Ireland
e-mail: edward.curry@insight-centre.org

W. Wahlster
German Research Centre for Artificial Intelligence (DFKI), Saarbrücken, Germany
e-mail: wahlster@dfki.de

© The Author(s) 2016

J.M. Cavanillas et al. (eds.), *New Horizons for a Data-Driven Economy*,
DOI 10.1007/978-3-319-21569-3_1

data within a number of key sectors. It discusses the need for a clear strategy to increase the competitiveness of European industries in order to drive innovation and competitiveness. Finally the chapter describes the key dimensions, including skills, legal, business, and social, that need to be addressed in a European Big Data Ecosystem.

1.2 Harnessing Big Data

The impacts of big data go beyond the commercial world; within the scientific community, the explosion of available data is producing what is called Data Science (Hey et al. 2009), a new data-intensive approach to scientific discovery. The capability of telescopes or particle accelerators to generate several petabytes of data per day is producing different problems in terms of storage and processing. Scientists do not have off-the-shelf solutions ready to analyse and properly compare disperse and huge datasets. Enabling this vision will require innovative big data technologies for data management, processing, analytics, discovery, and usage (Hey et al. 2009).

Data has become a new factor of production, in the same way as hard assets and human capital. Having the right technological basis and organizational structure to exploit data is essential. Europe must exploit the potential of big data to create value for society, citizens, and businesses. However, from an industry adoption point of view, Europe is lagging behind the USA in big data technologies and is not taking advantage of the potential benefits of big data across its industrial sectors. A clear strategy is needed to increase the competitiveness of European industries through big data. While US-based companies are widely recognized for their works in big data, very few European organizations are known for their works in the field. This currently makes Europe dependent on technologies coming from outside and may prevent European stakeholders from taking full advantage of big data technology. Being competitive in big data technologies and solutions will give Europe a new source of competitiveness and the potential to foster a new data-related industry that will generate new jobs.

Addressing the current problems requires a holistic approach, where technical activities work jointly with business, policy, and society aspects. Europe needs to define actions that support faster deployment and adoption of the technology in real cases. Support is needed not only to "build" the technology but also to "grow" the ecosystem that makes innovation possible. There are many technical challenges that will require further research, but this work has to be accompanied by a continuous understanding of how big data technologies support both business and societal challenges. How can data-driven innovation be integrated into an organization's processes, cultural values, and business strategy? Europe has a track record in joint research efforts, as well as strength in converging policies or eliminating adoption barriers. There is an opportunity to build upon these and other European strengths in order to enable a vision where big data contributes to making Europe the most competitive economy in the world in 2020.

1.3   A Vision for Big Data in 2020

The Information and Communications Technology (ICT) sector is directly responsible for 5 % of European GDP, with a market value of 660 billion euros annually; it also contributes significantly to overall productivity growth (20 % directly from the ICT sector and 30 % from ICT investments). Big data solutions can contribute to increase European competitiveness by delivering value adding tools, applications, and services. One estimate for 2020 puts the potential of big and open data to improve the European GDP by 1.9 %, an equivalent of one full year of economic growth in the EU (Buchholtz et al. 2014). International Data Corporation (IDC) forecasts that the big data technology and services market will grow at a 27 % compound annual growth rate (CAGR) to \$32.4 billion through 2017 (Vesset et al. 2013).

The European Commission launched in March 2010 the Europe 2020 Strategy (European Commission 2010) to exit the crisis and prepare the EU economy for the next challenges in terms of productivity, economy, and social cohesion. The Digital Agenda for Europe is one of the seven flagship initiatives of the Europe 2020 Strategy; it defines the key enabling role that the use of ICT will have to play if Europe wants to succeed in its ambitions for 2020. The paramount importance of big data was recognized by including a specific topic in the Digital Agenda to get maximum benefit from existing data and specifically the need to open up public data resources for re-use. As then EU Commissioner Kroes stated, "Big Data is the new Oil" that can be managed, manipulated, and used like never before thanks to high-performance digital tools, making big data the fuel for innovation.

1.3.1   Transformation of Industry Sectors

The potential for big data is expected to impact all sectors, from healthcare to media, from energy to retail (Manyika et al. 2011). The positive transformational potential has already been identified in a number of key sectors.

- **Healthcare:** In the early twenty-first century, Europe is an ageing society that places significant demands on its healthcare infrastructure. There is an urgent need for improvement in efficiency of the current healthcare system to make it more sustainable. The application of big data has significant potential in the sector with estimated savings in expenditure at 90 billion euros from national healthcare budgets in the EU (Manyika et al. 2011). Clinical applications of big data range from comparative effectiveness research where the clinical and financial effectiveness of interventions is compared to the next generation of clinical decision support systems that make use of comprehensive heterogeneous health datasets as well as advanced analytics of clinical operations. Healthcare R&D applications include predictive modelling, statistical tools, and algorithms to improve clinical trial design, personalized medicine, and analysing disease patterns.

- **Public Sector:** Europe's public sector accounts for almost half of GDP and can benefit significantly from big data to gain efficiency in administrative processes. Big data could reduce the costs of administrative activities by 15–20 %, creating the equivalent of 150 billion euros to 300 billion euros in new value (OECD 2013). Potential benefits in the public sector include improved transparency via open government and open data, improved public procurement, enhanced allocation of funding into programmes, higher quality services, increased public sector accountability, and a better-informed citizen. Crucial to the future is the definition of policies to share data across government agencies and to inform citizens about the trade-offs between the privacy and security risks of sharing data and the benefits they can gain. Big data will also change the relationship between citizens and government by empowering citizens to understand political and social issues in new transparent ways, enabling them to engage with local, regional, national, and global issues through participation.
- **Finance and Insurance:** There are a number of ways for financial service companies to achieve business advantages by mining and analysing data. These include enhanced retail customer service, detection of fraud, and improvement of operational efficiencies. Big data can be used to identify exposure in real time across a range of sophisticated financial instruments like derivatives. Predictive analysis of both internal and external data results in better, proactive management of a wide range of issues from credit and operational risk (e.g. fraud and reputational risk) to customer loyalty and profitability. A challenge for the financial sector is how to use the breadth and depth of data available to satisfy more demanding regulators while also providing personalized services for their customers.
- **Telecom, Media, and Entertainment:** Big data analysis and visualization techniques can enable the effective discovery and delivery of media content enabling users to dynamically interact with new media and content across multiple platforms. The domain of personal location data offers the potential for new value creation with applications, including location-based content delivery for individuals, smart personalized content routing, automotive telematics, mobile location-based services, and geo-targeted advertising.
- **Retail:** Significant opportunities for using big data technologies reside in the interactions between retailers and consumers. Data is playing an increasing role as consumers search, research, compare, buy, and obtain support online and the products sold by retailers increasingly generate their own data footprints. Big data can increase productivity and efficiency resulting in a potential 60 % increase in retailers' operating margins (Manyika et al. 2011). Big data can impact retail in areas such as marketing: cross-selling, location-based marketing, in-store behaviour analysis, customer micro-segmentation, customer sentiment

analysis, enhancement of multi-channel consumer experience; merchandizing: assortment optimization, pricing optimization, placement and design optimization; operations: performance transparency, labour inputs optimization; supply chain: inventory management, distribution and logistics optimization, informing supplier negotiations; new business models: price comparison services, web-based markets.

- **Manufacturing:** The manufacturing sector was an early adopter of IT to design, build, and distribute products. The next-generation of smart factories with intelligent and networked machinery (i.e. Internet of Things, Industry 4.0) will see further efficiency improvement in design, production, and product quality. Big data will enable fulfilment of customer needs through precisely targeted products and effective distribution. In addition to efficiency gains and predictive maintenance, big data will enable entirely new business models in the area of mass production of individualized products.

- **Energy and Transport:** Big data will open up new opportunities for innovative ways to monitor and control transportation and logistics networks using a variety of data sources and the Internet of Things. The potential for big data in the transport sector is estimated at USD 500 billion worldwide in the form of time and fuel savings, with the avoidance of 380 megatonnes of CO_2 emissions (OECD 2013). The digitization of energy systems enables the acquisition of real-time, high-resolution data via smart metres that can be leveraged within advanced analytics to improve the levels of efficiency within both the demand and supply sides of energy networks. Smart buildings and smart cities will be key drivers of enhanced efficiency in the energy sectors. Big data technology in the utilities sectors has the potential to reduce CO_2 emissions by more than 2 gigatonnes, equivalent to 79 billion euros (OECD 2013).

A successful data ecosystem would "bring together data owners, data analytics companies, skilled data professionals, cloud service providers, companies from the user industries, venture capitalists, entrepreneurs, research institutes and universities" (DG Connect 2013). A successful data ecosystem, which is a prominent feature of the data-driven economy, would see these stakeholders interact seamlessly within a Digital Single Market, leading to business opportunities, easier access to knowledge, and capital (European Commission 2014). "The Commission can contribute to this by bringing the relevant players together and by steering the available financial resources that facilitate collaboration among the various stakeholders in the European data economy" (DG Connect 2013).

Big data offers tremendous untapped potential value for many sectors; however, there is no coherent data ecosystem in Europe. As Commissioner Kroes explained, "The fragmentation concerns sectors, languages, as well as differences in laws and policy practices between EU countries" (European Commission 2013; Kroes 2013). During the ICT 2013 Conference, Commissioner Kroes called for a European public–private partnership on big data to create a coherent European data ecosystem that stimulates research and innovation around data, as well as the uptake of cross-sector, cross-lingual, and cross-border data services and products. She also noted the need for ensuring privacy "Mastering big data means mastering privacy too" (Kroes 2013). In order for this to occur, an interdisciplinary approach is required to create an optimal business environment for big data that will accelerate adoption within Europe.

1.4   A Big Data Innovation Ecosystem

In order to drive innovation and competitiveness, Europe needs to foster the development and wide adoption of big data technologies, value adding use cases, and sustainable business models. While no coherent data ecosystem exists at the European level (DG Connect 2013), the benefits of sharing and linking data across domains and industry are becoming obvious. An ecosystem approach allows organizations to create new value that no single organization could achieve by itself (Adner 2006). A European Big Data Ecosystem is an important factor for commercialization and commoditization of big data services, products, and platforms. Within a healthy business ecosystem, companies can work together in a complex business web where they can easily exchange and share vital resources (Kim et al. 2010). If a Big Data Ecosystem is to emerge in Europe, it is important that the different actors within the ecosystem "define a shared vision and jointly identify gaps in the current data landscape" (DG Connect 2013). A successful big data ecosystem would see all "stakeholders interact seamlessly within a Digital Single Market, leading to business opportunities, easier access to knowledge, and capital" (European Commission 2014).

1.4.1   The Dimensions of European Big Data Ecosystem

An efficient use and understanding of big data as an economic asset carries great potential for the EU economy and society. The challenges for establishing a Big Data Ecosystem in Europe have been defined into a set of key dimensions (Cavanillas et al. 2014) as illustrated in Fig. 1.1. Europe must address these multiple challenges (Cavanillas et al. 2014) to foster the development of a big data ecosystem.

- **Data:** Availability and access to data will be the foundation of any data-centric ecosystem. A healthy data ecosystem will consist of a wide spectrum of different data types: structured, unstructured, multi-lingual, machine and sensor generated, static, and real-time data. The data in the ecosystem should come from different sectors, including healthcare, energy, retail, and from both public and private sources. Value may be generated in many ways, by acquiring data, combining data from different sources and across sectors, providing low latency

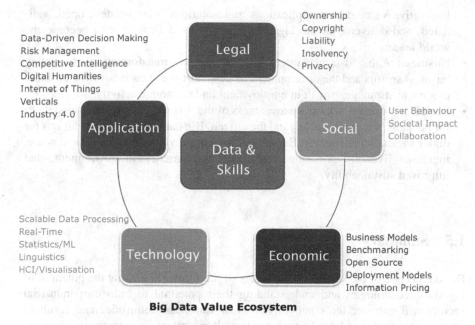

Data-Driven Decision Making
Risk Management
Competitive Intelligence
Digital Humanities
Internet of Things
Verticals
Industry 4.0

Ownership
Copyright
Liability
Insolvency
Privacy

User Behaviour
Societal Impact
Collaboration

Business Models
Benchmarking
Open Source
Deployment Models
Information Pricing

Scalable Data Processing
Real-Time
Statistics/ML
Linguistics
HCI/Visualisation

Big Data Value Ecosystem

Fig. 1.1 The dimensions of a Big Data Value Ecosystem [adapted from Cavanillas et al. (2014)]

access, improving data quality, ensuring data integrity, enriching data, extracting insights, and preserving privacy.

- **Skills:** A critical challenge for Europe will be ensuring the availability of skilled workers in the data ecosystem. An active ecosystem will require data scientists and engineers who have expertise in analytics, statistics, machine learning, data mining, and data management. Technical experts will need to be combined with data savvy business experts with strong domain knowledge and the ability to apply their data know-how within organizations for value creation.
- **Legal:** Appropriate regulatory environments are needed to facilitate the development of a pan-European big data marketplace. Legal clarity is needed on issues such as data ownership, usage, protection, privacy, security, liability, cybercrime, intellectual property rights, and the implications of insolvencies and bankruptcy.
- **Technical:** Key technical challenges need to be overcome including large scale and heterogeneous data acquisition, efficient data storage, massive real-time data processing and data analysis, data curation, advanced data retrieval and visualization, intuitive user interfaces, interoperability and linking data, information, and content. All of these topics need to be advanced to sustain or develop competitive advantages.
- **Application:** Big data has the potential to transform many sectors and domains including the health, public sector, finance, energy, and transport sectors.

Innovative value-driven applications and solutions must be developed, validated, and delivered in the big data ecosystems if Europe is to become the world leader.

- **Business:** A big data ecosystem can support the transformation of existing business sectors and the development of new start-ups with innovative business models to stimulate growth in employment and economic activity.
- **Social:** It is critical to increase awareness of the benefits that big data can deliver for business, the public sector, and the citizen. Big data will provide solutions for major societal challenges in Europe, such as improved efficiency in healthcare, increased liveability of cities, enhanced transparency in government, and improved sustainability.

1.5 Summary

Big data is one of the key economic assets of the future. Mastering the potential of big data technologies and understanding their potential to transform industrial sectors will enhance the competitiveness of European companies and result in economic growth and jobs. Europe needs a clear strategy to increase the competitiveness of European industries in order to drive innovation. Europe needs to foster the development and wide adoption of big data technologies, value adding use cases, and sustainable business models through a Big Data Ecosystem. Strategic investments are needed by both the public and private sector to enable Europe to be the leader in the global data-driven digital economy and to reap the benefits it offers with the creation of a European Big Data Ecosystem.

References

Adner, R. (2006). Match your innovation strategy to your innovation ecosystem. *Harvard Business Review, 84*, 98–107.

Buchholtz, S., Bukowski, M., & Śniegocki, A. (2014). Big and open data in Europe – A growth engine or a missed opportunity? Warsaw Institute for Economic Studies Report Commissioned by demosEUROPA.

Cavanillas, J., Markl, V., May, M., Platte, K-D., Urban, J., Wahlster, W., & Wrobel, S. (2014). *Framing a European partnership for a big data value ecosystem*. BIG NESSI Report.

DG Connect. (2013). *A European strategy on the data value chain.*

European Commission. (2010). *Communication from the Commission: Europe 2020 – A European strategy for smart, sustainable and inclusive growth*. COM 2020.

European Commission. (2013). *Digital Agenda for Europe, Session Reports, ICT for Industrial Leadership: Innovating by exploiting big and open data and digital content.*

European Commission. (2014). *Towards a thriving data-driven economy, Communication from the commission to the European Parliament, the council, the European economic and social Committee and the committee of the regions*, Brussels.

Hey, T., Tansley, S., & Tolle, K. M. (Eds.). (2009). *The fourth paradigm: Data-intensive scientific discovery*. Redmond, WA: Microsoft Research.

Kim, H., Lee, J.-N., & Han, J. (2010). The role of IT in business ecosystems. *Communications of the ACM, 53*, 151. doi:10.1145/1735223.1735260.

Kroes, N. (2013). *Big data for Europe – ICT 2013 Event – Session on Innovating by exploiting big and open data and digital content*, Vilnius.

Manyika, J., Chui, M., Brown, B., Bughin, J., Dobbs, R., Roxburgh, C., & Byers, A. H. (2011). *Big data: The next frontier for innovation, competition, and productivity*. McKinsey Global Institute, p. 156.

OECD. (2013). *Exploring Data-Driven Innovation as a New Source of Growth – mapping the policy issues raised by "Big Data."* Rep. from OECD.

Turner, V., Gantz, J. F., Reinsel, D., & Minton, S. (2014). *The digital universe of opportunities: rich data and the increasing value of the internet of things*. Rep. from IDC EMC.

Vesset, D., Nadkarni, A., Brothers, R., Christiansen, C. A., Conway, S., Dialani, M., Eastwood, M., Fleming, M., Grady, J., Grieser, T., McDonough, B., Mehra, R., Morris, H. D., Olofson, C. W., Schubmehl, D., Stolarski, K., Turner, M. J., Wardley, M., Webster, M., & Zaidi, A. (2013). Worldwide Big Data Technology and Services 2013–2017 Forecast (IDC #244979). IDC Mark Anal 34.

Chapter 2
The BIG Project

Edward Curry, Tilman Becker, Ricard Munné, Nuria De Lama, and Sonja Zillner

2.1 Introduction

The Big Data Public Private Forum (BIG) Project (http://www.big-project.eu/) was an EU coordination and support action to provide a roadmap for big data within Europe. The BIG project worked towards the definition and implementation of a clear big data strategy that tackled the necessary activities needed in research and innovation, technology adoption, and the required support from the European Commission necessary for the successful implementation of the big data economy. As part of this strategy, the outcomes of the project were used as input for Horizon 2020.

E. Curry (✉)
Insight Centre for Data Analytics, National University of Ireland Galway, Lower Dangan, Galway, Ireland
e-mail: edward.curry@insight-centre.org

T. Becker
German Research Centre for Artificial Intelligence (DFKI), Stuhlsatzenhausweg 3, 66123 Saarbrücken, Germany
e-mail: tilman.becker@dfki.de

R. Munné
Atos Spain, S.A., Av. Diagonal, 200, 08018 Barcelona, Spain
e-mail: ricard.munne@atos.net

N. De Lama
Atos Spain, S.A., Albarracín, 25, 28037 Madrid, Spain
e-mail: nuria.delama@atos.net

S. Zillner
Corporate Technology, Siemens AG, Munich, Germany

School of International Business and Entrepreneurship, Steinbeis University, Berlin, Germany
e-mail: sonja.zillner@siemens.com

© The Author(s) 2016
J.M. Cavanillas et al. (eds.), *New Horizons for a Data-Driven Economy*,
DOI 10.1007/978-3-319-21569-3_2

Foundational research technologies and innovative sectorial applications were analysed and assessed in the BIG project in order to create technology and strategy roadmaps so that business and operational communities understand the potential of big data technologies and are enabled to implement appropriate strategies and technologies for commercial benefit.

This chapter provides an overview of the BIG project detailing the project's mission and strategic objectives. The chapter describes the partners within the consortium and the overall structure of the project work. The three-phase methodology used in the project is described, including details on the techniques used within the technical working groups, sectorial forms, and road mapping activity. Finally, the project's role in setting up the Horizon 2020 Big Data Value contractual Public Private Partnership and Big Data Value Association is discussed.

2.2   Project Mission

In order to realize the vision of a data-driven society in 2020, Europe has to prepare the right ecosystem around big data. Public and private organizations need to have the necessary infrastructures and technologies to deal with the complexity of big data, but should also be able to use data to maximize their competitiveness and deliver business value.

Building an industrial community around big data in Europe was a key priority of the BIG project, together with setting up the necessary collaboration and dissemination infrastructure to link technology suppliers, integrators, and leading user organizations. The BIG project (from now on referred to as BIG) worked towards the definition and implementation of a strategy that includes research and innovation, but also technology adoption. The establishment of the community together with adequate resources to work at all levels (technical, business, political, etc.) is the basis for a long-term European strategy. Convinced that a strong reaction is needed, BIG defined its mission accordingly:

> The mission of BIG is setting up an ecosystem that will bring together all the relevant stakeholders needed to materialize a data-driven society in 2020. This ecosystem will ensure that Europe plays a leading role in the definition of the new context by building the necessary infrastructures and technologies, generating a suitable innovation space where all organizations benefit from data, and provides a pan-European framework to coherently address policy, regulatory, legal, and security barriers.

The BIG mission was broken down into a number of specific strategic objectives for the project.

2.3 Strategic Objectives

In September 2012, the project identified a set of strategic objectives to ensure it delivered on its mission. The specific objectives were:

- **BIG will set up an industrial-led initiative around Intelligent Information Management and Big Data to contribute to EU competitiveness and position it in Horizon 2020:** Industrial leadership will guide actions towards real business benefits, but will be complemented by the views of academia and research organizations, which will also take part in this endeavour. The project will take a long-term approach to represent the views and interests of IIM stakeholders, with a special focus on big data due to its relevance in the current and future context. Decisions such as establishing it as a legal entity will be considered, and potential mergers with relevant associations at the EU level will also be envisaged for the sake of sustainability and impact.
- **BIG will elaborate an integrated roadmap that takes into consideration technical, business, policy, and society aspects,** focusing not only on pure technical issues, but also establishing priorities based on expected impact. The BIG consortium will engage the necessary expertise to ensure contributions not only from project partners, but also from a wider community comprised of experts in relevant technical domains as well as experts in sectors or application domains where the use of these technologies is expected to produce a high impact.
- **BIG will ensure that technical research areas selected by the project cover the needs expressed by the industry in different application domains:** For this to happen, a sharp understanding is needed of how big data can be applied within industrial sectors. This understanding needs to be transmitted to domain experts to establish a clear path for the adoption of the technology in each of the selected sectors.
- **BIG will promote adoption of earlier waves of big data technology:** Instead of adopting only a futuristic approach, BIG will use as a starting point those technologies that are already in place. The objective is to reach a clear understanding of the level of maturity of different technical solutions as well as the feasibility of their implementation. This will be valuable information with respect to the state of the art and will be used as input for the elaboration of both the sectorial and the integrated roadmaps.
- **BIG will define and promote actions dealing with policy and regulation,** including aspects such as data security, intellectual property, privacy, liability, and data access. BIG will contribute to the entire ecosystem related to big data implementation without restricting its activities to only technical issues.
- **BIG will carry out dissemination actions targeting different stakeholders and players in the value chain:** Dissemination actions will be customized to the different communities (e.g. technical experts, data scientists, technical managers, business managers, and executives in both Multinational Corporation (MNC) and Small and Medium-sized Enterprises (SMEs)). BIG addressed all

the relevant communities with an ambitious strategy including presence in mass
media, relevant conferences, organization of workshops and events, and maxi-
mization of the use of web channels.
- All this will not have been possible without **providing the right collaboration
infrastructures**. Collaboration among projects, but also many discussions
between all the relevant stakeholders and actors in the value chain, including
major industrial organizations in the EU landscape, will take place. Bearing this
in mind BIG set up and maintained a support infrastructure that will enable
collaboration, information sharing, and customization of actions toward different targeted audiences.

2.4 Consortium

The participants of the BIG consortium (illustrated in Fig. 2.1) were carefully
selected to include key players with complementary skills in both industry and
academia. Each of the project partners had experience in cutting-edge European
projects and significant connections to key stakeholders in the big data marketplace.
The academic partners using their expert knowledge in the field lead the technical
investigations of big data technology. The industrial partners were well positioned
in their knowledge of large-scale data management products and services and their
application within different industrial sectors.

The partners of the BIG consortium were:

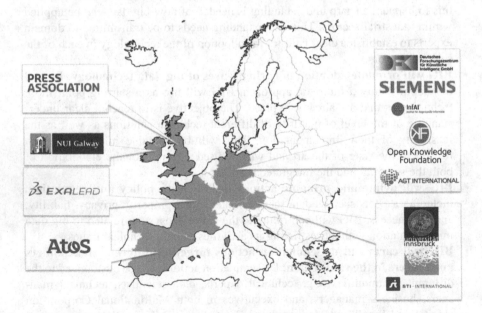

Fig. 2.1 BIG project consortium members

- **Industry:** Atos, Press Association (PA), Siemens, AGT International, Exalead, and the Open Knowledge Foundation (OKF)
- **Academia:** University of Innsbruck (UIBK), National University of Ireland Galway (NUIG), University of Leipzig, German Research Centre for Artificial Intelligence (DFKI), and STI International

2.5   Stakeholder Engagement

Essential for the success of a large-scale, cross-fertilization, and broad road mapping effort is the involvement of a large fraction of the community and industry, not only from the point of view of technology provision but also technology adoption. The project took an inclusive approach to stakeholder engagement and actively solicited inputs from the wider community composed of experts in technical domains as well as experts in business sectors. An open philosophy was applied to all the documents generated by the project, which were made public to the wider community for active contribution and content validation. The project held stakeholder workshops to engage the community within the project. The first workshop was held at the European Data Forum (EDF) 2013 in Dublin to announce the project to the community and gather participants. The second workshop took place at EDF 2014 in Athens to present the interim results of the project for feedback and further validation with stakeholders. Over the duration of the project a number of well-attended sector-specific workshops were held to gather needs and validate findings. At the end of the project a final workshop was convened to present the results of the project in October 2014 in Heidelberg.

2.6   Project Structure

The work of the BIG project was split into groups focusing on industrial sectors and technical areas. The project structure comprised of sectorial forums and technical working groups.

Sectorial forums examined how big data technologies can enable business innovation and transformation within different sectors. The sector forums were led by the industrial partners of the project. Their objective was to gather big data requirements from vertical industrial sectors, including health, public sector, finance, insurance, telecoms, media, entertainment, manufacturing, retail, energy, and transport (see Fig. 2.2).

Technical working groups focused on big data technologies for each activity in the data value chain to examine their capabilities, level of maturity, clarity, understandability, and suitability for implementation. The technical groups (see Fig. 2.3) were led by the academic partners in BIG and examined emerging technological and research trends for coping with big data.

Fig. 2.2 Sectorial forums within the BIG project

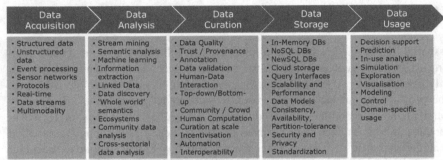

Fig. 2.3 Technical working groups within the BIG project

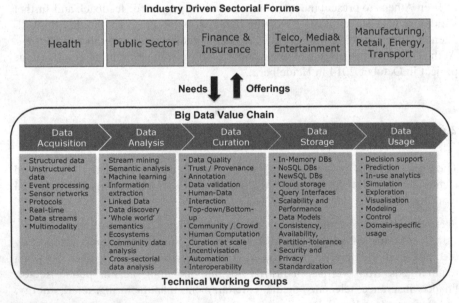

Fig. 2.4 The BIG project structure

As illustrated in Fig. 2.4, the needs identified by sector forums were used to understand the maturity and gaps in the capability offered by current big data technology. This analysis provided a clear picture on the limitations and expectations regarding big data technology deployment. The outputs of the analysis were used to produce a series of consensus-reflecting roadmaps that defined priorities and actions needed for big data in each sector.

2.7   Methodology

From an operational point of view, BIG defined a set of activities based on a three-phase approach as illustrated in Fig. 2.5. The three phases were:

1. Technology state of the art and sector analysis
2. Roadmapping activity
3. Big data public private partnership

2.7.1   Technology State of the Art and Sector Analysis

In the first phase of the project, the sectorial forums and the technical working groups performed a parallel investigation in order to identify:

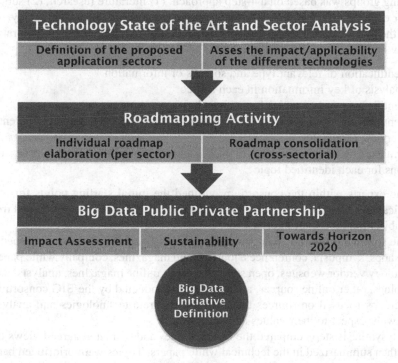

Fig. 2.5 Three-phase methodology of BIG

- Sectorial needs and requirements gathered from different stakeholders
- The state of the art of big data technologies as well as identifying research challenges

As part of the investigation, application sectors expressed their needs with respect to the technology as well as possible limitations and expectations regarding its current and future deployment.

Using the results of the investigation a gap analysis was performed between what technology capability was ready, with the sectorial expectations of what technological capability was currently required together with future requirements. The analysis produced a series of consensus-reflecting sectorial roadmaps that defined priorities and actions to guide further steps in big data research.

2.7.1.1 Technical Working Groups

The goal of the technical working groups was to investigate the state of the art in big data technologies to determine its level of maturity, clarity, understandability, and suitability for implementation. To allow for an extensive investigation and detailed mapping of developments, the technical working groups deployed a combination of a top-down and bottom-up approach, with a focus on the latter. The approach of the working groups was based on a 4-step approach: (1) literature research, (2) subject matter expert interviews, (3) stakeholder workshops, and (4) technical survey.

In the first step each technical working group performed a systematic literature review based on the following activities:

- Identification of relevant type and sources of information
- Analysis of key information in each source
- Identification of key topics for each technical working group
- Identification of the key subject matter experts for each topic as potential interview candidates
- Synthesizing the key message of each data source into state-of-the art descriptions for each identified topic

The experts within the consortium outlined the initial starting points for each technical area, and the topics were expanded through the literature search and from the subject matter expert interviews.

The following types of data sources were used: scientific papers published in workshops, symposia, conferences, journals and magazines, company white papers, technology vendor websites, open source projects, online magazines, analysts' data, web blogs, other online sources, and interviews conducted by the BIG consortium. The groups focused on sources that mention concrete technologies and analysed them with respect to their values and benefits.

The synthesis step compared the key messages and extracted agreed views that were then summarized in the technical white papers. Topics were prioritized based on the degree to which they are able to address business needs as identified by the sectorial forum working groups.

The literature survey was complemented with a series of interviews with subject matter experts for relevant topic areas. Subject matter expert interviews are a technique well suited to data collection and particularly for exploratory research because it allows expansive discussions that illuminate factors of importance (Oppenheim 1992; Yin 2009). The information gathered is likely to be more accurate than information collected by other methods since the interviewer can avoid inaccurate or incomplete answers by explaining the questions to the interviewee (Oppenheim 1992).

The interviews followed a semi-structured protocol. The topics of the interview covered different aspects of big data, with a focus on:

• Goals of big data technology
• Beneficiaries of big data technology
• Drivers and barriers for big data technologies
• Technology and standards for big data technologies

An initial set of interviewees was identified from the literature survey, contacts within the consortium, and a wider search of the big data ecosystem. Interviewees were selected to be representative of the different stakeholders within the big data ecosystem. The selection of interviewees covered (1) established providers of big data technology (typically MNCs), (2) innovative sectorial players who are successful at leveraging big data, (3) new and emerging SMEs in the big data space, and (4) world leading academic authorities in technical areas related to the Big Data Value Chain.

2.7.1.2 Sectorial Forums

The overall objective of the sectorial forums was to acquire a deep understanding of how big data technology can be used in the various industrial sectors, such as healthcare, public, finance and insurance, and media.

In order to identify the user needs and industrial requisites of each domain, the sectorial forums followed a research methodology encompassing the following three steps as illustrated in Fig. 2.6. For each industrial sector, the steps were accomplished separately. However, in the case where sectors were related (such as energy and transport) the results have been merged for those sectors in order to highlight differences and similarities.

The aim of the first steps was to identify both stakeholders and use cases for big data applications within the different sectors. Therefore, a survey was conducted including scientific reviews, market studies, and other Internet sources. This knowledge allowed the sectorial forums to identify and select potential interview partners and guided the development of the questionnaire for the domain expert interviews.

The questionnaire consisted of up to 12 questions that were clustered into three parts:

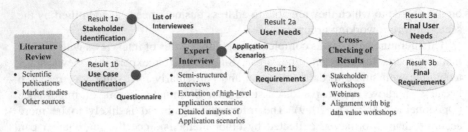

Fig. 2.6 The three steps of the sectorial forums research methodology

- Direct inquiry of specific user needs
- Indirect evaluation of user needs by discussing the relevance of the use cases identified at Step 1 as well as any other big data applications of which they were aware
- Reviewing constraints that need to be addressed in order to foster the implementation of big data applications in each sector

In the second step, semi-structured interviews were conducted using the developed questionnaire. At least one representative of each stakeholder group identified in Step 1 was interviewed. To derive the user needs from the collected material, the most relevant and frequently mentioned use cases were aggregated into high-level *application scenarios*. The data collection and analysis strategy was inspired by the triangulation approach (Flick 2004). Reviewing and quantitatively assessing the high-level application scenarios derived a reliable analysis of user needs. Examinations of the likely constraints of big data applications helped to identify the relevant requirements that needed to be addressed.

The third step involved a crosscheck and validation of the initial results of the first two steps by involving stakeholders of the domain. Some sectors conducted dedicated workshops and webinars with industrial stakeholders to discuss and review the outcomes. The results of the workshops were studied and integrated whenever appropriate.

2.7.2   Cross-Sectorial Roadmapping

Comparison among the different sectors enabled the identification of commonalities and differences at multiple levels, including technical, policy, business, and regulatory. The analysis was used to define an integrated cross-sectorial roadmap that provides a coherent holistic view of the big data domain. The cross-sectorial big data roadmap was defined using the following three steps:

1. **Consolidation** to establish a common understanding of requirements as well as technology descriptions and terms used across domains
2. **Mapping** to identify any technologies needed to address the identified cross-sector requirements

3. **Temporal alignment** to highlight which technologies need to be available at what point in time by incorporating the estimated adoption rate by the involved stakeholders

The remainder of this section describes each of these steps in more detail.

2.7.2.1   Consolidation

Alignment among the technical working groups, and between the technical working groups and the sectorial forums, was important and facilitated through early exchange of drafts, one-on-one meetings, and the collection of consolidated requirements through the SFs. In order to align the sector-specific labelling of requirements, a consolidated description was established. In doing so, each sector provided their requirements with the associated user needs. In dedicated meetings, similar and related requirements were clustered and then merged, aligned, or restructured. Thus, the initial list of 13 high-level requirements and 28 sub-level requirements could be reduced to 8 high-level requirements and 25 sub-level requirements. In summary the consolidation phase reduced the total number of requirements by 20 %.

2.7.2.2   Mapping

For mapping technology to requirements the technical working groups indicated which technology could be used to address the consolidated requirements. Besides providing a mapping between requirements and technologies, the technical working groups also indicated the associated research challenges.

Within a 1-day workshop, the initial mapping of technologies and requirements was consolidated in two steps. First, the indicated technological capabilities were analysed in further detail by describing how the sector-specific aspects of each cross-sector requirement can be handled. Second, for each cross-sector requirement it was investigated whether the technologies from various technical working groups need to be combined in order to address the full scope of the requirement. At the end of the discussion, any technologies that were requested by at least two sectors were included into the cross-sector roadmap.

2.7.2.3   Temporal Alignment

After identifying the key technologies, their temporal alignment needed to be defined. This was achieved by answering two questions:

- How long is the development time of the technology?
- When will the stakeholder involved adopt the technology?

The development time for each technology indicates how much time is needed to solve the associated research challenges. This time frame depends on the technical complexity of the challenge together with the extent to which sector-specific extensions are needed. In order to determine the adoption rate of big data technology (or the associated use case) non-technical requirements such as availability of business cases, suitable incentive structures, legal frameworks, potential benefits, as well as the total cost for all the stakeholders involved (Adner 2012) were considered.

2.8 Big Data Public Private Partnership

The Big Data Public Private Forum, as it was initially called, was intended to create the path towards implementation of the roadmaps. The path required two major elements: (1) a mechanism to include content of the roadmaps into real agendas supported by the necessary resources (economic investment of both public and private stakeholders) and (2) a community interested in the topics and committed to making the investment and collaborating towards the implementation of the agendas.

The BIG consortium was convinced that achieving this result would require creating a broad awareness and commitment outside the project. BIG took the necessary steps to contact major players and to liaise with the NESSI European Technology Platform to jointly work towards this endeavour. The collaboration was set up in the summer of 2013 and allowed the BIG partners to establish the necessary high-level connections at both industrial and political levels. This collaboration led to the following outcomes:

- **The Strategic Research & Innovation Agenda (SRIA) on Big Data Value** that was initially fed by the BIG technical papers and roadmaps and has been extended with the input of a public consultation that included hundreds of additional stakeholders representing both the supply and the demand side.
- **A cPPP (contractual PPP) proposal** as the formal step to set up a PPP on Big Data Value. The cPPP proposal builds on the SRIA by adding additional content elements such as potential instruments that could be used for the implementation of the agenda.
- The formation of a **representative community of stakeholders** that has endorsed the SRIA and expressed an interest and commitment in getting involved in the cPPP. The identification of an industrially led core group ready to commit to the objectives of the cPPP with a willingness to invest money and time.
- The **establishment of a legal entity based** in Belgium: a non-profit organization named Big Data Value Association (BDVA) to represent the private side of the cPPP. The BDVA had 24 founding members, including many partners of the BIG project.

- And finally, the **signature of the Big Data Value cPPP** between the BDVA and
  the European Commission. The cPPP was signed by Vice President Neelie
  Kroes, the then EU Commissioner for the Digital Agenda, and Jan Sundelin,
  the president of the Big Data Value Association (BDVA), on 13 October 2014 in
  Brussels. The BDV cPPP provides a framework that guarantees the industrial
  leadership, investment, and commitment of both the private and the public side
  to build a data-driven economy across Europe, mastering the generation of value
  from big data and creating a significant competitive advantage for European
  industry that will boost economic growth and jobs.

2.9   Summary

The Big Data Public Private Forum (BIG) Project was an EU coordination and
support action to provide a roadmap for big data within Europe. The BIG project
worked towards the definition and implementation of a clear big data strategy that
tackled the necessary activities needed in research and innovation, technology
adoption, and the required support from the European Commission necessary for
the successful implementation of the big data economy.

The BIG project used a three-phase methodology with technical working groups
examining foundational technologies, sectorial forums examining innovative sectorial applications, and a road mapping activity to create technology and strategy
roadmaps so that business and operational communities understand the potential of
big data technologies and are enabled to implement appropriate strategies and
technologies for commercial benefit. The project was a key contributor to setting
up the Horizon 2020 Big Data Value Association contractual Public Private Partnership (cPPP) and Big Data Value Association.

References

Adner, R. (2012). *The wide lens: A new strategy for innovation*. London: Penguin.
Flick, U. (2004). Triangulation in qualitative research. In U. Flick, E. V. Kardorff, & I. Steinke
(Eds.), *A companion to qualitative research* (p. 432). London: Sage.

Oppenheim, A. N. (1992). *Questionnaire design, interviewing and attitude measurement*. London: Continuum.

Yin, R. K. (2009). Case study research: Design and methods. In L. Bickman & D. J. Rog (Eds.), *Essential guide to qualitative methods in organization research*. London: Sage. doi:10.1097/FCH.0b013e31822dda9e.

Part II
The Big Data Value Chain: Enabling and Value Creating Technologies

Chapter 3
The Big Data Value Chain: Definitions, Concepts, and Theoretical Approaches

Edward Curry

3.1 Introduction

The emergence of a new wave of data from sources, such as the Internet of Things, Sensor Networks, Open Data on the Web, data from mobile applications, social network data, together with the natural growth of datasets inside organisations (Manyika et al. 2011), creates a demand for new data management strategies which can cope with these new scales of data environments. Big data is an emerging field where innovative technology offers new ways to reuse and extract value from information. The ability to effectively manage information and extract knowledge is now seen as a key competitive advantage, and many organisations are building their core business on their ability to collect and analyse information to extract business knowledge and insight. Big data technology adoption within industrial sectors is not a luxury but an imperative need for most organisations to gain competitive advantage.

This chapter examines definitions and concepts related to big data. The chapter starts by exploring the different definitions of "Big Data" which have emerged over the last number of years to label data with different attributes. The Big Data Value Chain is introduced to describe the information flow within a big data system as a series of steps needed to generate value and useful insights from data. The chapter explores the concept of Ecosystems, its origins from the business community, and how it can be extended to the big data context. Key stakeholders of a big data ecosystem are identified together with the challenges that need to be overcome to enable a big data ecosystem in Europe.

E. Curry (✉)
Insight Centre for Data Analytics, National University of Ireland Galway, Lower Dangan, Galway, Ireland
e-mail: edward.curry@insight-centre.org

© The Author(s) 2016
J.M. Cavanillas et al. (eds.), *New Horizons for a Data-Driven Economy*,
DOI 10.1007/978-3-319-21569-3_3

29

3.2   What Is Big Data?

Over the last years, the term "Big Data" was used by different major players to label data with different attributes. Several definitions of big data have been proposed over the last decade; see Table 3.1. The first definition, by Doug Laney of META Group (then acquired by Gartner), defined big data using a three-dimensional perspective: "Big data is high volume, high velocity, and/or high variety information assets that require new forms of processing to enable enhanced decision-making, insight discovery and process optimization" (Laney 2001). Loukides (2010) defines big data as "when the size of the data itself becomes part of the problem and traditional techniques for working with data run out of steam". Jacobs (2009) describes big data as "data whose size forces us to look beyond the tried-and-true methods that are prevalent at that time".

Big data brings together a set of data management challenges for working with data under new scales of size and complexity. Many of these challenges are not new. What is new however are the challenges raised by the specific characteristics of big data related to the 3 Vs:

- **Volume (amount of data)**: dealing with large scales of data within data processing (e.g. Global Supply Chains, Global Financial Analysis, Large Hadron Collider).
- **Velocity (speed of data):** dealing with streams of high frequency of incoming real-time data (e.g. Sensors, Pervasive Environments, Electronic Trading, Internet of Things).
- **Variety (range of data types/sources)**: dealing with data using differing syntactic formats (e.g. Spreadsheets, XML, DBMS), schemas, and meanings (e.g. Enterprise Data Integration).

The Vs of big data challenge the fundamentals of existing technical approaches and require new forms of data processing to enable enhanced decision-making, insight discovery, and process optimisation. As the big data field matured, other Vs have been added such as Veracity (documenting quality and uncertainty), Value, etc. The value of big data can be described in the context of the dynamics of knowledge-based organisations (Choo 1996), where the processes of decision-making and organisational action are dependent on the process of sense-making and knowledge creation.

3.3   The Big Data Value Chain

Within the field of Business Management, Value Chains have been used as a decision support tool to model the chain of activities that an organisation performs in order to deliver a valuable product or service to the market (Porter 1985). The value chain categorises the generic value-adding activities of an organisation

Table 3.1 Definitions of big data

Big data definition	Source
"Big data is high volume, high velocity, and/or high variety information assets that require new forms of processing to enable enhanced decision making, insight discovery and process optimization"	Laney (2001), Manyika et al. (2011)
"When the size of the data itself becomes part of the problem and traditional techniques for working with data run out of steam"	Loukides (2010)
Big Data is "data whose size forces us to look beyond the tried-and-true methods that are prevalent at that time"	Jacobs (2009)
"Big Data technologies [are] a new generation of technologies and architectures designed to extract value economically from very large volumes of a wide variety of data by enabling high-velocity capture, discovery, and/or analysis"	IDC (2011)
"The term for a collection of datasets so large and complex that it becomes difficult to process using on-hand database management tools or traditional data processing applications"	Wikipedia (2014)
"A collection of large and complex data sets which can be processed only with difficulty by using on-hand database management tools"	Mike 2.0 (2014)
"Big Data is a term encompassing the use of techniques to capture, process, analyse and visualize potentially large datasets in a reasonable timeframe not accessible to standard IT technologies." By extension, the platform, tools and software used for this purpose are collectively called "Big Data technologies"	NESSI (2012)
"Big data can mean big volume, big velocity, or big variety"	Stonebraker (2012)

allowing them to be understood and optimised. A value chain is made up of a series of subsystems each with inputs, transformation processes, and outputs. Rayport and Sviokla (1995) were one of the first to apply the value chain metaphor to information systems within their work on Virtual Value Chains. As an analytical tool, the value chain can be applied to information flows to understand the value creation of data technology. In a Data Value Chain, information flow is described as a series of steps needed to generate value and useful insights from data. The European Commission sees the data value chain as the "centre of the future knowledge economy, bringing the opportunities of the digital developments to the more traditional sectors (e.g. transport, financial services, health, manufacturing, retail)" (DG Connect 2013).

The Big Data Value Chain (Curry et al. 2014), as illustrated in Fig. 3.1, can be used to model the high-level activities that comprise an information system. The Big Data Value Chain identifies the following key high-level activities:

Data Acquisition is the process of gathering, filtering, and cleaning data before it is put in a data warehouse or any other storage solution on which data analysis can be carried out. Data acquisition is one of the major big data challenges in terms of infrastructure requirements. The infrastructure required to support the acquisition of big data must deliver low, predictable latency in both capturing data and in executing queries; be able to handle very high transaction volumes, often in a

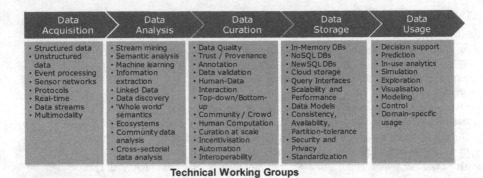

Data Acquisition	Data Analysis	Data Curation	Data Storage	Data Usage
• Structured data • Unstructured data • Event processing • Sensor networks • Protocols • Real-time • Data streams • Multimodality	• Stream mining • Semantic analysis • Machine learning • Information extraction • Linked Data • Data discovery • 'Whole world' semantics • Ecosystems • Community data analysis • Cross-sectorial data analysis	• Data Quality • Trust / Provenance • Annotation • Data validation • Human-Data Interaction • Top-down/Bottom-up • Community / Crowd • Human Computation • Curation at scale • Incentivisation • Automation • Interoperability	• In-Memory DBs • NoSQL DBs • NewSQL DBs • Cloud storage • Query Interfaces • Scalability and Performance • Data Models • Consistency, Availability, Partition-tolerance • Security and Privacy • Standardization	• Decision support • Prediction • In-use analytics • Simulation • Exploration • Visualisation • Modeling • Control • Domain-specific usage

Technical Working Groups

Fig. 3.1 The Big Data Value Chain as described within (Curry et al. 2014)

distributed environment; and support flexible and dynamic data structures. Data acquisition is further detailed in this chapter.

Data Analysis is concerned with making the raw data acquired amenable to use in decision-making as well as domain-specific usage. Data analysis involves exploring, transforming, and modelling data with the goal of highlighting relevant data, synthesising and extracting useful hidden information with high potential from a business point of view. Related areas include data mining, business intelligence, and machine learning. Chapter 4 covers data analysis.

Data Curation is the active management of data over its life cycle to ensure it meets the necessary data quality requirements for its effective usage (Pennock 2007). Data curation processes can be categorised into different activities such as content creation, selection, classification, transformation, validation, and preservation. Data curation is performed by expert curators that are responsible for improving the accessibility and quality of data. Data curators (also known as scientific curators, or data annotators) hold the responsibility of ensuring that data are trustworthy, discoverable, accessible, reusable, and fit their purpose. A key trend for the curation of big data utilises community and crowd sourcing approaches (Curry et al. 2010). Further analysis of data curation techniques for big data is provided in Chap. 5.

Data Storage is the persistence and management of data in a scalable way that satisfies the needs of applications that require fast access to the data. Relational Database Management Systems (RDBMS) have been the main, and almost unique, solution to the storage paradigm for nearly 40 years. However, the ACID (Atomicity, Consistency, Isolation, and Durability) properties that guarantee database transactions lack flexibility with regard to schema changes and the performance and fault tolerance when data volumes and complexity grow, making them unsuitable for big data scenarios. NoSQL technologies have been designed with the scalability goal in mind and present a wide range of solutions based on alternative data models. A more detailed discussion of data storage is provided in Chap. 6.

Data Usage covers the data-driven business activities that need access to data, its analysis, and the tools needed to integrate the data analysis within the business activity. Data usage in business decision-making can enhance competitiveness through reduction of costs, increased added value, or any other parameter that can be measured against existing performance criteria. Chapter 7 contains a detailed examination of data usage.

3.4   Ecosystems

The term *ecosystem* was coined by Tansley in 1935 to identify a basic ecological unit comprising of both the environment and the organisms that use it. Within the context of business, James F. Moore (1993, 1996, 2006) exploited the biological metaphor and used the term to describe the business environment. Moore defined a business ecosystem as an "economic community supported by a foundation of interacting organizations and individuals" (Moore 1996). A strategy involving a company attempting to succeed alone has proven to be limited in terms of its capacity to create valuable products or services. It is crucial that businesses collaborate among themselves to survive within a business ecosystem (Moore 1993; Gossain and Kandiah 1998). Ecosystems allow companies to create new value that no company could achieve by itself (Adner 2006). Within a healthy business ecosystem, companies can work together in a complex business web where they can easily exchange and share vital resources (Kim et al. 2010).

The study of Business Ecosystems is an active area of research where researchers are investigating many facets of the business ecosystem metaphor to explore aspects such as community, cooperation, interdependency, co-evolution, eco-systemic functions, and boundaries of business environments. Koening (2012) provides a simple typology of Business Ecosystems based on the degree of key resource control and type of member interdependence. Types of business ecosystems include supply systems (i.e. Nike), platforms (Apple iTunes), communities of destiny (i.e. Sematech in the semiconductor industry), and expanding communities.

3.4.1   Big Data Ecosystems

In natural ecosystems, smart organisms control their energy. In business ecosystems, a smart company manages information and its flows (Kim et al. 2010). In terms of data, the ecosystem metaphor is useful to describe the data environment supported by a community of interacting organisations and individuals. Big Data Ecosystems can form in different ways around an organisation, community technology platforms, or within or across sectors. Big Data Ecosystems exist within many industrial sectors where vast amount of data move between actors within complex information supply chains. Sectors with established or emerging data ecosystems include Healthcare, Finance (O'Riáin et al. 2012), Logistics, Media, Manufacturing, and Pharmaceuticals (Curry et al. 2010). In addition to the data itself, Big Data Ecosystems can also be supported by data management platforms, data infrastructure (e.g. Various Apache open source projects), and data services.

3.4.2 European Big Data Ecosystem

While no coherent data ecosystem exists at the European-level (DG Connect 2013), the benefits of sharing and linking data across domains and industry sectors are becoming obvious. Initiatives such as smart cities are showing how different sectors (i.e. energy and transport) can collaborate to maximise the potential for optimisation and value return. The cross-fertilisation of stakeholder and datasets from different sectors is a key element for advancing the big data economy in Europe.

A European big data business ecosystem is an important factor for commercialisation and commoditisation of big data services, products, and platforms. A successful big data ecosystem would see all "stakeholders interact seamlessly within a Digital Single Market, leading to business opportunities, easier access to knowledge and capital" (European Commission 2014).

A well-functioning working data ecosystem must bring together the key stakeholders with a clear benefit for all. The key actors in a big data ecosystem, as illustrated in Fig. 3.2, are:

- **Data Suppliers:** Person or organisation [Large and small and medium-sized enterprises (SME)] that create, collect, aggregate, and transform data from both public and private sources
- **Technology Providers:** Typically organisations (Large and SME) as providers of tools, platforms, services, and know-how for data management
- **Data End Users:** Person or organisation from different industrial sectors (private and public) that leverage big data technology and services to their advantage.
- **Data Marketplace:** Person or organisation that host data from publishers and offer it to consumers/end users.
- **Start-ups and Entrepreneurs:** Develop innovative data-driven technology, products, and services.
- **Researchers and Academics:** Investigate new algorithms, technologies, methodologies, business models, and societal aspects needed to advance big data.
- **Regulators** for data privacy and legal issues.
- **Standardisation Bodies:** Define technology standards (both official and de facto) to promote the global adoption of big data technology.
- **Investors, Venture Capitalists, and Incubators:** Person or organisation that provides resources and services to develop the commercial potential of the ecosystem.

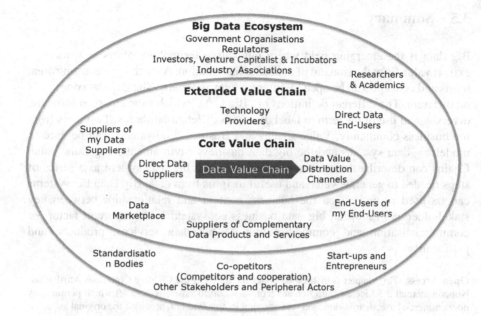

Fig. 3.2 The Micro, Meso, and Macro Levels of a Big Data Ecosystem [adapted from Moore (1996)]

3.4.3   Toward a Big Data Ecosystem

Enabling a European wide data ecosystem will require a number of technical challenges to be overcome associated with the cost and complexity of publishing and utilising data. Current ecosystems face a number of problems such as data discovery, curation, linking, synchronisation, distribution, business modelling, and sales and marketing. A number of key societal and environmental challenges need to be overcome to establish effective big data ecosystems; these include but are not limited to:

- Understanding the value and contribution of big data technology
- Determining the value of data
- Identification of business models that will support a data-driven ecosystem
- Enabling entrepreneurs and venture capitalists to easily access the ecosystem
- Preservation of privacy and security for all actors in the ecosystem
- Reducing fragmentation of languages, intellectual property rights, laws, and policy practices between EU countries

3.5   Summary

Big data is the emerging field where innovative technology offers new ways to extract value from the tsunami of available information. As with any emerging area, terms and concepts can be open to different interpretations. The Big Data domain is no different. The different definitions of "Big Data" which have emerged show the diversity and use of the term to label data with different attributes. Two tools from the business community, Value Chains and Business Ecosystems, can be used to model big data systems and the big data business environments. Big Data Value Chains can describe the information flow within a big data system as a series of steps needed to generate value and useful insights from data. Big Data Ecosystems can be used to understand the business context and relationships between key stakeholders. A European big data business ecosystem is an important factor for commercialisation and commoditisation of big data services, products, and platforms.

References

Adner, R. (2006). Match your innovation strategy to your innovation ecosystem. *Harvard Business Review, 84*, 98–107.
Choo, C. W. (1996). The knowing organization: How organizations use information to construct meaning, create knowledge and make decisions. *International Journal of Information Management, 16*, 329–340. doi:10.1016/0268-4012(96)00020-5.
Curry, E., Ngonga, A., Domingue, J., Freitas, A., Strohbach, M., Becker, T., et al. (2014). D2.2.2. Final version of the technical white paper. Public deliverable of the EU-Project BIG (318062; ICT-2011.4.4).
Curry, E., Freitas, A., & O'Riáin, S. (2010). The role of community-driven data curation for enterprises. In D. Wood (Ed.), *Linking enterprise data* (pp. 25–47). Boston, MA: Springer US.
DG Connect. (2013). *A European strategy on the data value chain.*
European Commission. (2014). *Towards a thriving data-driven economy, Communication from the commission to the European Parliament, the council, the European economic and social Committee and the committee of the regions*, Brussels.
Gossain, S., & Kandiah, G. (1998). Reinventing value: The new business ecosystem. *Strategy and Leadership, 26*, 28–33.
IDC. (2011). *IDC's worldwide big data taxonomy.*

Jacobs, A. (2009). The pathologies of big data. *Communications of the ACM, 52*, 36–44. doi:10. 1145/1536616.1536632.

Kim, H., Lee, J.-N., & Han, J. (2010). The role of IT in business ecosystems. *Communications of the ACM, 53*, 151. doi:10.1145/1735223.1735260.

Koenig, G. (2012). Business ecosystems revisited. *Management, 15*, 208–224.

Laney, D. (2001). *3D data management: Controlling data volume, velocity, and variety*. Technical report, META Group.

Loukides, M. (2010). What is data science? *O'Reily Radar*.

Manyika, J., Chui, M., Brown, B., Bughin, J., Dobbs, R., Roxburgh, C., & Byers, A. H. (2011). *Big data: The next frontier for innovation, competition, and productivity*. McKinsey Global Institute, p. 156.

Mike 2.0. (2014). Big data definition – Mike 2.0.

Moore, J. F. (1993). Predators and prey: A new ecology of competition. *Harvard Business Review, 71*, 75–86.

Moore, J. F. (1996). *The death of competition: Leadership and strategy in the age of business ecosystems*. New York: HarperCollins.

Moore, J. F. (2006). Business ecosystems and the view from the firm. *Antitrust Bulletin, 51*, 31–75.

NESSI. (2012). Big data: A new world of opportunities. NESSI White Paper.

O'Riáin, S., Curry, E., & Harth, A. (2012). XBRL and open data for global financial ecosystems: A linked data approach. *International Journal of Accounting Information Systems, 13*, 141–162. doi:10.1016/j.accinf.2012.02.002.

Pennock, M. (2007). Digital curation: A life-cycle approach to managing and preserving usable digital information. *Library and Archives Journal, 1*, 1–3.

Porter, M. E. (1985). *Competitive advantage: Creating and sustaining superior performance*. New York: Free Press. doi:10.1182/blood-2005-11-4354.

Rayport, J. F., & Sviokla, J. J. (1995). Exploiting the virtual value chain. *Harvard Business Review, 73*, 75–85. doi:10.1016/S0267-3649(00)88914-1.

Stonebraker, M. (2012). What does 'big data' mean. *Communications of the ACM*, BLOG@ ACM.

Tansley, A. G. (1935). The use and abuse of vegetational concepts and terms. *Ecology, 16*, 284–307.

Wikipedia. (2014) Big data. Wikipedia article. http://en.wikipedia.org/wiki/Big_data

Chapter 4
Big Data Acquisition

Klaus Lyko, Marcus Nitzschke, and Axel-Cyrille Ngonga Ngomo

4.1 Introduction

Over the last years, the term big data was used by different major players to label
data with different attributes. Moreover, different data processing architectures for
big data have been proposed to address the different characteristics of big data.
Overall, data acquisition has been understood as the process of gathering, filtering,
and cleaning data before the data is put in a data warehouse or any other storage
solution.

The position of big data acquisition within the overall big data value chain can be
seen in Fig. 4.1. The acquisition of big data is most commonly governed by four of
the Vs: volume, velocity, variety, and value. Most data acquisition scenarios
assume high-volume, high-velocity, high-variety, but low-value data, making it
important to have adaptable and time-efficient gathering, filtering, and cleaning
algorithms that ensure that only the high-value fragments of the data are actually
processed by the data-warehouse analysis. However, for some organizations, most
data is of potentially high value as it can be important to recruit new customers. For
such organizations, data analysis, classification, and packaging on very high data
volumes play the most central role after the data acquisition.

The goals of this chapter are threefold: First, it aims to identify the present
general requirements for data acquisition by presenting open state-of-the-art frameworks and protocols for big data acquisition for companies. Our second goal is then
to unveil the current approaches used for data acquisition in the different sectors.
Finally, it discusses how the requirements to data acquisition are met by current
approaches as well as possible future developments in the same area.

K. Lyko (✉) • M. Nitzschke • A.-C. Ngonga Ngomo
University of Leipzig, Augustusplatz 10, 04109 Leipzig, Germany
e-mail: lyko@informatik.uni-leipzig.de; nitzschke@informatik.uni-leipzig.de;
ngonga@informatik.uni-leipzig.de

© The Author(s) 2016   39
J.M. Cavanillas et al. (eds.), *New Horizons for a Data-Driven Economy*,
DOI 10.1007/978-3-319-21569-3_4

Big Data Value Chain

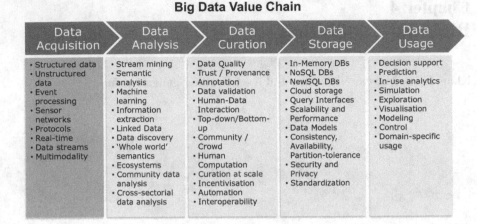

Data Acquisition	Data Analysis	Data Curation	Data Storage	Data Usage
• Structured data • Unstructured data • Event processing • Sensor networks • Protocols • Real-time • Data streams • Multimodality	• Stream mining • Semantic analysis • Machine learning • Information extraction • Linked Data • Data discovery • 'Whole world' semantics • Ecosystems • Community data analysis • Cross-sectorial data analysis	• Data Quality • Trust / Provenance • Annotation • Data validation • Human-Data Interaction • Top-down/Bottom-up • Community / Crowd • Human Computation • Curation at scale • Incentivisation • Automation • Interoperability	• In-Memory DBs • NoSQL DBs • NewSQL DBs • Cloud storage • Query Interfaces • Scalability and Performance • Data Models • Consistency, Availability, Partition-tolerance • Security and Privacy • Standardization	• Decision support • Prediction • In-use analytics • Simulation • Exploration • Visualisation • Modeling • Control • Domain-specific usage

Fig. 4.1 Data acquisition in the big data value chain

4.2 Key Insights for Big Data Acquisition

To get a better understanding of data acquisition, the chapter will first take a look at the different big data architectures of Oracle, Vivisimo, and IBM. This will integrate the process of acquisition within the big data processing pipeline.

The big data processing pipeline has been abstracted in numerous ways in previous works. Oracle (2012) relies on a three-step approach for data processing. In the first step, the content of different data sources is retrieved and stored within a scalable storage solution such as a NoSQL database or the Hadoop Distributed File System (HDFS). The stored data is subsequently processed by first being reorganized and stored in an SQL-capable big data analytics software and finally analysed by using big data analytics algorithms.

Velocity (Vivisimo 2012) relies on a different view on big data. Here, the approach is more search-oriented. The main component of the architecture is a connector layer, in which different data sources can be addressed. The content of these data sources is gathered in parallel, converted, and finally added to an index, which builds the basis for data analytics, business intelligence, and all other data-driven applications. Other big players such as IBM rely on architectures similar to Oracle's (IBM 2013).

Throughout the different architectures to big data processing, the core of data acquisition boils down to gathering data from distributed information sources with the aim of storing them in scalable, big data-capable data storage. To achieve this goal, three main components are required:

1. Protocols that allow the gathering of information for distributed data sources of any type (unstructured, semi-structured, structured)
2. Frameworks with which the data is collected from the distributed sources by using different protocols

3. Technologies that allow the persistent storage of the data retrieved by the frameworks

4.3   Social and Economic Impact of Big Data Acquisition

Over the last years, the sheer amount of data that is produced in a steady manner has increased. Ninety percent of the data in the world today was produced over the last 2 years. The source and nature of this data is diverse. It ranges from data gathered by sensors to data depicting (online) transactions. An ever-increasing part is produced in social media and via mobile devices. The type of data (structured vs. unstructured) and semantics are also diverse. Yet, all this data must be aggregated to help answer business questions and form a broad picture of the market.

For business this trend holds several opportunities and challenges to both creating new business models and improving current operations, thereby generating market advantages. Tools and methods to deal with big data driven by the four Vs can be used for improved user-specific advertisement or market research in general. For example, smart metering systems are tested in the energy sector. Furthermore, in combination with new billing systems these systems could also be beneficial in other sectors such as telecommunication and transport.

Big data has already influenced many businesses and has the potential to impact all business sectors. While there are several technical challenges, the impact on management and decision-making and even company culture will be no less great (McAfee and Brynjolfsson 2012).

There are still several boundaries though. Namely privacy and security concerns need to be addressed by these systems and technologies. Many systems already generate and collect large amounts of data, but only a small fragment is used actively in business processes. In addition, many of these systems lack real-time requirements.

4.4   Big Data Acquisition: State of the Art

The bulk of big data acquisition is carried out within the message queuing paradigm, sometimes also called the streaming paradigm, publish/subscribe paradigm (Carzaniga et al. 2000), or event processing paradigm (Cugola and Margara 2012; Luckham 2002). Here, the basic assumption is that manifold volatile data sources generate information that needs to be captured, stored, and analysed by a big data processing platform. The new information generated by the data source is forwarded to the data storage by means of a data acquisition framework that implements a predefined protocol. This section describes the two core technologies for acquiring big data.

4.4.1 Protocols

Several of the organizations that rely internally on big data processing have devised enterprise-specific protocols of which most have not been publicly released and can thus not be described in this chapter. This section presents the commonly used open protocols for data acquisition.

4.4.1.1 AMQP

The reason for the development of Advanced Message Queuing Protocol (AMQP) was the need for an open protocol that would satisfy the requirements of large companies with respect to data acquisition. To achieve this goal, 23 companies compiled a sequence of requirements for a data acquisition protocol. The resulting AMQP (Advanced Message Queuing Protocol) became an OASIS standard in October 2012. The rationale behind AMQP (Bank of America et al. 2011) was to provide a protocol with the following characteristics:

- **Ubiquity:** This property of AMQP refers to its ability to be used across different industries within both current and future data acquisition architectures. AMQP's ubiquity was achieved by making it easily extensible and simple to implement. The large number of frameworks that implement it, including SwiftMQ, Microsoft Windows Azure Service Bus, Apache Qpid, and Apache ActiveMQ, reflects how easy the protocol is to implement.
- **Safety:** The safety property was implemented across two different dimensions. First, the protocol allows the integration of message encryption to ensure that even intercepted messages cannot be decoded easily. Thus, it can be used to transfer business-critical information. The protocol is robust against the injection of spam, making the AMQP brokers difficult to attack. Second, the AMQP ensures the durability of messages, meaning that it allows messages to be transferred even when the sender and receiver are not online at the same time.
- **Fidelity:** This third characteristic is concerned with the integrity of the message. AMQP includes means to ensure that the sender can express the semantics of the message and thus allow the receiver to understand what it is receiving. The protocol implements reliable failure semantics that allow systems to detect errors from the creation of the message at the sender's end before the storage of the information by the receiver.
- **Applicability:** The intention behind this property is to ensure that AMQP clients and brokers can communicate by using several of the protocols of the Open Systems Interconnection (OSI) model layers such as Transmission Control Protocol (TCP), User Datagram Protocol (UDP), and also Stream Control Transmission Protocol (SCTP). By these means, AMQP is applicable in many scenarios and industries where not all the protocols of the OSI model layers are required and used. Moreover, the protocol was designed to support different messaging patterns including direct messaging, request/reply, publish/subscribe, etc.

- **Interoperability:** The protocol was designed to be independent of particular implementations and vendors. Thus, clients and brokers with fully independent implementations, architectures, and ownership can interact by means of AMQP. As stated above, several frameworks from different organizations now implement the protocol.
- **Manageability:** One of the main concerns during the specification of the AMQP was to ensure that frameworks that implement it could scale easily. This was achieved by ensuring that AMQP is a fault-tolerant and lossless wire protocol through which information of all types (e.g. XML, audio, video) can be transferred.

To implement these requirements, AMQP relies on a type system and four different layers: a transport layer, a messaging layer, a transaction layer, and a security layer. The type system is based on primitive types from databases (integers, strings, symbols, etc.), described types as known from programming, and descriptor values that can be extended by the users of the protocol. In addition, AMQP allows the use of encoding to store symbols and values as well as the definition of compound types that consist of combinations of several primary types.

The transport layer defines how AMQP messages are to be processed. An AMQP network consists of nodes that are connected via links. Messages can originate from (senders), be forwarded by (relays), or be consumed by nodes (receivers). Messages are only allowed to travel across a link when this link abides by the criteria defined by the source of the message. The transport layer supports several types of route exchanges including message fanout and topic exchange.

The messaging layer of AMQP describes the structure of valid messages. A bare message is a message as submitted by the sender to an AMQP network.

The transaction layer allows for the "coordinated outcome of otherwise independent transfers" (Bank of America et al. 2011, p. 95). The basic idea behind the architecture of the transactional messaging approach followed by the layer lies in the sender of the message acting as controller while the receiver acts as a resource as messages are transferred as specified by the controller. By these means, decentralized and scalable message processing can be achieved.

The final AMQP layer is the security layer, which enables the definition of means to encrypt the content of AMQP messages. The protocols for achieving this goal are supposed to be defined externally from AMQP itself. Protocols that can be used to this end include transport layer security (TSL) and simple authentication and security layer (SASL).

Due to its adoption across several industries and its high flexibility, it is likely that AMQP will become the standard approach for message processing in industries that cannot afford to implement their own dedicated protocols. With the upcoming data-as-a-service industry, it also promises to be the go-to solution for implementing services around data streams. One of the most commonly used AMQP brokers is RabbitMQ, whose popularity is mostly due to the fact that it implements several messaging protocols including JMS.

4.4.1.2   Java Message Service

Java Message Service (JMS) API was included in the Java 2 Enterprise Edition on 18 March 2002, after the Java Community Process in its final version 1.1 ratified it as a standard.

According to the 1.1 specification JMS "provides a common way for Java programs to create, send, receive and read an enterprise messaging system's messages". Administrative tools allow one to bind destinations and connection factories into a Java Naming and Directory Interface (JNDI) namespace. A JMS client can then use resource injection to access the administered objects in the namespace and then establish a logical connection to the same objects through the JMS provider.

The JNDI serves in this case as the moderator between different clients who want to exchange messages. Note that the term "client" is used here (as the spec does) to denote the sender as well as receiver of a message, because JMS was originally designed to exchange message peer-to-peer. Currently, JMS offers two messaging models: point-to-point and publisher-subscriber, where the latter is a one-to-many connection.

AMQP is compatible with JMS, which is the de facto standard for message passing in the Java world. While AMQP is defined at the format level (i.e. byte stream of octets), JMS is standardized at API level and is therefore not easy to implement in other programing languages (as the "J" in "JMS" suggests). Also JMS does not provide functionality for load balancing/fault tolerance, error/advisory notification, administration of services, security, wire protocol, or message type repository (database access).

A considerable advantage of AMQP is, however, the programming language independence of the implementation that avoids vendor-lock in and platform compatibility.

4.4.2   Software Tools

With respect to software tools for data acquisition, many of them are well known and many use cases are available all over the web so it is feasible to have a first approach to them. Despite this, the correct use of each tool requires a deep knowledge on the internal working and the implementation of the software. Different paradigms of data acquisition have appeared depending on the scope these tools have been focused on. The architectural diagram in Fig. 4.2 shows an overall picture of the complete big data workflow highlighting the data acquisition part.

In the remainder of this section, these tools and others relating to data acquisition are described in detail.

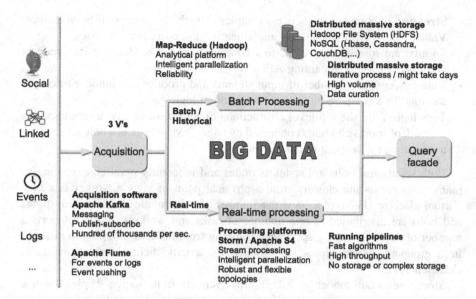

Fig. 4.2 Big data workflow

4.4.2.1   Storm

Storm is an open-source framework for the robust distributed real-time computation on streams of data. It started off as an open-source project and now has a large and active community. Storm supports a wide range of programming languages and storage facilities (relational databases, NoSQL stores, etc.). One of the main advantages of Storm is that it can be utilized in many data gathering scenarios including stream processing and distributed RPC for solving computationally intensive functions on-the-fly, and continuous computation applications (Gabriel 2012). Many companies and applications are using Storm to power a wide variety of production systems processing data, including Groupon, The Weather Channel, fullcontact.com, and Twitter.

The logical network of Storm consists of three types of nodes: a master node called Nimbus, a set of intermediate Zookeeper nodes, and a set of Supervisor nodes.

- **The Nimbus:** is equivalent to Hadoop's JobTracker: it uploads the computation for execution, distributes code across the cluster, and monitors computation.
- **The Zookeepers:** handle the complete cluster coordination. This cluster organization layer is based upon the Apache ZooKeeper project.
- **The Supervisor Daemon:** spawns worker nodes; it is comparable to Hadoop's TaskTracker. This is the place where most of the work of application developers goes into. The worker nodes communicate with the Nimbus via the Zookeepers to determine what to run on the machine, starting and stopping workers.

A computation is called topology in Storm. Once deployed, topologies run indefinitely. There are four concepts and abstraction layers within Storm:

- **Streams:** unbounded sequence of tuples, which are named lists of values. Values can be arbitrary objects implementing a serialization interface.
- **Spouts:** are sources of streams in a computation, e.g. readers for data sources such as the Twitter Streaming APIs.
- **Bolts:** process any number of input streams and produce any number of output streams. This is where most of the application logic goes.
- **Topologies:** are the top-level abstractions of Storm. Basically, a topology is a network of spouts and bolts connected by edges. Every edge is a bolt subscribing to the stream of a spout or another bolt.

Both spouts and bolts are stateless nodes and inherently parallel, executing as many tasks across the cluster. From a physical point of view a worker is a Java Virtual Machine (JVM) process with a number of tasks running within. Both spouts and bolts are distributed over a number of tasks and workers. Storm supports a number of stream grouping approaches ranging from random grouping to tasks, to field grouping, where tuples are grouped by specific fields to the same tasks (Madsen 2012).

Storm uses a pull model; each bolt pulls events from its source. Tuples traverse the entire network within a specified time window or are considered as failed. Therefore, in terms of recovery the spouts are responsible to keep tuples ready for replay.

4.4.2.2   S4

S4 (simply scalable streaming system) is a distributed, general-purpose platform for developing applications that process streams of data. Started in 2008 by Yahoo! Inc., since 2011 it is an Apache Incubator project. S4 is designed to work on commodity hardware, avoiding I/O bottlenecks by relying on an all-in-memory approach (Neumeyer 2011).

In general keyed data events are routed to processing elements (PE). PEs receive events and either emit resulting events and/or publish results. The S4 engine was inspired by the MapReduce model and resembles the Actors model (encapsulation semantics and location transparency). Among others it provides a simple programming interface for processing data streams in a decentralized, symmetric, and pluggable architecture.

A stream in S4 is a sequence of elements (events) of both tuple-valued keys and attributes. A basic computational unit PE is identified by the following four components: (1) its functionality provided by the PE class and associated configuration, (2) the event types it consumes, (3) the keyed attribute in this event, and (4) the value of the keyed attribute of the consuming events. A PE is instantiated by the platform for each value of the key attribute. Keyless PEs are a special class of PEs with no keyed attribute and value. These PEs consume all events of the corresponding type and are typically at the input layer of an S4 cluster. There is a large number of standard PEs available for a number of typical tasks such as aggregate and join. The logical hosts of PEs are the processing nodes (PNs). PNs listen to events, execute operations for incoming events, and dispatch events with the assistance of the communication layer.

S4 routes each event to PNs based on a hash function over all known values of the keyed attribute in the event. There is another special type of PE object: the PE prototype. It is identified by the first three components. These objects are configured upon initialization and for any value it can clone itself to create a fully qualified PE. This cloning event is triggered by the PN for each unique value of the keyed attribute. An S4 application is a graph composed of PE prototypes and streams that produce, consume, and transmit messages, whereas PE instances are clones of the corresponding prototypes containing the state and are associated with unique keys (Neumeyer et al. 2011).

As a consequence of this design S4 guarantees that all events with a specific value of the keyed attribute arrive at the corresponding PN and within it are routed to the specific PE instance (Bradic 2011). The current state of a PE is inaccessible to other PEs. S4 is based upon a push model: events are routed to the next PE as fast as possible. Therefore, if a receiver buffer fills up events may be dropped. Via lossy checkpointing S4 provides state recovery. In the case of a node crash a new one takes over its task from the most recent snapshot. The communication layer is based upon the Apache ZooKeeper project. It manages the cluster and provides failover handling to stand-by nodes. PEs are built in Java using a fairly simple API and are assembled into the application using the Spring framework.

4.4.2.3 Kafka

Kafka is a distributed publish-subscribe messaging system designed to support mainly persistent messaging with high-throughput. Kafka aims to unify offline and online processing by providing a mechanism for a parallel load into Hadoop as well as the ability to partition real-time consumption over a cluster of machines. The use for activity stream processing makes Kafka comparable to Apache Flume, though the architecture and primitives are very different and make Kafka more comparable to a traditional messaging system.

Kafka was originally developed at LinkedIn for tracking the huge volume of activity events generated by the website. These activity events are critical for monitoring user engagement as well as improving relevancy in their data-driven products. The previous diagram gives a simplified view of the deployment topology at LinkedIn.

Note that a single Kafka cluster handles all activity data from different sources. This provides a single pipeline of data for both online and offline consumers. This tier acts as a buffer between live activity and asynchronous processing. Kafka can also be used to replicate all data to a different data centre for offline consumption.

Kafka can be used to feed Hadoop for offline analytics, as well as a way to track internal operational metrics that feed graphs in real time. In this context, a very appropriate use for Kafka and its publish-subscribe mechanism would be processing related stream data, from tracking user actions on large-scale websites to relevance and ranking tasks.

In Kafka, each stream is called a "topic". Topics are partitioned for scaling purposes. Producers of messages provide a key which is used to determine the partition the message is sent to. Thus, all messages partitioned by the same key are guaranteed to be in the same topic partition. Kafka brokers handle some partitions and receive and store messages sent by producers.

Kafka consumers read from a topic by getting messages from all partitions of the topic. If a consumer wants to read all messages with a specific key (e.g. a user ID in case of website clicks) he only has to read messages from the partition the key is on, not the complete topic. Furthermore, it is possible to reference any point in a brokers log file using an offset. This offset determines where a consumer is in a specific topic/partition pair. The offset is incremented once a consumer reads the topic/partition pair.

Kafka provides an at-least-once messaging guarantee and highly available partitions. To store and cache messages Kafka relies on file systems, whereas all data is written immediately to a persistent log without necessarily flushing to disk. In combination the protocol is built upon a message set abstraction, which groups messages together. Therewith, it minimizes the network overhead and sequential disk operations. Both consumer and producer share the same message format.

4.4.2.4   Flume

Flume is a service for efficiently collecting and moving large amounts of log data. It has a simple and flexible architecture based on streaming data flows. It is robust and fault tolerant with tuneable reliability mechanisms and many failover and recovery mechanisms. It uses a simple extensible data model that allows online analytic applications. The system was designed with these four key goals in mind: reliability, scalability, manageability, and extensibility

The purpose of Flume is to provide a distributed, reliable, and available system for efficiently collecting, aggregating, and moving large amounts of log data from many different sources to a centralized data store. The architecture of Flume NG is based on a few concepts that together help achieve this objective:

- **Event:** a byte payload with optional string headers that represent the unit of data that Flume can transport from its point of origin to its final destination.
- **Flow:** movement of events from the point of origin to their final destination is considered a data flow, or simply flow.
- **Client:** an interface implementation that operates at the point of origin of events and delivers them to a Flume agent.
- **Agent:** an independent process that hosts flume components such as sources, channels, and sinks, and thus has the ability to receive, store, and forward events to their next-hop destination.

- **Source:** an interface implementation that can consume events delivered to it via a specific mechanism.
- **Channel:** a transient store for events, where events are delivered to the channel via sources operating within the agent. An event put in a channel stays in that channel until a sink removes it for further transport.
- **Sink:** an interface implementation that can remove events from a channel and transmit them to the next agent in the flow, or to the event's final destination.

These concepts help in simplifying the architecture, implementation, configuration, and deployment of Flume.

A flow in Flume NG starts from the client. The client transmits the event to its next-hop destination. This destination is an agent. More precisely, the destination is a source operating within the agent. The source receiving this event will then deliver it to one or more channels. The channels that receive the event are drained by one or more sinks operating within the same agent. If the sink is a regular sink, it will forward the event to its next-hop destination, which will be another agent. If instead it is a terminal sink, it will forward the event to its final destination. Channels allow for the decoupling of sources from sinks using the familiar producer-consumer model of data exchange. This allows sources and sinks to have different performance and runtime characteristics and yet be able to effectively use the physical resources available to the system.

The primary use case for Flume is as a logging system that gathers a set of log files on every machine in a cluster and aggregates them to a centralized persistent store such as the Hadoop Distributed File System (HDFS). Also, Flume can be used as an HTTP event manager that deals with different types of requests and drives each of them to any specific data store during a data acquisition process, such as an NoSQL databases like HBase.

Therefore, Apache Flume is not a pure data acquisition system but acts in a complementary fashion by managing the different data types acquired and transforming them to specific data stores or repositories.

4.4.2.5 Hadoop

Apache Hadoop is an open-source project developing a framework for reliable, scalable, and distributed computing on big data using clusters of commodity hardware. It was derived from Google's MapReduce and the Google File System (GFS) and written in JAVA. It is used and supported by a large community and is both used in production and research environments by many organizations, most notably: Facebook, a9.com, AOL, Baidu, IBM, Imageshack, and Yahoo. The Hadoop project consists of four modules:

- **Hadoop Common:** for common utilities used throughout Hadoop.
- **Hadoop Distributed File System (HDFS):** a highly available and efficient file system.

- **Hadoop YARN (Yet Another Resource Negotiator):** a framework for job scheduling and cluster management.
- **Hadoop MapReduce:** a system to parallel processing large amounts of data.

A Hadoop cluster is designed according to the master-slave principle. The master is the name node. It keeps track of the metadata about the file distribution. Large files are typically split into chunks of 128 MB. These parts are copied three times and the replicas are distributed through the cluster of data nodes (slave nodes). In the case of a node failure its information is not lost; the name node is able to allocate the data again. To monitor the cluster every slave node regularly sends a heartbeat to the name node. If a slave is not recognized over a specific period it is considered dead. As the master node is a single point of failure it is typically run on highly reliable hardware. And, as precaution a secondary name node can keep track of changes in the metadata; with its help it is possible to rebuild the functionality of the name node and thereby ensure the functionality of the cluster.

YARN is Hadoop's cluster scheduler. It allocates a number of containers (which are essential processes) in a cluster of machines and executes arbitrary commands on them. YARN consists of three main pieces: a ResourceManager, a NodeManager, and an ApplicationMaster. In a cluster each machine runs a NodeManager, responsible for running processes on the local machine. Resource-Managers tell NodeManagers what to run, and Applications tell the ResourceManager when to run something on the cluster.

Data is processed according to the MapReduce paradigm. MapReduce is a framework for parallel-distributed computation. As data storage processing works in a master-slave fashion, computation tasks are called jobs and are distributed by the job tracker. Instead of moving the data to the calculation, Hadoop moves the calculation to the data. The job tracker functions as a master distributing and administering jobs in the cluster. Task trackers carry out the actual work on jobs. Typically each cluster node is running a task tracker instance and a data node. The MapReduce framework eases programming of highly distributed parallel programs. A programmer can focus on writing the more simpler map() and reduce() functions dealing with the task at hand while the MapReduce infrastructure takes care of running and managing the tasks in the cluster.

In the orbit of the Hadoop project a number of related projects have emerged. The Apache Pig project for instance is built upon Hadoop and simplifies writing and maintaining Hadoop implementations. Hadoop is very efficient for batch processing. The Apache HBase project aims to provide real-time access to big data.

4.5   Future Requirements and Emerging Trends for Big Data Acquisition

Big data acquisition tooling has to deal with high-velocity, variety, and real-time data acquisition. Thus, tooling for data acquisition has to ensure a very high throughput. This means that data can come from multiple resources (social networks, sensors, web mining, logs, etc.) with different structures, or be unstructured (text, video, pictures, and media files) and at a very high pace (tens or hundreds of thousands events per second). Therefore, the main challenge in acquiring big data is to provide frameworks and tools that ensure the required throughput for the problem at hand without losing any data in the process.

In this context, emerging challenges for the acquisition of big data include the following:

- Data acquisition is often started by tools that provide some kind of input data to the system, such as social networks and web mining algorithms, sensor data acquisition software, logs periodically injected, etc. Typically the data acquisition process starts with single or multiple end points where the data comes from. These end points could take different technical appearances, such as log importers, Storm-based algorithms, or even the data acquisition may offer APIs to the external world to inject the data, by using RESTful services or any other programmatic APIs. Hence, any technical solution that aims to acquire data from different sources should be able to deal with this wide range of different implementations.

- To provide the mechanisms to connect the data acquisition with the data pre- and post-processing (analysis) and storage, both in the historical and real-time layers. In order to do so, the batch and real-time processing tools (i.e. Storm and Hadoop) should be able to be contacted by the data acquisition tools. This is implemented in different ways. For instance Apache Kafka uses a publish-subscribe mechanism where both Hadoop and Storm can be subscribed, and therefore the messages received will be available to them. Apache Flume on the other hand follows a different approach, storing the data in a NoSQL key-value store to ensure velocity, and pushing the data to one or several receivers (i.e. Hadoop and Storm). There is a red thin line between data acquisition, storage, and analysis in this process, as data acquisition typically ends by storing the raw data in an appropriate master dataset, and connecting with the analytical pipeline (especially for real-time, but also batch processing).

- To come up with a structured or semi-structured model valid for data analysis, to effectively pre-process acquired data, especially unstructured data. The borders between data acquisition and analysis are blurred in the pre-processing stage. Some may argue that pre-processing is part of processing, and therefore of data analysis, while others believe that data acquisition does not end with the actual gathering, but also with cleaning the data and providing a minimal set of coherence and metadata on top of it. Data cleaning usually takes several steps, such as boilerplate removal (i.e. removing HTML headers in web mining acquisition), language detection and named entities recognition (for textual resources), and providing extra metadata such as timestamp, provenance information (yet another overlap with data curation), etc.

- The acquisition of media (pictures, video) is a significant challenge, but it is an even bigger challenge to perform the analysis and storage of video and images.
- Data variety requires processing the semantics in the data in order to correctly and effectively merge data from different sources while processing. Works on semantic event processing such as semantic approximations (Hasan and Curry 2014a), thematic event processing (Hasan and Curry 2014b), and thingsonomy tagging (Hasan and Curry 2015) are emerging approaches in this area, within this context.
- In order to perform post- and pre-processing of acquired data, the current state-of the art provides a set of open-source and commercial tools and frameworks. The main goal when defining a correct data acquisition strategy is therefore to understand the needs of the system in terms of data volume, variety, and velocity, and take the right decision on which tool is best to ensure the acquisition and desired throughput.

4.6 Sector Case Studies for Big Data Acquisition

This section analyses the use of big data acquisition technology within a number of sectors.

4.6.1 Health Sector

Within the health sector big data technology aims to establish a holistic approach whereby clinical, financial, and administrative data as well as patient behavioural data, population data, medical device data, and any other related health data are combined and used for retrospective, real-time, and predictive analysis.

In order to establish a basis for the successful implementation of big data health applications, the challenge of data digitalization and acquisition (i.e. putting health data in a form suitable as input for analytic solutions) needs to be addressed.

As of today, large amounts of health data are stored in data silos and data exchange is only possible via Scan, Fax, or email. Due to inflexible interfaces and missing standards, the aggregation of health data relies on individualized solutions with high costs.

In hospitals patient data is stored in CIS (clinical information system) or EHR (electronic health record) systems. However, different clinical departments might use different systems, such as RIS (radiology information system), LIS (laboratory information system), or PACS (picture archiving and communication system) to store their data. There is no standard data model or EHR system. Existing mechanisms for data integration are either adaptations of standard data warehouse solutions from horizontal IT providers like Oracle Healthcare Data Model, Teradata's Healthcare Logical Data Model, IBM Healthcare Provider Data Model, or new solutions like the i2b2 platform. While the first three are mainly used to generate benchmarks regarding the performance of the overall hospital organization, the i2b2 platform establishes a data warehouse that allows the integration of data from different clinical departments in order to support the task of identifying patient cohorts. In doing so, structured data such as diagnoses and lab values are mapped to standardized coding systems. However, unstructured data is not further labelled with semantic information. Besides its main functionality of patient cohorts identification, the i2b2 hive offers several additional modules. Besides specific modules for data import, export, and visualization tasks, modules to create and use additional semantics are available. For example, the natural language processing (NLP) tool offers a means to extract concepts out of specific terms and connect them with structured knowledge.

Today, data can be exchanged by using exchange formats such as HL7. However, due to non-technical reasons such as privacy, health data is commonly not shared across organizations (phenomena of organizational silos). Information about diagnoses, procedures, lab values, demographics, medication, provider, etc., is in general provided in a structured format, but not automatically collected in a standardized manner. For example, lab departments use their own coding system for lab values without an explicit mapping to the LOINC (Logical Observation Identifiers Names and Codes) standard. Also, different clinical departments often use different but customized report templates without specifying the common semantics. Both scenarios lead to difficulties in data acquisition and consequent integration.

Regarding unstructured data like texts and images, standards for describing high-level meta-information are only partially collected. In the imaging domain, the DICOM (Digital Imaging and Communications in Medicine) standard for specifying image metadata is available. However, for describing meta-information of clinical reports or clinical studies a common (agreed) standard is missing. To the best of our knowledge, for the representation of the content information of unstructured data like images, texts, or genomics data, no standard is available. Initial efforts to change this situation are initiatives such as the structured reporting initiative by RSNA or semantic annotations using standardized vocabularies. For example, the Medical Subject Headings (MeSH) is a controlled vocabulary thesaurus of the US National Library of Medicine to capture topics of texts in the medical and biological domain. There also exist several translations to other languages.

Since each EHR vendor provides their own data model, there is no standard data model for the usage of coding systems to represent the content of clinical reports. In terms of the underlying means for data representation, existing EHR systems rely on a case-centric rather than on a patient-centric representation of health data. This hinders longitudinal health data acquisition and integration.

Easy to use structured reporting tools are required which do not create extra work for clinicians, i.e. these systems need to be seamlessly integrated into the clinical workflow. In addition, available context information should be used to assist the clinicians. Given that structured reporting tools are implemented as easy-to-use tools, they can gain acceptance by clinicians such that most of the clinical documentation is carried out in a semi-structured form and the quality and quantity of semantic annotations increases.

From an organizational point of view, the storage, processing, access, and protection of big data has to be regulated on several different levels: institutional, regional, national, and international level. There is a need to define who authorizes which processes, who changes processes, and who implements process changes. Therefore, a proper and consistent legal framework or guidelines [e.g. ISO/IEC 27000] for all four levels are required.

IHE (integrating the healthcare enterprise) enables plug-and-play and secure access to health information whenever and wherever it is needed. It provides different specifications, tools, and services. IHE also promotes the use of well-established and internationally accepted standards (e.g. Digital Imaging and Communications in Medicine, Health Level 7). Pharmaceutical and R&D data that encompass clinical trials, clinical studies, population and disease data, etc. is typically owned by the pharmaceutical companies, research labs/academia, or the government. As of today, a lot of manual effort is taken to collect all the datasets for conducting clinical studies and related analysis. The manual effort for collecting the data is quite high.

4.6.2   Manufacturing, Retail, and Transport

Big data acquisition in the context of the retail, transportation, and manufacturing sectors becomes increasingly important. As data processing costs decrease and storage capacities increase, data can now be continuously gathered. Manufacturing companies as well as retailers may monitor channels like Facebook, Twitter, or news for any mentions and analyse these data (e.g. customer sentiment analysis). Retailers on the web are also collecting large amounts of data by storing log files and combining that information with other data sources such as sales data in order to analyse and predict customer behaviour. In the field of manufacturing, all participating devices are nowadays interconnected (e.g. sensors, RFID), such that vital information is constantly gathered in order to predict defective parts at an early stage.

All three sectors have in common that the data comes from very heterogeneous sources (e.g. log files, data from social media that needs to be extracted via proprietary APIs, data from sensors, etc.). Data comes in at a very high pace, requiring that the right technologies be chosen for extraction (e.g. MapReduce). Challenges may also include data integration. For example, product names used by customers on social media platforms need to be matched against IDs used for product pages on the web and then matched against internal IDs used in Enterprise Resource Planning (ERP) systems. Tools used for data acquisition in retail can be grouped by the two types of data typically collected in retail:

- Sales data from accounting and controlling departments
- Data from the marketing departments

The dynamite data channel monitor, recently bought by Market Track LLC, provides a solution to gather information about product prices on more than 1 billion "buy" pages at more than 4000 global retailers in real time, and thus allows to study the impact of promotional investments, monitor prices, and track consumer sentiment on brands and products.

The increasing use of social media not only empowers consumers to easily compare services and products both with respect to price and quality, but also enables retailers to collect, manage, and analyse large volumes and velocity of data, providing a great opportunity for the retail industry. To gain competitive advantages, real-time information is essential for accurate prediction and optimization models. From a data acquisition perspective means for stream data computation are necessary, which can deal with the challenges of the Vs of the data.

In order to bring a benefit for the transportation sector (especially multimodal urban transportation), tools that support big data acquisition have to achieve mainly two tasks (DHL 2013; Davenport 2013). First, they have to handle large amounts of personalized data (e.g. location information) and deal with the associated privacy issues. Second, they have to integrate data from different service providers, including geographically distributed sensors (i.e. Internet of Things (IoT)) and open data sources.

Different players benefit from big data in the transport sector. Governments and public institutions use an increasing amount of data for traffic control, route planning, and transport management. The private sector exploits increasing amounts of date for route planning and revenue management to gain competitive advantages, save time, and increase fuel efficiency. Individuals increasingly use data via websites, mobile device applications, and GPS information for route planning to increase efficiency and save travel time.

In the manufacturing sector, tools for data acquisition need to mainly process large amounts of sensor data. Those tools need to handle sensor data that may be incompatible with other sensor data and thus data integration challenges need to be tackled, especially when sensor data is passed through multiple companies in a value chain.

Another category of tools needs to address the issue of integrating data produced by sensors in a production environment with data from, e.g. ERP systems within enterprises. This is best achieved when tools produce and consume standardized metadata formats.

4.6.3 Government, Public, Non-profit

Integrating and analysing large amounts of data play an increasingly important role in today's society. Often, however, new discoveries and insights can only be attained by integrating information from dispersed sources. Despite recent advances in structured data publishing on the web (such as using RDF in attributes (RDFa) and the schema.org initiative), the question arises how larger datasets can be published in a manner that makes them easily discoverable and facilitates integration as well as analysis.

One approach for addressing this problem is data portals, which enable organizations to upload and describe datasets using comprehensive metadata schemes. Similar to digital libraries, networks of such data portals can support the description, archiving, and discovery of datasets on the web. Recently, a rapid growth has been seen of data catalogues being made available on the web. The data catalogue registry datacatalogs.org lists 314 data catalogues worldwide. Examples for the increasing popularity of data catalogues are Open Government Data portals, data portals of international organizations and NGOs, as well as scientific data portals. In the public and governmental sector a few catalogues and data hubs can be used to find metadata or at least to find locations (links) to interesting media files such as publicdata.eu.

The public sector is centred around the activities of the citizens. Data acquisition in the public sector includes tax collection, crime statistics, water and air pollution data, weather reports, energy consumption, Internet business regulation: online gaming, online casinos, intellectual property protection, and others.

The open data initiatives of the governments (data.gov, data.gov.uk for open public data, or govdata.de) are recent examples of the increasing importance of public and non-profit data. There exist similar initiatives in many countries. Most data collected by public institutions and governments of these countries is in principle available for reuse. The W3C guidance on opening up government data (Bennett and Harvey 2009) suggests that data should be published as soon as available in the original raw format, then to enhance it with semantics and metadata. However, in many cases governments struggle to publish certain data, due to the fact that the data needs to be strictly non-personal and non-sensitive and compliant with data privacy and protection regulations. Many different sectors and players can benefit from this public data.

The following presents several case studies for implementing big data technologies in different areas of the public sector.

4.6.3.1 Tax Collection Area

One key area for big data solutions is for the tax revenue recovery of millions of dollars per year. The challenge for such an application is to develop a fast, accurate identity resolution and matching capability for a budget-constrained, limited-staffed state tax department in order to determine where to deploy scarce auditing resources and enhance tax collection efficiency. The main implementation highlights are:

- Rapidly identify exact and close matches
- Enable de-duplication from data entry errors
- High throughput and scalability handles growing data volumes
- Quickly and easily accommodate file format changes, and addition of new data sources

One solution is based on software developed by the Pervasive Software company: the Pervasive DataRush engine, the Pervasive DataMatcher, and the Pervasive Data Integrator. Pervasive DataRush provides simple constructs to:

- Create units of work (processes) that can each individually be made parallel.
- Tie processes together in a dataflow graph (assemblies), but then enable the reuse of complex assemblies as simple operators in other applications.
- Further tie operators into new, broader dataflow applications.
- Run a compiler that can traverse all sub-assemblies while executing customizers to automatically define parallel execution strategies based on then-current resources and/or more complex heuristics (this will only improve over time).

This is achieved using techniques such as fuzzy matching, record linking, and the ability to match any combination of fields in a dataset. Other key techniques include data integration and Extract, Transform, Load (ETL) processes that save and store all design metadata in an open XML-based design repository for easy metadata interchange and reuse. This enables fast implementation and deployment and reduces the cost of the entire integration process.

4.6.3.2 Energy Consumption

An article reports on the problems in the regulation of energy consumption. The main issue is that when energy is put on the distribution network it must be used at that time. Energy providers are experimenting with storage devices to assist with this problem, but they are nascent and expensive. Therefore the problem is tackled with smart metering devices.

When collecting data from smart metering devices, the first challenge is to store the large volume of data. For example, assuming that 1 million collection devices retrieve 5 kB of data per single collection, the potential data volume growth in a year can be up to 2920 TB.

The consequential challenges are to analyse this huge volume of data, cross-reference that data with customer information, network distribution, and capacity information by segment, local weather information, and energy spot market cost data.

Harnessing this data will allow the utilities to better understand the cost structure and strategic options within their network, which could include:

- Adding generation capacity versus purchasing energy off the spot market (e.g. renewables such as wind, solar, electric cars during off-peak hours)
- Investing in energy storage devices within the network to offset peak usage and reduce spot purchases and costs
- Provide incentives to individual consumers, or groups of consumers, to change energy consumption behaviours

One such approach from the Lavastorm company is a project that explores analytics problems with innovative companies such as FalbygdensEnergi AB (FEAB) and Sweco. To answer key questions, the Lavastorm Analytic Platform is utilized. The Lavastorm Analytics Engine is a self-service business analytics solution that empowers analysts to rapidly acquire, transform, analyse, and visualize data, and share key insights and trusted answers to business questions with non-technical managers and executives. The engine offers an integrated set of analytics capabilities that enables analysts to independently explore enterprise data from multiple data sources, create and share trusted analytic models, produce accurate forecasts, and uncover previously hidden insights in a single, highly visual and scalable environment.

4.6.4   Media and Entertainment

Media and entertainment is centred on knowledge included in the media files. With the significant growth of media files and associated metadata, due to evolution of the Internet and the social web, data acquisition in this sector has become a substantial challenge.

According to a Quantum report, managing and sharing content can be a challenge, especially for media and entertainment industries. With the need to access video footage, audio files, high-resolution images, and other content, a reliable and effective data sharing solution is required.

Commonly used tools in the media and entertainment sector include:

- Specialized file systems that are used as a high-performance alternative to NAS and network shares
- Specialized archiving technologies that allow the creation of a digital archive that reduces costs and protects content
- Specialized clients that enable both LAN-based applications and SAN-based applications to share a single content pool
- Various specialized storage solutions (for high-performance file sharing, cost-effective near-line storage, offline data retention, for high-speed primary storage)

Digital on-demand services have radically changed the importance of schedules for both consumers and broadcasters. The largest media corporations have already invested heavily in the technical infrastructure to support the storage and streaming of content. For example, the number of legal music download and streaming sites, and Internet radio services, has increased rapidly in the last few years—consumers have an almost-bewildering choice of options depending on what music genres, subscription options, devices, Digital rights management (DRM) they like. Over 391 million tracks were sold in Europe in 2012, and 75 million tracks played on online radio stations.

According to Eurostat, there has been a massive increase in household access to broadband in the years since 2006. Across the "EU27" (EU member states and six other countries in the European geographical area) broadband penetration was at around 30 % in 2006 but stood at 72 % in 2012. For households with high-speed broadband, media streaming is a very attractive way of consuming content. Equally, faster upload speeds mean that people can create their own videos for social media platforms.

There has been a huge shift away from mass, anonymized mainstream media, towards on-demand, personalized experiences. Large-scale shared consumer experiences such as major sporting events, reality shows, and soap operas are now popular. Consumers expect to be able to watch or listen to whatever they want, whenever they want.

Streaming services put control in the hands of users who choose when to consume their favourite shows, web content, or music. The largest media corporations have already invested heavily in the technical infrastructure to support the storage and streaming of content.

Media companies hold significant amounts of personal data, whether on customers, suppliers, content, or their own employees. Companies have responsibility not just for themselves as data controllers, but also their cloud service providers (data processors). Many large and small media organizations have already suffered catastrophic data breaches—two of the most high-profile casualties were Sony and LinkedIn. They incurred not only the costs of fixing their data breaches, but also fines from data protection bodies such as the Information Commissioner's Office (ICO) in the UK.

4.6.5   Finance and Insurance

Integrating large amounts of data with business intelligence systems for analysis plays an important role in financial and insurance sectors. Some of the major areas for acquiring data in these sectors are exchange markets, investments, banking, customer profiles, and behaviour.

According to McKinsey Global Institute Analysis, "Financial Services has the most to gain from big data". For ease of capturing and value potential, "financial players get the highest marks for value creation opportunities". Banks can add value by improving a number of products, e.g., customizing UX, improved targeting, adapting business models, reducing portfolio losses and capital costs, office efficiencies, and new value propositions. Some of the publicly available financial data are provided by international statistical agencies like Eurostat, World Bank, European Central Bank, International Monetary Fund, International Financial Corporation, Organization for Economic Co-operation and Development. While these data sources are not as time sensitive in comparison to exchange markets, they provide valuable complementary data.

Fraud detection is an important topic in finance. According to the Global Fraud Study 2014, a typical organization loses about 5 % of revenues each year to fraud. The banking and financial services sector has a great number of frauds. Approximately 30 % of fraud schemes were detected by tip off and up to 10 % by accident, but only up to 1 % by IT controls (ACFE 2014). Better and improved fraud detection methods rely on real-time analysis of big data (Sensmeier 2013). For more accurate and less intrusive fraud detection method, banks and financial service institutions are increasingly using algorithms that rely on real-time data about transactions. These technologies make use of large volumes of data being generated at a high velocity and from hybrid sources. Often, data from mobile sources and social data such as geographical information is used for prediction and detection (Krishnamurthy 2013). By using machine-learning algorithms, modern systems are able to detect fraud more reliably and faster (Sensmeier 2013). But there are limitations for such systems. Because financial services operate in a regulatory environment, the use of customer data is subject to privacy laws and regulations.

4.7 Conclusions

Data acquisition is an important process and enables the subsequent tools of the data value chain to do their work properly (e.g. data analysis tools). The state of the art regarding data acquisition tools showed that there are plenty of tools and protocols, including open-source solutions that support the process of data acquisition. Many of these tools have been developed and are operational within production environments or major players such as Facebook or Amazon.

Nonetheless there are many open challenges to successfully deploy effective big data solutions for data acquisition in the different sectors (see section "Future Requirements and Emerging Trends for Big Data Acquisition"). The main issue remains producing highly scalable robust solutions for today and researching next generation systems for the ever-increasing industrial requirements.

References

ACFE Association of Certified Fraud Examiners. (2014). *Report to the nations on occupational fraud and abuse*, Global fraud Study 2014. Available online at: http://www.acfe.com/rttn/docs/2014-report-to-nations.pdf

Bank of America et al. AMQP v1.0. (2011). Available online at http://www.amqp.org/sites/amqp.org/files/amqp.pdf

Bennett, D., & Harvey, A. (2009). *Publishing Open Government Data. W3C, Technical Report, 2009.* Available online at: http://www.w3.org/TR/gov-data/

Bradic, A. (2011) *S4: Distributed stream computing platform*, Slides@Software Scalability Belgrad. Available online at: http://de.slideshare.net/alekbr/s4-stream-computing-platform

Carzaniga, A., Rosenblum, D. S., & Wolf, A. L. (2000). Achieving scalability and expressiveness in an internet-scale event notification service. In *Proceedings of the Nineteenth Annual ACM Symposium on Principles of Distributed Computing*, pp 219–27.

Cugola, G., & Margara, A. (2012). Processing flows of information. *ACM Computing Surveys, 44* (3), 1–62. doi:10.1145/2187671.2187677.

Davenport, T. H. (2013). *At the Big Data Crossroads: turning towards a smarter travel experience.* Amadeus IT Group. Available online at: http://blogamadeus.com/wp-content/uploads/Amadeus-Big-Data-Report.pdf

DHL Solutions & Innovation Trend Research. (2013). *Big Data in Logistics. A DHL perspective on how to move beyond the hype.* Available online at: http://www.delivering-tomorrow.com/wp-content/uploads/2014/02/CSI_Studie_BIG_DATA_FINAL-ONLINE.pdf

Gabriel, G. (2012) Storm: The Hadoop of Realtime Stream Processing. *PyConUs.* Available online at http://pyvideo.org/video/675/storm-the-hadoop-of-realtime-stream-processing

Hasan, S., & Curry, E. (2014a). Approximate semantic matching of events for the internet of things. *ACM Transactions on Internet Technology* 14(1):1–23. doi:10.1145/2633684.

Hasan, S., & Curry, E. (2014b). Thematic event processing. In *Proceedings of the 15th International Middleware Conference on – Middleware '14*, ACM Press, New York, NY, pp. 109–120. doi:10.1145/2663165.2663335.

Hasan, S., & Curry, E. (2015). Thingsonomy: Tackling variety in internet of things events. *IEEE Internet Computing, 19*(2), 10–18. doi:10.1109/MIC.2015.26.

IBM. (2013). *Architecture of the IBM Big Data Platform.* Available online at http://public.dhe.ibm.com/software/data/sw-library/big-data/ibm-bigdata-platform-19-04-2012.pdf

Krishnamurthy, K. (2013). *Leveraging big data to revolutionize fraud detection, information week bank systems & technology.* Available online at: http://www.banktech.com/leveraging-big-data-to-revolutionize-fraud-detection/a/d-id/1296473?

Luckham, D. (2002). *The power of events: An introduction to complex event processing in distributed enterprise systems.* Boston, MA: Addison-Wesley Longman Publishing Co.

Madsen, K. (2012) *Storm: Comparison-introduction-concepts, slides*, March. Available online at: http://de.slideshare.net/KasperMadsen/storm-12024820

McAfee, A., & Brynjolfsson, E. (2012). Big Data: The management revolution. *Harvard Business Review, 90*(10), 60–66. Available online at http://automotivedigest.com/wp-content/uploads/2013/01/BigDataR1210Cf2.pdf.

Neumeyer, L. (2011). Apache S4: A distributed stream computing platform, *Slides Stanford Infolab*, Nov. Available online at: http://de.slideshare.net/leoneu/20111104-s4-overview

Neumeyer, L., Robbins, B., Nair, A., & Kesari, A. (2011). S4: Distributed stream computing platform, *KDCloud.* Available online at: http://www.4lunas.org/pub/2010-s4.pdf

Oracle. (2012). *Oracle information architecture: An architect's guide to big data.* http://www.oracle.com/technetwork/topics/entarch/articles/oea-big-data-guide-1522052.pdf

Sensmeier, L. (2013). How Big Data is revolutionizing Fraud Dedection in Financial Services. *Hortonworks Blog.* Available online at: http://hortonworks.com/blog/how-big-data-is-revolutionizing-fraud-detection-in-financial-services/

Vivisimo. (2012). Big Data White Paper.

Chapter 5
Big Data Analysis

John Domingue, Nelia Lasierra, Anna Fensel, Tim van Kasteren,
Martin Strohbach, and Andreas Thalhammer

5.1 Introduction

Data comes in many forms and one dimension to consider and compare differing data formats is the amount of *structure* contained therein. The more structure a dataset has the more amenable it will be to machine processing. At the extreme, semantic representations will enable machine reasoning. Big data analysis is the sub-area of big data concerned with adding structure to data to support decision-making as well as supporting domain-specific usage scenarios. This chapter outlines key insights, state of the art, emerging trends, future requirements, and sectorial case studies for data analysis.

The position of big data analysis within the overall big data value chain can be seen in Fig. 5.1. 'Raw' data which may or may not be structured and which will usually be composed of many different formats is transformed to be ready for data curation, data storage, and data usage. That is why without big data analysis most of the acquired data would be useless.

J. Domingue (✉)
STI International, Neubaugasse 10/15 A, 1070 Vienna, Austria

Knowledge Media Institute, The Open University, Walton Hall, Milton Keynes MK7 6AA, UK
e-mail: john.domingue@open.ac.uk

N. Lasierra • A. Fensel
University of Innsbruck, Technikerstraße 21a, 6020 Innsbruck, Austria
e-mail: nelia.lasierra@sti2.at; anna.fensel@sti2.at

T. van Kasteren • M. Strohbach
AGT International, Hilpertstr, 35, 64295 Darmstadt, Germany
e-mail: TKasteren@agtinternational.com; MStrohbach@agtinternational.com

A. Thalhammer
Institute for Applied Informatics and Formal Description Methods, Karlsruhe Institute of Technology, Kaiserstraße 89, 76133 Karlsruhe, Germany
e-mail: Thalhammer@kit.edu

© The Author(s) 2016   63
J.M. Cavanillas et al. (eds.), *New Horizons for a Data-Driven Economy*,
DOI 10.1007/978-3-319-21569-3_5

Big Data Value Chain

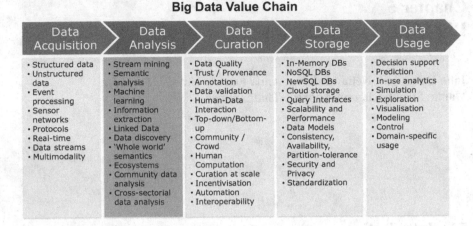

Data Acquisition	Data Analysis	Data Curation	Data Storage	Data Usage
• Structured data • Unstructured data • Event processing • Sensor networks • Protocols • Real-time • Data streams • Multimodality	• Stream mining • Semantic analysis • Machine learning • Information extraction • Linked Data • Data discovery • 'Whole world' semantics • Ecosystems • Community data analysis • Cross-sectorial data analysis	• Data Quality • Trust / Provenance • Annotation • Data validation • Human-Data Interaction • Top-down/Bottom-up • Community / Crowd • Human Computation • Curation at scale • Incentivisation • Automation • Interoperability	• In-Memory DBs • NoSQL DBs • NewSQL DBs • Cloud storage • Query Interfaces • Scalability and Performance • Data Models • Consistency, Availability, Partition-tolerance • Security and Privacy • Standardization	• Decision support • Prediction • In-use analytics • Simulation • Exploration • Visualisation • Modeling • Control • Domain-specific usage

Fig. 5.1 Data analysis in the big data value chain

The analysis found that the following generic techniques are either useful today or will be in the short to medium term: reasoning (including stream reasoning), semantic processing, data mining, machine learning, information extraction, and data discovery.

These generic areas are not new. What is new however are the challenges raised by the specific characteristics of big data related to the three Vs:

- **Volume**—places scalability at the centre of all processing. Large-scale reasoning, semantic processing, data mining, machine learning, and information extraction are required.
- **Velocity**—this challenge has resulted in the emergence of the areas of stream data processing, stream reasoning, and stream data mining to cope with high volumes of incoming raw data.
- **Variety**—may take the form of differing syntactic formats (e.g. spreadsheet vs. csv) or differing data schemas or differing meanings attached to the same syntactic forms (e.g. 'Paris' as a city or person). Semantic techniques, especially those related to Linked Data, have proven to be the most successful applied thus far although scalability issues remain to be addressed.

5.2 Key Insights for Big Data Analysis

Interviews with various stakeholders related to big data analysis have identified the following key insights. A full list of interviewees is given in Table 3.1.

Old Technologies Applied in a New Context Individual and combinations of old technologies being applied in the Big Data context. The difference is the scale (volume) and the amount of heterogeneity encountered (variety). Specifically, in

Table 3.1 Big data analysis interviewees

No.	First name	Last name	Organization	Role/Position
1	Sören	Auer	Leipzig	Professor
2	Ricardo	Baeza-Yates	Yahoo!	VP of Research
3	François	Bancilhon	Data Publica	CEO
4	Richard	Benjamins	Telefoncica	Director Biz Intel
5	Hjalmar	Gislason	datamarket.com	Founder
6	Alon	Halvey	Google	Research Scientist
7	Usman	Haque	Cosm (Pachube)	Director Urban Project Division
8	Steve	Harris	Garlik/Experian	CTO
9	Jim	Hendler	RPI	Professor
10	Alek	Kołcz	Twitter	Data Scientist
11	Prasanna	Lal Das	World Bank	Snr Prog. Officer, Head of Open Financial Data Program
12	Peter	Mika	Yahoo!	Researcher
13	Andreas	Ribbrock	Teradata GmbH	Team Lead Big Data Analytics and Senior Architect
14	Jeni	Tennison	Open Data Institute	Technical Director
15	Bill	Thompson	BBC	Head of Partner Development
16	Andraž	Tori	Zemanta	Owner and CTO
17	Frank	van Harmelen	Amsterdam	Professor
18	Marco	Viceconti	University of Sheffield and the VPH Institute	Professor and Director
19	Jim	Webber	Neo	Chief Scientist

the web context a focus is seen on large semantically based datasets such as Freebase and on the extraction of high-quality data from the web. Besides scale there is novelty in the fact that these technologies come together at the same time.

Stream Data Mining This is required to handle high volumes of stream data that will come from sensor networks or online activities from high numbers of users. This capability would allow organizations to provide highly adaptive and accurate personalization.

'Good' Data Discovery Recurrent questions asked by users and developers are: Where can we get the data about X? Where can we get information about Y? It is hard to find the data and found data is often out of date and not in the right format. Crawlers are needed to find big datasets, metadata for big data, meaningful links between related datasets, and a dataset ranking mechanism that performs as well as Page Rank does for web documents.

Dealing with Both Very Broad and Very Specific Data A near feature about information extraction from the web is that the web is about everything so coverage is broad. Pre-web the focus was on specific domains when building databases and knowledge bases. This can no longer be done in the context of the web. The whole notion of "conceptualizing the domain" is altered: Now the domain is everything in the world. On the positive side, the benefit is you get a lot of breadth, and the research challenge is how one can go deeper into a domain while maintaining the broad context.

Simplicity Leads to Adoptability Hadoop[1] succeeded because it is the easiest tool to use for developers, changing the game in the area of big data. It did not succeed because it was the best but because it was the easiest to use (along with HIVE).[2] Hadoop managed to successfully balance dealing with complexity (processing big data) and simplicity for developers. Conversely, semantic technologies are often hard to use. Hjalmar Gislason, one of our interviewees advocates the need for the "democratisation of semantic technologies".

Ecosystems Built around Collections of Tools Have a Significant Impact These are often driven by large companies where a technology is created to solve an internal problem and then is given away. Apache Cassandra[3] is an example of this initially developed by Facebook to power their inbox search feature until 2010. The ecosystem around Hadoop is perhaps the best known.

Communities and Big Data Will Be Involved in New and Interesting Relationships Communities will be engaged with big data in all stages of the value chain and in a variety of ways. In particular, communities will be involved intimately in data collection, improving data accuracy and data usage. Big data will also enhance community engagement in society in general.

Cross-sectorial Uses of Big Data Will Open Up New Business Opportunities The retail section of future requirements and emerging trends describes an example for this. O2 UK together with Telefónica Digital has recently launched a service that maps and repurposes mobile data for the retail industry. This service allows retailers to plan where to site retail outlets based upon the daily movement of potential customers. This service highlights the importance of internal big data (in this case mobile records) that is later combined with external data sources (geographical and preference data) to generate new types of business. In general aggregating data across organizations and across sectors will enhance the competitiveness of European industry.

The biggest challenge for most industries is now to incorporate big data technologies in their processes and infrastructures. Many companies identify the need for doing big data analysis, but do not have the resources for setting up an infrastructure for analysing and maintaining the analytics pipeline (Benjamins). Increasing the simplicity of the technology will aid the adoption rate. On top of this a large body of domain knowledge has to be built up within each industry on how

---

[1] http://hadoop.apache.org/

[2] https://hive.apache.org/

[3] http://cassandra.apache.org/

data can be used: What is valuable to extract and what output can be used in daily operations.

The costs of implementing big data analytics are a business barrier for big data technology adoption. Anonymity, privacy, and data protection are cross-sectorial requirements highlighted for big data technologies. Additional information can be found in the final analysis of sector's requisites (Zillner et al. 2014). Examples of some sectorial case studies can be found in Sect. 5.5.

5.3 Big Data Analysis State of the Art

Industry is today applying large-scale machine learning and other algorithms for the analysis of huge datasets, in combination with complex event processing and stream processing for real-time analytics. It was also found that the current trends on Linked Data, semantic technologies, and large-scale reasoning are some of the topics highlighted by the interviewed experts in relation to the main research challenges and main technological requirements for big data.

This section presents a state-of-the-art review regarding big data analysis and published literature, outlining a variety of topics ranging from working efficiently with data to large-scale data management.

5.3.1 Large-Scale: Reasoning, Benchmarking, and Machine Learning

The size and heterogeneity of the web precludes performing full reasoning and requires new technological solutions to satisfy the requested inference capabilities. This requested feature has also been extended to machine-learning technologies and these technologies are required in order to extract useful information from huge amounts of data. Specifically, François Bancilhon mentioned in his interview how machine learning is important for topic detection and document classification at Data Publica. Then, Ricardo Baeza-Yates highlighted in his interview the need for standards in big data computation in order to allow big data providers to compare their systems.

5.3.1.1 Large-Scale Reasoning

The promise of reasoning as promoted within the context of the semantic web does not currently match the requirements of big data due to scalability issues. Reasoning is defined by certain principles, such as soundness and completeness, which are far from the practical world and the characteristics of the web, where data is often contradictory, incomplete, and of an overwhelming size. Moreover, there exists a gap between reasoning at web scale and the more tailored reasoning over simplified subsets of first-order logic, due to the fact that many aspects are assumed, which differ from reality (e.g. small set of axioms and facts, completeness and correctness of inference rules).

State-of-the-art approaches (Fensel 2007) propose a combination of reasoning and information retrieval methods (based on search techniques), to overcome the problems of web scale reasoning. Incomplete and approximate reasoning was highlighted by Frank van Harmelen as an important topic in his interview.

Querying and reasoning over structured data can be supported by semantic models automatically built from word co-occurrence patterns from large text collections (distributional semantic models) (Turney and Pantel 2010). Distributional semantic models provide a complementary layer of meaning for structured data, which can be used to support semantic approximation for querying and reasoning over heterogeneous data (Novacek et al. 2011; Freitas et al. 2013; Freitas and Curry 2014).

The combination of logic-based reasoning with information retrieval is one of the key aspects to these approaches and also machine-learning techniques, which provide a trade-off between the full-fledged aspects of reasoning and the practicality of these in the web context. When the topic of scalability arises, storage systems play an important role as well, especially the indexing techniques and retrieval strategies. The trade-off between online (backward) reasoning and offline (forward) reasoning was mentioned by Frank van Harmelen in his interview. Peter Mika outlined as well the importance of efficient indexing techniques in his interview.

Under the topic of large-scale systems, LarKC (Fensel et al. 2008) is a flagship project. LarKC[4] was an EU FP7 Large-Scale Integrating Project and the aim of it was to deal with large scalable reasoning systems and techniques using semantic technologies.

5.3.1.2 Benchmarking for Large-Scale Repositories

Benchmarking is nascent for the area of large-scale semantic data processing, and in fact currently they are only now being produced. Particularly, the Linked Data Benchmark Council (LDBC) project[5] aims to "create a suite of benchmarks for large-scale graph and RDF (Resource Description Framework) data management as well as establish an independent authority for developing benchmarks". A part of the suite of benchmarks created in LDBC is the benchmarking and testing of data integration and reasoning functionalities as supported by RDF systems. These benchmarks are focused on testing: (1) instance matching and Extract, Transform and Load that play a critical role in *data integration*; and (2) the *reasoning*

---

[4] LarKC Homepage, http://www.larkc.eu, last visited 3/03/2015.
[5] LDBC Homepage, http://www.ldbc.eu/, last visited 3/05/2015.

capabilities of existing RDF engines. Both topics are very important in practice, and they have both been largely ignored by existing benchmarks for Linked Data processing. In creating such benchmarks LDBC analyses various available scenarios to identify those that can best showcase the data integration and reasoning functionalities of RDF engines. Based on these scenarios, the limitations of existing RDF systems are identified in order to gather a set of requirements for RDF data integration and reasoning benchmarks. For instance, it is well known that existing systems do not perform well in the presence of non-standard reasoning rules (e.g. advanced reasoning that considers negation and aggregation). Moreover, existing reasoners perform inference by materializing the closure of the dataset (using backward or forward chaining). However, this approach might not be applicable when application-specific reasoning rules are provided and hence it is likely that improving the state of the art will imply support for hybrid reasoning strategies involving both backward and forward chaining, and query rewriting (i.e. incorporating the ruleset in the query).

5.3.1.3   Large-Scale Machine Learning

Machine-learning algorithms use data to automatically learn how to perform tasks such as prediction, classification, and anomaly detection. Most machine-learning algorithms have been designed to run efficiently on a single processor or core. Developments in multi-core architectures and grid computing have led to an increasing need for machine learning to take advantage of the availability of multiple processing units. Many programming interfaces and languages dedicated to parallel programming exist such as Orca MPI or OpenACC, which are useful for general purpose parallel programming. However, it is not always obvious how existing machine-learning algorithms can be implemented in a parallelized manner. There is a large body of research on distributed learning and data mining (Bhaduri et al. 2011), which encompasses machine-learning algorithms that have been designed specifically for distributed computing purposes.

Rather than creating specific parallel versions of algorithms, more generalized approaches involve frameworks for programming machine learning on multiple processing units. One approach is to use a high-level abstraction that significantly simplifies the design and implementation of a restricted class of parallel algorithms. In particular the MapReduce abstraction has been successfully applied to a broad range of machine-learning applications. Chu et al. (2007) show that any algorithm fitting the statistical query model can be written in a certain summation form, which can be easily implemented in a MapReduce fashion and achieves a near linear speed-up with the number of processing units used. They show that this applies to a variety of learning algorithms (Chu et al. 2007). The implementations shown in the paper led to the first version of the MapReduce machine learning library Mahout.

Low et al. (2010) explain how the MapReduce paradigm restricts users to using overly simple modelling assumptions to ensure there are no computational dependencies in processing the data. They propose the Graphlab abstraction that insulates users from the complexities of parallel programming (i.e. data races, deadlocks), while maintaining the ability to express complex computational dependencies using a data graph.

The programming languages, toolkits, and frameworks discussed allow many different configurations for carrying out large-scale machine learning. The ideal configuration to use is application dependent, since different applications will have different sets of requirements. However, one of the most popular frameworks used in recent years is that of Apache Hadoop, which is an open-source and free implementation of the MapReduce paradigm discussed above. Andraž Tori, one of our interviewees, identifies the simplicity of Hadoop and MapReduce as the main driver of its success. He explains that a Hadoop implementation can be outperformed in terms of computation time by, for example, an implementation using OpenMP, but Hadoop won in terms of popularity because it was easy to use.

The parallelized computation efforts described above make it possible to process large amounts of data. Besides the obvious application of applying existing methods to increasingly large datasets, the increase in computation power also leads to novel large-scale machine-learning approaches. One example is the recent work from Le et al. (2011) in which a dataset of ten million images was used to teach a face detector using only unlabelled data. Using the resulting features in an object recognition task resulted in a performance increase of 70 % over the state of the art (Le et al. 2011). Utilizing large amounts of data to overcome the need for labelled training data could become an important trend. By using only unlabelled data, one of the biggest bottlenecks to the broad adoption of machine learning is bypassed. The use of unsupervised learning methods has its limitations though and it remains to be seen if similar techniques can also be applied in other application domains.

5.3.2   Stream Data Processing

Stream data mining was highlighted as a promising area of research by Ricardo Baeza-Yates in his interview. This technique relates to the technological capabilities needed to deal with data streams with high volume and high velocity, coming from sensors networks, or other online activities where a high number of users are involved.

5.3.2.1   RDF Data Stream Pattern Matching

Motivated by the huge amount of structured and unstructured data available on the web as continuous streams, streaming processing techniques using web technologies have recently appeared. In order to process data streams on the web, it is important to cope with openness and heterogeneity. A core issue of data stream processing systems is to process data in a certain time frame and to be able to query for patterns. Additional desired features include static data support that will not change over time and can be used to enhance dynamic data. Temporal operators and time-based windows are also typically found in these systems, used to combine several RDF graphs with time dependencies. Some major developments in this area are C-SPARQL (Barbieri et al. 2010) ETALIS (Anicic et al. 2011), and SPARKWAVE (Komazec et al. 2012).

C-SPARQL is a language based on SPARQL (SPARQL Protocol and RDF Query Language) and extended with definitions for streams and time windows. Incoming triples are first materialized based on RDFS and then fed into the evaluation system. C-SPARQL does not provide true continuous pattern evaluation, due to the usage of RDF snapshots, which are evaluated periodically. However C-SPARQL's strength is in situations with significant amounts of static knowledge, which need to be combined with dynamic incoming data streams.

ETALIS is an event-processing system on top of SPARQL. As the pattern language component of SPARQL was extended with event-processing syntax, the pattern language is called EP-SPARQL. The supported features are temporal operators, out-of-order evaluation, aggregate functions, several garbage collection modes, and different consumption strategies.

SPARKWAVE provides continuous pattern matching over schema-enhanced RDF data streams. In contrast to the C-SPARQL and EP-SPARQL, SPARKWAVE is fixed regarding the utilized schema and does not support temporal operators or aggregate functions. The benefit of having a fixed schema and no complex reasoning is that the system can optimize and pre-calculate at the initialization phase the used pattern structure in memory, thus leading to high throughput when processing incoming RDF data.

5.3.2.2 Complex Event Processing

One insight of the interviews is that big data stream technologies can be classified according to (1) complex event-processing engines, and (2) highly scalable stream processing infrastructures. Complex event-processing engines focus on language and execution aspects of the business logic, while stream processing infrastructure provides the communication framework for processing asynchronous messages on a large scale.

Complex event processing (CEP) describes a set of technologies that are able to process events "in stream", i.e. in contrast to batch processing where data is inserted into a database and polled at regular intervals for further analysis. The advantages of CEP systems are their capability to process potentially large amounts of events in real time. The name complex event processing is due to the fact that simple events, e.g. from sensors or other operational data, can be correlated and processed generating more complex events. Such processing may happen in multiple steps, eventually generating an event of interest triggering a human operator or some business intelligence.

As Voisard and Ziekow point out, an event-based system "encompasses a large range of functionalities on various technological levels (e.g., language, execution, or communication)" (Voisard and Ziekow 2011). They provide a comprehensive survey that aids the understanding and classification of complex event-processing systems.

For big data stream analytics, it is a key capability that complex event-processing systems are able to scale out in order to process all incoming events in a timely fashion as required by the application domain. For instance the smart meter data of a large utility company may generate millions or even billions of events per second that may be analysed in order to maintain the operational reliability of the electricity grid. Additionally, coping with the semantic heterogeneity behind multiple data sources in a distributed event generation environment is a fundamental capability for big data scenarios. There are emerging automated semantic event-matching approaches (Hasan and Curry 2014) that target scenarios with heterogeneous event types. Examples of complex event-processing engines include the SAP Sybase Event Stream Processor, IBM InfoSphere Stream,[6] and ruleCore[7] to name just a few.

5.3.3 Use of Linked Data and Semantic Approaches to Big Data Analysis

According to Tim Berners-Lee and his colleagues (Bizer et al. 2009), "Linked Data is simply about using the Web to create typed links between data from different sources". Linked data refers to machine-readable data, linked to other datasets and published on the web according to a set of best practices built upon web technologies such as HTTP (Hypertext Transfer Protocol), RDF, and URIs (Uniform Resource Identifier).[8] Semantic technologies such as SPARQL, OWL, and RDF allow one to manage and deal with these. Building on the principles of Linked Data, a dataspace groups all relevant data sources into a unified shared repository (Heath and Bizer 2011). Hence, a dataspace offers a good solution to cover the heterogeneity of the web (large-scale integration) and deal with broad and specific types of data.

Linked data and semantic approaches to big data analysis have been highlighted by a number of interviewees including Sören Auer, François Bancilhon, Richard Benjamins, Hjalmar Gislason, Frank van Harmelen, Jim Hendler, Peter Mika, and Jeni Tennison. These technologies were highlighted as they address important challenges related to big data including efficient indexing, entities extraction and classification, and search over data found on the web.

---

[6] http://www-01.ibm.com/software/data/infosphere/streams, last visited 25/02/2014.

[7] RuleCore Homepage, http://www.rulecore.com/, last visited 13/02/2014.

[8] http://www.w3.org/standards/semanticweb/data

5.3.3.1   Entity Summarization

To the best of our knowledge, entity summarization was first mentioned in Cheng et al. (2008). The authors present Falcons which "... provides keyword-based search for Semantic Web entities". Next to features such as concept search, ontology and class recommendation, and keyword-based search, the system also describes a popularity-based approach for ranking statements an entity is involved in. Further, the authors also describe the use of the MMR technique (Carbonell and Jade 1998) to re-rank statements to account for diversity. In a later publication (Cheng 2011), entity summarization requires "... ranking data elements according to how much they help identify the underlying entity". This statement accounts for the most common definition of entity summarization: the ranking and selection of statements that identify or define an entity.

In Singhal (2012), the author introduces Google's Knowledge Graph. Next to entity disambiguation ("Find the right thing") and exploratory search ("Go deeper and broader"), the knowledge graph also provides summaries of entities, i.e. "get the best summary". Although not explained in detail, Google points out that they use the search queries of users for the summaries.[9] For the knowledge graph summaries, Google uses a unique dataset of millions of daily queries in order to provide concise summaries. Such a dataset is, however, not available to all content providers.

As an alternative, Thalhammer et al. (2012b) suggest using the background data of consumption patterns of items in order to derive summaries of movie entities. The idea stems from the field of recommender systems where item neighbourhoods can be derived by the co-consumption behaviour of users (i.e. through analysing the user-item matrix).

A first attempt to standardize the evaluation of entity summarization is provided by Thalhammer et al. (2012a). The authors suggest a game with a purpose (GWAP) in order to produce a reference dataset for entity summarization. In the description, the game is designed as a quiz about movie entities from Freebase. In their evaluation, the authors compare the summaries produced by Singhal (2012) and the summaries of Thalhammer et al. (2012b).

5.3.3.2   Data Abstraction Based on Ontologies and Communication Workflow Patterns

The problem of communication on the web, as well as beyond it, is not trivial, considering the rapidly increasing amount of channels (content sharing platforms, social media and networks, variety of devices) and audiences to be reached. To address this problem, technological solutions are being developed such as the one presented by Fensel et al. (2012) based on semantics. Data management via

---

[9] http://insidesearch.blogspot.co.at/2012/05/introducing-knowledge-graph-things-not.html

semantic techniques can certainly facilitate the communication abstraction and also increase automation and reduce the overall effort.

Inspired by the work of Mika (2005), eCommunication workflow patterns (e.g. typical query response patterns for online communication), which are usable and adaptable to the needs of the social web, can be defined (Stavrakantonakis 2013a, b). Moreover, there is an interest in social network interactions (Fuentes-Fernandez et al. 2012). The authors of the last work coined "social property" as a network of activity theory concepts with a given meaning. Social properties are considered as "patterns that represent knowledge grounded in the social sciences about motivation, behaviour, organization, interaction" (Fuentes-Fernandez et al. 2012). The results of this research direction combined with the generic work flow patterns described in Van Der Aalst et al. (2003) are highly relevant with the materialization of the communication patterns. The design of the patterns is also related to the collaboration among the various agents as described in Dorn et al. (2012) in the scope of the social workflows. Aside from the social properties, the work described in Rowe et al. (2011) introduces the usage of ontologies in the modelling of the user's activities in conjunction with content and sentiment. In the context of the approach, modelling behaviours enable one to identify patterns in communication problems and understand the dynamics in discussions in order to discover ways of engaging more efficiently with the public in the social web. Several researchers have proposed the realization of context-aware work flows (Wieland et al. 2007) and social collaboration processes (Liptchinsky et al. 2012), which are related to the idea of modelling the related actors and artefacts in order to enable adaptiveness and personalization in the communication patterns infrastructure.

5.4 Future Requirements and Emerging Trends for Big Data Analysis

5.4.1 Future Requirements for Big Data Analysis

5.4.1.1 Next Generation Big Data Technologies

Current big data technologies such as Apache Hadoop have matured well over the years into platforms that are widely used within various industries. Several of our interviewees have identified future requirements that the next generation of big data technologies should address:

- *Handle the growth of the Internet* (Baeza-Yates)—as more users come online big data technologies will need to handle larger volumes of data.
- *Process complex data types* (Baeza-Yates)—data such as graph data and possible other types of more complicated data structures need to be easily processed by big data technologies.

- *Real-time processing* (Baeza-Yates)—big data processing was initially carried out in batches of historical data. In recent years, stream processing systems such as Apache Storm have become available and enable new application capabilities. This technology is relatively new and needs to be developed further.
- *Concurrent data processing* (Baeza-Yates)—being able to process large quantities of data concurrently is very useful for handling large volumes of users at the same time.
- *Dynamic orchestration of services in multi-server and cloud contexts* (Tori)—most platforms today are not suitable for the cloud and keeping data consistent between different data stores is challenging.
- *Efficient indexing* (Mika)—indexing is fundamental to the online lookup of data and is therefore essential in managing large collections of documents and their associated metadata.

5.4.1.2 Simplicity

The simplicity of big data technologies refers to how easily developers are able to acquire the technology and use it in their specific environment. Simplicity is important as it leads to a higher adoptability of the technology (Baeza-Yates). Several of our interviewees have identified the critical role of simplicity in current and future big data technologies.

The success of Hadoop and MapReduce is mainly due to its simplicity (Tori). Other big data platforms are available that can be considered as more powerful, but have a smaller community of users because their adoption is harder to manage. Similarly, Linked Data technologies, for example, RDF SPARQL, have been reported as overly complex and containing too steep a learning curve (Gislason). Such technologies seem to be over-designed and overly complicated—suitable only for use by specialists.

Overall, there exist some very mature technologies for big data analytics, but these technologies need to be industrialized and made accessible to everyone (Benjamins). People outside of the core big data community should become aware of the possibilities of big data, to obtain wider support (Das). Big data is moving beyond the Internet industry and into other non-technical industries. An easy-to-use big data platform will help in the adoption of big data technologies by non-technical industries.

5.4.1.3 Data

An obvious key ingredient to big data solutions is the data itself. Our interviewees identified several issues that need to be addressed.

Large companies such as Google and Facebook are working on big data and they will focus their energies on certain areas and not on others. EU involvement could support a big data ecosystem that encourages a variety of small, medium, and large players, where regulation is effective and data is open (Thompson).

In doing so, it is important to realize that there is far more data out there than most people realize and this data could help us to make better decisions to identify threats and see opportunities. A lot of the data needed already exists, but it is not easy to find and use this data. Solving this issue will help businesses, policy makers, and end users in decision-making. Just making more of the world's data available at people's fingertips will have a substantial effect overall. There will be a significant impact for this item in emergency situations such as earthquakes and other natural disasters (Halevy) (Gislason).

However, making data available in pre-Internet companies and organizations is difficult. In Internet companies, there was a focus on using collected data for analytic purposes from the very beginning. Pre-Internet companies face issues with privacy, legal as well as technical, and process restrictions in repurposing the data. This holds even for data that is already available in digital form, such as call detail records for telephone companies. The processes around storing and using such data were never set up with the intention of using the data for analytics (Benjamins).

Open data initiatives can play an important role in helping companies and organizations get the most out of data. Once a dataset has gone through the necessary validations with regard to privacy and other restrictions, it can be reused for multiple purposes by different companies and organizations and can serve as a platform for new business (Hendler). It is therefore important to invest in processes and legislation that support open data initiatives. Achieving an acceptable policy seems challenging. As one of our interviewees' notes, there is an inherent tension between open data and privacy—it may not be possible to truly have both (Tori). But also closed datasets should be addressed. A lot of valuable information, such as cell phone data, is currently closed and owned by the telecom industry. The EU should look into ways to make such data available to the big data community, while taking into account the associated cost of making the data open. Also, how the telecom industry can benefit from making data open while taking into account any privacy concerns (Das). The web can also serve as an important data source. Companies such as Data Publica rely on snapshots of the web (which are 60–70 terabytes) to support online services. Freely available versions of web snapshots are available, but more up-to-date versions are preferred. These do not necessarily have to be free, but cheap. The big web players such as Google and Facebook have access to data related to searches and social networks that have important societal benefit. For example, dynamic social processes such as the spread of disease or rates of employment are often most accurately tracked by Google searches. The EU may want to prioritize the European equivalent of these analogous to the way the Chinese have cloned Google and Twitter (Bancilhon).

As open datasets become more common, it becomes increasingly challenging to discover the dataset needed. One prediction estimates that by 2015 there will be over 10 million datasets available on the web (Hendler). Valuable lessons can be learnt from how document discovery evolved on the web. Early on there was a registry—all of the web could be listed on a single web page; then users and organizations had their own lists; then lists of lists. Later Google came to dominate by providing metrics on how documents link to other documents. If an analogy is drawn to the data area, it is currently in the registry era. It needs crawlers to find big datasets, good dataset metadata on contents, links between related datasets, and a relevant dataset ranking mechanism (analogous to page rank). A discovery mechanism that can only work with good quality data will drive data owners to publish their data in a better way, analogous to the way that search engine optimization (SEO) drives the quality of the current web (Tennison).

5.4.1.4 Languages

Most of the big data technologies originated in the United States and therefore have primarily been created with the English language in mind. The majority of the Internet companies serve an international audience and many of their services are eventually translated into other languages. Most services are initially launched in English though and are only translated once they gain popularity. Furthermore, certain language-related technology optimizations (e.g. search engine optimizations) might work well for English, but not for other languages. In any case, languages need to be taken into account at the very beginning, especially in Europe, and should play an import role in creating big data architectures (Halevy).

5.4.2 Emerging Paradigms for Big Data Analysis

5.4.2.1 Communities

The rise of the Internet makes it possible to quickly reach a large audience and grow communities around topics of interest. Big data is starting to play an increasingly important role in that development. Our interviewees have mentioned this emerging paradigm on a number of occasions.

- **Rise of data journalists:** Who are able to write interesting articles based on data uploaded by the public to infrastructure such as the Google Fusion Tables. The Guardian journalist Simon Rogers won the Best UK Internet Journalist award for his work[10] based on this platform. A feature of journalistic take-up is that data blogs typically have a high dissemination impact (Halevy).
- **Community engagement in local political issues:** Two months after the school massacre in Connecticut[11] local citizens started looking at data related to gun

---

[10] http://www.oii.ox.ac.uk/news/?id=576

[11] http://en.wikipedia.org/wiki/Sandy_Hook_Elementary_School_shooting

permit applications in two locations and exposed this on a map.[12] This led to a huge discussion on the related issues (Halevy).

- **Engagement through community data collection and analysis:** The company COSM (formerly Pachube) has been driving a number of community-led efforts. The main idea behind these is that the way data is collected introduces specific slants on how the data can be interpreted and used. Getting communities involved has various benefits: the number of data collection points can be dramatically increased; communities will often create bespoke tools for the particular situation and to handle any problems in data collection; and citizen engagement is increased significantly.

   In one example, the company crowd sourced real-time radiation monitoring in Japan following the problem with reactors in Fukushima. There are now hundreds of radiation-related feeds from Japan on Pachube, monitoring conditions in real time and underpinning more than half a dozen incredibly valuable applications built by people around the world. These combine "official" data, "unofficial" data, and also real-time networked Geiger counter measurements contributed by concerned citizens (Haque).

- **Community engagement to educate and improve scientific involvement:** Communities can be very useful in collecting data. Participation in such projects allows the public to obtain a better understanding of certain scientific activities and therefore helps to educate people in these topics. That increase in understanding will further stimulate the development and appreciation of upcoming technologies and therefore result in a positive self-reinforcing cycle (Thompson).

- **Crowdsourcing to improve data accuracy:** Through crowdsourcing the precision of released UK Government data on the location of bus stops was dramatically increased (Hendler).

These efforts play well into the future requirements section on data. A community-driven approach to creating datasets will stimulate data quality and lead to even more datasets becoming publicly available.

5.4.2.2 Academic Impact

The availability of large datasets will impact academia (Tori) for two reasons. First, public datasets can be used by researchers from disciplines such as social science and economics to support their research activities. Second, a platform for sharing academic dataset will stimulate reuse and improve the quality of studied datasets. Sharing datasets also allows others to add additional annotations to the data, which is generally an expensive task.

[12] http://tinyurl.com/kvlv64l

Next to seeing big data technologies affecting other scientific disciplines, other scientific disciplines are being brought into computer science. Big Internet companies like Yahoo are hiring social scientists, including psychologists and economists, to increase the effectiveness of analysis tools (Mika). More generally speaking, as the analysis of data in various domains continues an increasing need for domain experts arises.

5.5 Sectors Case Studies for Big Data Analysis

This section describes several big data case studies outlining the stakeholders involved, where applicable, and the relationship between technology and the overall sector context. In particular, it covers the following sectors: the public sector, health sector, retail sector, logistics, and finally the financial sector. In many cases the descriptions are supported by the interviews that were conducted, and add further evidence of the enormous potential for big data.

5.5.1 Public Sector

Smart cities generate data from sensors, social media, citizen mobile reports, and municipality data such as tax data. Big data technologies are used to process the large datasets that cities generate to impact society and businesses (Baeza-Yates). This section discusses how big data technologies utilize smart city data to provide applications in traffic and emergency response.

5.5.1.1 Traffic

Smart city sensors that can be used for applications in traffic include induction loop detection, traffic cameras, and license plate recognition cameras (LPR). Induction loops can be used for counting traffic volume at a particular point. Traffic cameras can be combined with video analytic solutions to automatically extract statistics such as the number of cars passing and average speed of traffic. License plate recognition is a camera-based technology that can track license plates throughout the city using multiple cameras. All these forms of sensing help in estimating traffic statistics, although they vary in degree of accuracy and reliability.

Deploying such technology on a city-wide level results in large datasets that can be used for day-to-day operations, as well as applications such as anomaly detection and support in planning operations. In terms of big data analysis, the most interesting application is anomaly detection. The system can learn from historical data what is considered to be normal traffic behaviour for the time of the day and the day of the week and detect deviations from the norm to inform operators in a command

and control centre of possible incidents that require attention (Thajchayapong and Barria 2010). Such an approach becomes even more powerful when combining the data from multiple locations using data fusion to get more accurate estimates of the traffic statistics that allow the detection of more complex scenarios.

5.5.1.2 Emergency Response

Cities equipped with sensors can benefit during emergencies by obtaining actionable information that can aid in decision-making. Of particular interest is the possibility to use social media analytics during emergency response. Social media networks provide a constant flow of information that can be used as a low-cost global sensing network for gathering near real-time information about an emergency. Although people post a lot of unrelated information on social media networks, any information about the emergency can be very valuable to emergency response teams. Accurate data can help in obtaining the correct situational awareness picture of the emergency, consequently enabling a more efficient and faster response that can reduce casualties and overall damage (Van Kasteren et al. 2014).

Social media analytics is used to process large volumes of social media posts, such as tweets, to identify clusters of posts centred around the same topic (high content overlap), same area (for posts that contain GPS tags), and around the same time. Clusters of posts are the result of high social network activity in an area. This can be an indication of a landmark (e.g. the Eiffel tower), a planned event (e.g. a sports match), or an unplanned event (e.g. an accident). Landmark sites have high tweet volumes throughout the year and can therefore be easily filtered out. For the remaining events machine-learning classifiers are used to automatically recognize which clusters are of interest for an emergency response operator (Walther and Kaisser 2013).

Using social media data for purposes that it was not originally intended for is just a single example of the significant impact that can occur when the right data is presented to the right people at the right time. Some of our interviewees explained that there is far more data out there than most people realize and this data could help us to make better decisions to identify threats and see opportunities. A lot of the data needed already exists, but it is not always easy to find and use this data (Gislason) (Halevy).

5.5.2   Health

The previous section spoke of the data that is repurposed in applications that differ strongly from the original application that generated the data. Such cases also exist in the healthcare sector. For example, dynamic social processes such as the spread of disease can be accurately tracked by Google searches (Bancilhon) and call detail records from Telefonica have been used to measure the impact of epidemic alerts on human mobility (Frias-Martinez et al. 2012).

Big data analytics can be used to solve significant problems globally. The EU is therefore advised to produce solutions that solve global problems rather than focus solely on problems that affect the EU (Thompson). An example is the construction of clean water wells in Africa. The decision on where to locate wells is based on spreadsheets that may contain data that has not been updated for 2 years. Given that new wells can stop working after 6 months this causes unnecessary hardship and more (Halevy). Technology might offer a solution, either by allowing citizen reports or by inferring the use of wells from other data sources.

The impact in local healthcare is expected to be enormous. Various technological projects are aimed at realizing home healthcare, where at the very least people are able to record health-related measurements in their own homes. When combined with projects such as smart home solutions, it is possible to create rich datasets consisting of both health data and all kinds of behavioural data that can help tremendously in establishing a diagnosis, as well as getting a better understanding of disease onset and development.

There are, however, very strong privacy concerns in the healthcare sector that are likely to block many of these developments until they are resolved. Professor Marco Viceconti from the University of Sheffield outlined in his interview how certain recent developments such as k-anonymity can help protect privacy. A dataset has k-anonymity protection if the information for each individual in the dataset cannot be distinguished from at least $k-1$ individuals whose information also appears in the dataset (Sweeney 2002). Professor Viceconti envisions a future system that can automatically protect privacy by serving as a membrane between a patient and an institute using the data, where data can flow both ways and all the necessary privacy policies and anonymization processes are executed automatically in between. Such a system would benefit both the patient, by providing a more accurate diagnosis, and the institute, by allowing research using real-world data.

5.5.3 Retail

O2 UK together with Telefónica Digital recently launched a service called Telefónica Dynamic Insights. This service takes all UK mobile data, including location, timing of calls and texts, and also when customers move from one mast to another. This data is mapped and repurposed for the retail industry. The data is first anonymized, aggregated, and placed in the cloud. Then analytics are run which calculate where people live, where they work, and where they are in transit. If this data is then combined with anonymized customer relationship management (CRM) data, it can determine the type of people who pass by a particular shop at a specific time-point. It can also calculate the type of people who visit a shop, where they live, and where else they shop (termed catchment).

This service supports real-estate management for retailers and contrasts well with present practice. What retailers do today is that they hire students with clickers just to count the number of people who walk past the shop, leading to data that is far less detailed. The service is thus solving an existing problem in a new way. The service can be run on a weekly or daily basis and provides completely new business opportunities. In addition to retail the service could be run in other sectors, for example, within the public sector it could analyse who walks past an underground station. Combining mobile data with preference data could open up new propositions for existing and new industries. This example is a taste of what is to come, the sum of which will definitely improve the competitiveness of European industry (Benjamins).

5.5.4 Logistics

In the United States, 45 % of fruits and vegetables reach the plate of the consumer and in Europe 55 % reaches the plate. Close to half of what is produced is lost. This is a big data problem: collecting data over the overall supply chain, analysing systems related to the distributed food, and identifying leaks and bottlenecks in the process would have an enormous impact. If implemented there would be a better handle on prices and a fairer distribution of wealth among all the agents in the food supply chain. Big data technology is important and so is access to the right data and data sources (Bancilhon).

5.5.5 Finance

The World Bank is an organization that aims to end extreme poverty and promote shared prosperity. Their operations strongly rely on accurate information and they are using big data analytics to support their activities. They plan to organize competitions to drive the analytic capabilities to obtain an alternative measure for poverty and to detect financial corruption and fraud at an early stage.

In terms of poverty, an important driver is to get more real-time estimates of poverty, which make it possible to make better short-term decisions. Three examples of information sources that are currently being explored to obtain the information needed are: (1) Twitter data can be used to look for indicators of social and economic well-being; (2) poverty maps can be merged with alternative data sources such as satellite imagery to identify paved roads and support decisions in micro financing; and (3) web data can be scraped to get pricing data from supermarkets that help in poverty estimation.

Corruption is currently dealt with reactively, meaning actions are only taken once corruption has been reported to the Worldbank. On average only 30 % of the money is retrieved in corruption cases when dealt with reactively. Big data analytics will make more proactive approaches feasible, resulting in higher returns. This requires creating richer profiles of the companies and the partners that they work with. Data mining this in-depth profile data together with other data sources would make it possible to identify risk-related patterns.

Overall, it is important for the Worldbank to be able to make decisions, move resources, and make investment options available as fast as possible through the right people at the right time. Doing this based on limited sets of old data is not sustainable in the medium to long term. Accurate and real-time information is critical during the decision-making process. For example, if there is a recession looming, one needs to respond before it happens. If a natural disaster occurs, making decisions based on data available directly from the field rather than a 3-year-old dataset is highly desirable (Das).

5.6 Conclusions

Big data analysis is a fundamental part of the big data value chain. We can caricature this process using an old English saying that what this component achieves is to "turn lead into gold". Large volumes of data which may be heterogeneous with respect to encoding mechanism, format, structure, underlying semantics, provenance, reliability, and quality is turned into data which is usable.

As such big data analysis comprises a collection of techniques and tools some of which are old mechanisms recast to face the challenges raised by the three Vs (e.g. large-scale reasoning) and some of which are new (e.g. stream reasoning).

The insights gathered on big data analysis presented here are based upon 19 interviews with leading players in large and small industries and visionaries from Europe and the United States. The choice was taken to interview senior staff members who have a leadership role in large multinationals, technologists who work at the coalface with big data, founders and CEOs of the new breed of SMEs that are already producing value from big data, and academic leaders in the field.

From our analysis it is clear that delivering highly scalable data analysis and reasoning mechanisms that are associated with an ecosystem of accessible and usable tools will produce significant benefits for Europe. The impact will be both economic and social. Current business models and process will be radically transformed for economic and social benefit. The case study of reducing the amount of food wasted within the global food production life cycle is a prime example of this type of potential for big data.

To summarize, big data analysis is an essential part of the overall big data value chain which promises to have significant economic and social impact in the European Union in the near to medium term. Without big data analysis the rest of the chain does not function. As one of our interviewees stated in a recent discussion on the relationship between data analysis and data analytics:

Analytics without data is worthless. Analytics with bad data is dangerous. Analytics with good data is the objective.[13]

We wholeheartedly agree.

References

Anicic, D., Fodor, P., Rudolph, S., Stühmer, R., Stojanovic, N., & Studer, R. (2011). ETALIS: Rule-based reasoning in event processing. In: *Reasoning in event-based distributed systems* (pp. 99–124). Studies in Computational Intelligence, vol. 347, Springer.

Baeza-Yates, R. (2013). Yahoo. *BIG Project Interviews Series.*

Bancilhon, F. (2013). Data Publica. *BIG Project Interviews Series.*

Barbieri, D. F., Braga, D., Ceri, S., Della Valle, E., & Grossniklaus, M. (2010). C-SPARQL: A continuous query language for RDF data streams. *International Journal of Semantic Computing, 4*(1), 3–125.

Benjamins, R. (2013). Telefonica. *BIG Project Interviews Series.*

Bhaduri, K., Das, K., Liu, K., Kargupta, H., & Ryan, J. (2011). *Distributed data mining bibliography.* http://www.cs.uinbc.edu/-hillol/DDM-BIB.

Bizer, C., Heath, T., & Berners-Lee, T. (2009). Linked data-the story so far. *International Journal on Semantic Web and Information Systems, 5*(3), 1–22.

Carbonell, J., & Jade, G. (1998). The use of MMR, diversity-based reranking for reodering documents and producing summaries. *SIGIR* (pp. 335–336). Melbourne, Australia: ACM.

Cheng, G. T. (2011). RELIN: Relatedness and informativeness-based centrality for entity summarization. In L. W. In: Aroyo, *ISCW, Part I. LNCS vol. 7031* (pp. 114–129). Heidelberg: Springer.

Cheng, G., Ge, W., & Qu, Y. (2008). Falcons: Searching and browsing entities on the semantic web. In *Proceedings of the 17th International Conference on World Wide Web* (pp. 1101–1102). Beijing, China: ACM.

Chu, C., Kim, S. K., Lin, Y.-A., Yu, Y., Bradski, G., Ng, A. Y., et al. (2007). Map-reduce for machine learning on multicore. *Advances in Neural Information Processing Systems, 19*, 281.

Das, P. L. (2013).Worldbank. *BIG Project Interviews Series.*

Dorn, C., Taylor, R., & Dustdar, S. (2012). Flexible social workflows: Collaborations as human architecture. *IEEE Internet Computing, 16*(2), 72–77.

Fensel, D. (2007). Unifying reasoning and search to web scale. *IEEE Internet Computing, 11*(2), 94–96.

---

[13] Richard Benjamins in a personal communication.

Fensel, A., Fensel, D., Leiter, B., Thalhammer, A. (2012). Effective and efficient online communication: The channel model. In *Proceedings of International Conference on Data Technologies and Applications (DATA '12)* (pp. 209–215), SciTePress, Rome, Italy, 25–27 July, 2012.

Fensel, D., van Harmelen, F., Andersson, B., Brennan, P., Cunningham, H., Della Valle, E., et al. (2008). *Towards LarKC: A platform for web-scale reasoning.* Los Alamitos, CA: IEEE Computer Society Press.

Freitas, A., & Curry, E. (2014). Natural language queries over heterogeneous linked data graphs: A distributional-compositional semantics approach. In *Proceedings of the 19th International Conference on Intelligent User Interfaces (IUI)*, Haifa.

Freitas, A., da Silva, J. C. P, O'Riain, S., & Curry, E. (2013). Distributional relational networks. In *Proceedings AAAI Fall Symposium*, Arlington.

Frias-Martinez, V., Rubio, A., & Frias-Martinez, E. (2012). Measuring the impact of epidemic alerts on human mobility (Vol. 12). Pervasive Urban Applications – PURBA.

Fuentes-Fernandez, R., Gomez-Sanz, J. J., & Pavon, J. (2012). User-oriented analysis of interactions in online social networks. *IEEE Intelligent Systems, 27*, 18–25.

Gislason, H. (2013). Datamarket.com. *BIG Project Interviews Series*.

Halevy, A. (2013). Google. *BIG Project Interviews Series*.

Haque, U. (2013). Cosm. *BIG Project Interviews Series*.

Hasan, S., & Curry, E. (2014). Approximate semantic matching of events for the internet of things. *ACM Trans Internet Technology, 14*, 1–23. doi:10.1145/2633684.

Heath, T., & Bizer, C. (2011) Linked data: Evolving the web into a global data space (1st edn). In *Synthesis Lectures on the Semantic Web: Theory and Technology*, 1(1): 1–136. Morgan & Claypool.

Hendler, J. (2012). RPI. *BIG Project Interviews Series*.

Komazec, S., Cerri, D., & Fensel, D. (2012). Sparkwave: Continuous schema-enhanced pattern matching over RDF data streams. In *Proceedings of the 6th ACM International Conference on Distributed Event-Based Systems* (DEBS '12) (pp. 58–68). New York, NY: ACM. doi:10.1145/2335484.2335491.

Le, Q. V, Monga, R., Devin, M., Chen, K., Corrado, G. S., Dean, J., et al. (2011). Building high-level features using large-scale unsupervised learning. *International Conference on Machine Learning*.

Liptchinsky, V., Khazankin, R., Truong, H., & Dustdar, S. (2012). A novel approach to mod eling context-aware and social collaboration processes. In: *Advanced Information Systems Engineering*, (pp. 565–580), Springer.

Low, Y., Gonzalez, J., Kyrola, A., Bickson, D., Guestrin, C., & Hellerstein, J. M. (2010). GraphLab: A new framework for parallel machine learning. *The 26th Conference on Uncertainty in Artificial Intelligence (UAI 2010)*, Catalina Island, California, July 8–11.

Mika, P. (2005). Ontologies are us: A unified model of social networks and semantics. (pp. 522–536). *The Semantic Web - ISWC*.

Mika, P. (2013). Yahoo. *BIG Project Interviews Series*.

Novacek, V., Handschuh, S., & Decker S., (2011). Getting the meaning right: A complementary distributional layer for the web semantics. *International Semantic Web Conference* (1):504–519.

Rowe, M., Angeletou, S., & Alani, H. (2011). Predicting discussions on the social semantic web (pp. 405–420). *The Semantic Web: Research and Applications*.

Singhal, A. (2012). Introducing the knowledge graph. Retrieved from googleblog: http://googleblog.blogspot.com/2012/05/introducing-knowledge-graphthings

Stavrakantonakis, I. (2013a). Personal data and user modelling in tourism. In: *Information and Communication Technologies in Tourism 2013* (pp 507–518).

Stavrakantonakis, I. (2013b). Semantically assisted Workflow Patterns for the Social Web. In *Proceedings of the 10th Extended Semantic Web Conference ESWC 2013 PhD Symposium track*. (pp. 692–696).

Sweeney, L. (2002). k-anonymity: A model for protecting privacy. *International Journal of Uncertainty, Fuzziness and Knowledge-Based Systems, 10*(5), 557–570.

Tennison, J. (2013). Open data institute. *BIG Project Interviews Series.*

Thajchayapong, S., & Barria, J. A. (2010). Anomaly detection using microscopic traffic variables on freeway segments. *Transportation Research Board of the National Academies*, 10-2393.

Thalhammer, A., Knuth, M., & Sack, H. (2012a). Evaluating entity summarization using a game-based ground truth. *International Semantic Web Conference (2)* (pp. 350–361). Boston: Springer.

Thalhammer, A., Toma, I., Roa-Valverde, A. J., Fensel, D. (2012b). Leveraging usage data for linked data movie entity summarization. In *Proceedings of the 2nd International Workshop on Usage Analysis and the Web of Data.* Lyon, France: USEWOD co-located with WWW.

Thompson, B. (2013). BBC. *BIG Project Interviews Series.*

Tori, A. (2013). *BIG Project Interviews Series.*

Turney, P. D., & Pantel, P. (2010). From frequency to meaning: vector space models of semantics. *Journal of Artificial Intelligence Research, 37*(1), 141–188.

Van Der Aalst, W., Ter Hofstede, A., Kiepuszewski, B., & Barros, A. (2003). Workflow patterns. *Distributed and Parallel Databases, 14*(1), 5–51.

Van Kasteren, T., Ulrich, B., Srinivasan, V., & Niessen, M. (2014). Analyzing tweets to aid situational awareness. In *36th European Conference on Information Retrieval.*

Voisard, A., & Ziekow, H. (2011). ARCHITECT: A layered framework for classifying technologies of event-based systems. *Information Systems, 36*(6), 937–957. doi:10.1016/j.is.2011.03. 006.

Walther, M., & Kaisser, M. (2013). Geo-spatial event detection in the twitter stream. *Advances in Information Retrieval*, 356–367.

Wieland, M., Kopp, O., Nicklas, D., & Leymann, F (2007). Towards context-aware workflows. *In: CAiSE.* pp. 11–15.

Zillner, S., Rusitschka, S., Munne, R., Lippell, H., Vilela, F. L., Hussain, K., et al. (2014). D2.3.2. Final version of the sectorial requisites. Public deliverable of the EU-Project BIG (318062; ICT-2011.4.4).

Chapter 6
Big Data Curation

André Freitas and Edward Curry

6.1 Introduction

One of the key principles of data analytics is that the quality of the analysis is dependent on the quality of the information analysed. Gartner estimates that more than 25 % of critical data in the world's top companies is flawed (Gartner 2007). Data quality issues can have a significant impact on business operations, especially when it comes to the decision-making processes within organizations (Curry et al. 2010).

The emergence of new platforms for decentralized data creation such as sensor and mobile platforms, the increasing availability of open data on the web (Howe et al. 2008), added to the increase in the number of data sources inside organizations (Brodie and Liu 2010), brings an unprecedented volume of data to be managed. In addition to the data volume, data consumers in the big data era need to cope with data variety, as a consequence of the decentralized data generation, where data is created under different contexts and requirements. Consuming third-party data comes with the intrinsic cost of repurposing, adapting, and ensuring data quality for its new context.

Data curation provides the *methodological* and *technological* data management support to address *data quality issues* maximizing the usability of the data. According to Cragin et al. (2007), "Data curation is the active and on-going management of data through its lifecycle of interest and usefulness; ... curation activities enable data discovery and retrieval, maintain quality, add value, and provide for re-use over time". Data curation emerges as a key data management process where there is an increase in the number of data sources and platforms for data generation.

A. Freitas (✉) • E. Curry
Insight Centre for Data Analytics, National University of Ireland Galway, Lower Dangan, Galway, Ireland
e-mail: andre.freitas@insight-centre.org; edward.curry@insight-centre.org

© The Author(s) 2016
J.M. Cavanillas et al. (eds.), *New Horizons for a Data-Driven Economy*,
DOI 10.1007/978-3-319-21569-3_6

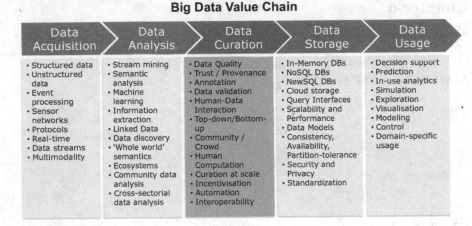

Fig. 6.1 Data curation in the big data value chain

The position of big data curation within the overall big data value chain can be seen in Fig. 6.1. Data curation processes can be categorized into different activities such as *content creation, selection, classification, transformation, validation,* and *preservation.* The selection and implementation of a data curation process is a multi-dimensional problem, depending on the interaction between the *incentives, economics, standards,* and *technological* dimensions. This chapter analyses the data dynamics in which data curation is inserted, investigates future requirements and emerging trends for data curation, and briefly describes exemplar case studies.

6.2 Key Insights for Big Data Curation

eScience and eGovernment are the innovators while biomedical and media companies are the early adopters. The demand for data interoperability and reuse on eScience and the demand for effective transparency through open data in the context of eGovernment are driving data curation practices and technologies. These sectors play the roles of visionaries and innovators in the data curation technology adoption lifecycle. From the industry perspective, organizations in the biomedical space, such as pharmaceutical companies, play the role of early adopters, driven by the need to reduce the time-to-market and lower the costs of the drug discovery pipelines. Media companies are also early adopters, driven by the need to organize large unstructured data collections, to reduce the time to create new products, repurposing existing data, and to improve accessibility and visibility of information artefacts.

The core impact of data curation is to enable more complete and high-quality data-driven models for knowledge organizations. More complete models support a larger number of answers through data analysis. Data curation practices and technologies will progressively become more present in contemporary data management environments, facilitating organizations and individuals to reuse third-party data in different contexts, reducing the barriers for generating content with high data quality. The ability to efficiently *cope with data quality and heterogeneity issues at scale* will support data consumers on the creation of more sophisticated models, *highly impacting the productivity of knowledge-driven organizations*.

Data curation depends on the creation of an incentives structure. As an emergent activity, there is still vagueness and poor understanding on the role of data curation inside the big data lifecycle. In many projects the data curation costs are not estimated or are underestimated. The individuation and recognition of the *data curator role* and of data curation activities depends on realistic estimates of the costs associated with producing high-quality data. Funding boards can support this process by requiring an explicit estimate of the data curation resources on public funded projects with data deliverables and by requiring the publication of high-quality data. Additionally, the improvement of the tracking and recognition of data and infrastructure as a first-class scientific contribution is also a fundamental driver for methodological and technological innovation for data curation and for maximizing the return of investment and reusability of scientific outcomes. Similar recognition is needed within the enterprise context.

Emerging economic models can support the creation of data curation infrastructures. *Pre-competitive* and *public-private partnerships* are emerging economic models that can support the creation of data curation infrastructures and the generation of high-quality data. Additionally, the justification for the investment on data curation infrastructures can be supported by a better quantification of the economic impact of high-quality data.

Curation at scale depends on the interplay between automated curation platforms and collaborative approaches leveraging large pools of data curators. Improving the scale of data curation depends on reducing the cost per data curation task and increasing the pool of data curators. Hybrid human-algorithmic data curation approaches and the ability to compute the uncertainty of the results of algorithmic approaches are fundamental for improving the automation of complex curation tasks. Approaches for automating data curation tasks such as curation by demonstration can provide a significant increase in the scale of automation. Crowdsourcing also plays an important role in scaling-up data curation, allowing access to large pools of potential data curators. The improvement of crowdsourcing platforms towards more specialized, automated, reliable, and sophisticated platforms and the improvement of the integration between organizational systems and crowdsourcing platforms represent an exploitable opportunity in this area.

The improvement of human–data interaction is fundamental for data curation. Improving approaches in which *curators can interact with data* impacts curation efficiency and reduces the barriers for domain experts and casual users to curate data. Examples of key functionalities in human–data interaction include natural language interfaces, semantic search, data summarization and visualization, and intuitive data transformation interfaces.

Data-level trust and permission management mechanisms are fundamental to supporting data management infrastructures for data curation. Provenance management is a key enabler of trust for data curation, providing curators the context to select data that they consider trustworthy and allowing them to capture their data curation decisions. Data curation also depends on mechanisms to assign permissions and digital rights at the data level.

Data and conceptual model standards strongly reduce the data curation effort. A standards-based data representation reduces syntactic and semantic heterogeneity, improving interoperability. Data model and conceptual model standards (e.g. vocabularies and ontologies) are available in different domains. However, their adoption is still growing.

There is the need for improved theoretical models and methodologies for data curation activities. Theoretical models and methodologies for data curation should concentrate on supporting the transportability of the generated data under different contexts, facilitating the detection of data quality issues and improving the automation of data curation workflows.

Better integration between algorithmic and human computation approaches is required. The growing maturity of data-driven statistical techniques in fields such as Natural Language Processing (NLP) and Machine Learning (ML) is shifting their use from academic to industry environments. Many NLP and ML tools have uncertainty levels associated with their results and are dependent on training over large datasets. Better integration between statistical approaches and human computation platforms is essential to allow the continuous evolution of statistical models by the provision of additional training data and also to minimize the impact of errors in the results.

6.3 Emerging Requirements for Big Data Curation

Many big data scenarios are associated with reusing and integrating data from a number of different data sources. This perception is recurrent across data curation experts and practitioners and it is reflected in statements such as: "a lot of big data is a lot of small data put together", "most of big data is not a uniform big block", "each data piece is very small and very messy, and a lot of what we are doing there is dealing with that variety" (Data Curation Interview: Paul Groth 2014).

Reusing data that was generated under different requirements comes with the intrinsic price of coping with *data quality* and *data heterogeneity* issues. Data can be incomplete or may need to be transformed in order to be rendered useful. Kevin Ashley, director of Digital Curation Centre, summarizes the mind-set behind data reuse: "... [it is] when you simply use what is there, which may not be what you would have collected in an ideal world, but you may be able to derive some useful knowledge from it" (Kevin Ashley 2014). In this context, data shifts from a resource that is tailored from the start to a certain purpose, to a raw material that will need to be repurposed in different contexts in order to satisfy a particular requirement.

In this scenario *data curation* emerges as a key data management activity. Data curation can be seen from a *data generation* perspective (curation at source), where data is represented in a way that maximizes its quality in different contexts. Experts emphasize this as an important aspect of data curation: From the *data science* aspect, methodologies are needed to describe data so that it is actually reusable outside its original context (Kevin Ashley 2014). This points to the demand to investigate approaches which maximize the quality of the data in multiple contexts with a minimum curation effort: "we are going to curate data in a way that makes it usable ideally for any question that somebody might try to ask the data" (Kevin Ashley 2014). Data curation can also be done at the *data consumption* side where data resources are selected and transformed to fit a set of requirements from the data consumption side.

Data curation activities are heavily dependent on the challenges of scale, in particular data variety, that emerges in the big data context. James Cheney, research fellow at the University of Edinburgh, observes *"Big Data seems to be about addressing challenges of scale, in terms of how fast things are coming out at you versus how much it costs to get value out of what you already have"*. Coping with data variety can be costly even for smaller amounts of data: *"you can have Big Data challenges not only because you have Petabytes of data but because data is incredibly varied and therefore consumes a lot of resources to make sense of it"*.

While in the big data context the expression *data variety* is used to express the data management trend of coping with data from different sources, the concepts of *data quality* (Wang and Strong 1996; Knight and Burn 2005) and *data heterogeneity* (Sheth 1999) have been well established in the database literature and provide a precise ground for understanding the tasks involved in data curation.

Despite the fact that data heterogeneity and data quality were concerns already present before the big data scale era (Wang and Strong 1996; Knight and Burn 2005), they become more prevalent in data management tasks with the *growth in the number of data sources*. This growth brought the need to define *principles* and *scalable approaches* for *coping with data quality issues*. It also brought data curation from a niche activity, restricted to a small community of scientists and analysts with high data quality standards, to a routine data management activity, which will progressively become more present within the average data management environment.

The growth in the number of data sources and the scope of databases defines a *long tail of data variety* (Curry and Freitas 2014). Traditional relational data management

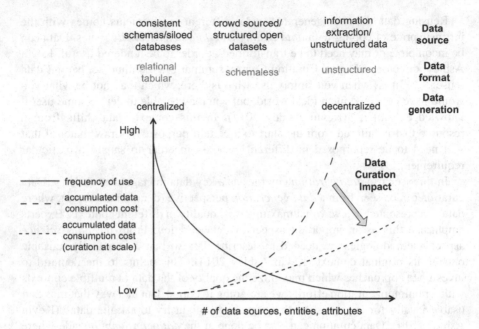

Fig. 6.2 The long tail of data curation and the scalability of data curation activities

environments were focused on data that mapped to frequent business processes and were regular enough to fit into a relational model. The *long tail of data variety* (see Fig. 6.2) expresses the shift towards expanding the data coverage of data management environments towards data that is less frequently used, more decentralized, and less structured. The long tail allows data consumers to have a more comprehensive model of their domain that can be *searched*, *queried*, *analysed*, and *navigated*.

The central challenge of data curation models in the big data era is to deal with the long tail of data and to *improve data curation scalability*, by *reducing the cost* of data curation and *increasing the number of data curators* (Fig. 6.2), allowing data curation tasks to be addressed under limited time constraints.

Scaling up data curation is a multidisciplinary problem that requires the development of *economic models*, *social structures*, *incentive models*, and *standards*, in coordination with *technological solutions*. The connection between these dimensions and data curation scalability is at the centre of the future requirements and future trends for data curation.

6.4   Social and Economic Impact of Big Data Curation

The growing availability of data brings the opportunity for people to use them to inform their decision-making process, allowing data consumers to have a more complete *data-supported* picture of reality. While some big data use cases are based on large scale but small schema and regular datasets, other decision-making scenarios depend on the integration of complex, multi-domain, and distributed data. The extraction of value from information coming from different data sources is dependent on the feasibility of integrating and analysing these data sources.

Decision-makers can range from molecular biologists to government officials or marketing professionals and they have in common the need to discover patterns and create models to address a specific task or a business objective. These models need to be supported by quantitative evidence. While unstructured data (such as text resources) can support the decision-making process, *structured data provides users greater analytical capabilities, by defining a structured representation associated with the data*. This allows users to compare, aggregate, and transform data. With more data available, the barrier of data acquisition is reduced. However, to extract value from it, data needs to be systematically processed, transformed, and repurposed into a new context.

Areas that depend on the representation of multi-domain and complex models are leading the data curation technology lifecycle. eScience projects lead the experimentation and innovation on data curation and are driven by the need to create infrastructures for improving reproducibility and large-scale multidisciplinary collaboration in science. They play the role of *visionaries* in the *technology adoption lifecycle for advanced data curation technologies* (see Use Cases Section).

In the *early adopter* phase of the lifecycle, the biomedical industry (in particular, the pharmaceutical industry) is the main player, *driven by the need of reducing the costs and time-to-market of drug discovery pipelines* (Data Curation Interview: Nick Lynch 2014). For pharmaceutical companies data curation is central to organizational data management and third-party data integration. Following a different set of requirements, *the media industry is also positioned as early adopters*, using data curation pipelines to classify large collections of unstructured resources (text and video), improving the data consumption experience through better accessibility and maximizing its reuse under different contexts. *The third major early adopters are governments*, targeting transparency through open data projects (Shadbolt et al. 2012).

Data curation enables the extraction of value from data, and it is a capability that is required for areas that are dependent on complex and/or continuous data integration and classification. The improvement of data curation tools and methods directly provides greater efficiency of the knowledge discovery process, maximizes return of investment per data item through reuse, and improves organizational transparency.

6.5   Big Data Curation State of the Art

This section concentrates on briefly describing the technologies that are widely adopted and established approaches for data curation, while the next section focuses on the future requirements and emerging approaches.

Master Data Management is composed of the processes and tools that support a single point of reference for the data of an organization, an authoritative data source. Master Data Management (MDM) tools can be used to remove duplicates and standardize data syntax, as an authoritative source of master data. MDM focuses on ensuring that an organization does not use multiple and inconsistent versions of the same master data in different parts of its systems. Processes in MDM include source identification, data transformation, normalization, rule administration, error detection and correction, data consolidation, data storage, classification, taxonomy services, schema mapping, and semantic enrichment.

Master data management is highly associated with data quality. According to Morris and Vesset (2005), the three main objectives of MDM are:

1. Synchronizing master data across multiple instances of an enterprise application
2. Coordinating master data management during an application migration
3. Compliance and performance management reporting across multiple analytic systems

Rowe (2012) provides an analysis on how 163 organizations implement MDM and its business impact.

Curation at Source *Sheer curation or curation-at-source* is an approach to curate data where lightweight curation activities are integrated into the normal workflow of those creating and managing data and other digital assets (Curry et al. 2010). Sheer curation activities can include lightweight categorization and normalization activities. An example would be vetting or "rating" the results of a categorization process performed by a curation algorithm. Sheer curation activities can also be composed with other curation activities, allowing more immediate access to curated data while also ensuring the quality control that is only possible with an expert curation team.

The following are the high-level objectives of sheer curation described by Hedges and Blanke (2012):

• Avoid data deposit by integrating with normal workflow tools
• Capture provenance information of the workflow
• Seamless interfacing with data curation infrastructure

Crowdsourcing Data curation can be a resource-intensive and complex task, which can easily exceed the capacity of a single individual. Most non-trivial data curation efforts are dependent of a collective data curation set-up, where participants are able to share the costs, risks, and technical challenges. Depending on the domain, data scale, and type of curation activity, data curation efforts can utilize relevant communities through invitation or crowds (Doan et al. 2011). These systems can range from systems with a large and open participation base such as Wikipedia (crowds-based) to systems or more restricted domain expert groups, such as Chemspider.

The notion of "wisdom of crowds" advocates that potentially large groups of non-experts can solve complex problems usually considered to be solvable only by experts (Surowiecki 2005). Crowdsourcing has emerged as a powerful paradigm for outsourcing work at scale with the help of online people (Doan et al. 2011). Crowdsourcing has been fuelled by the rapid development in web technologies that facilitate contributions from millions of online users. The underlying assumption is that large-scale and cheap labour can be acquired on the web. The effectiveness of crowdsourcing has been demonstrated through websites like Wikipedia,[1] Amazon Mechanical Turk,[2] and Kaggle.[3] Wikipedia follows a volunteer crowdsourcing approach where the general public is asked to contribute to the encyclopaedia creation project for the benefit of everyone (Kittur et al. 2007). Amazon Mechanical Turk provides a labour market for crowdsourcing tasks against money (Ipeirotis 2010). Kaggle enables organization to publish problems to be solved through a competition between participants against a predefined reward. Although different in terms of incentive models, all these websites allow access to large numbers of workers, therefore, enabling their use as recruitment platforms for human computation (Law and von Ahn 2011).

General-purpose crowdsourcing service platforms such as CrowdFlower (CrowdFlower Whitepaper 2012) or Amazon Mechanical Turk (Ipeirotis 2010) allow projects to route tasks for a paid crowd. The user of the service is abstracted from the effort of gathering the crowd and offers its tasks for a price in a market of crowd-workers. Crowdsourcing service platforms provide a flexible model and can be used to address ad hoc small-scale data curation tasks (such as a simple classification of thousands of images for a research project), peak data curation volumes (e.g. mapping and translating data in an emergency response situation), or at regular curation volumes (e.g. continuous data curation for a company).

Collaboration spaces such as Wiki platforms and Content Management Systems (CMSs) allow users to collaboratively create and curate unstructured and structured data. While CMSs focuses on allowing smaller and more restricted groups to collaboratively edit and publish online content (such as News, blogs, and eCommerce platforms), Wikis have proven to scale to very large user bases. As of 2014, Wikipedia counted more than 4,000,000 articles and has a community with more than 130,000 active registered contributors.

---

[1] "Wikipedia" 2005. 12 Feb 2014. https://www.wikipedia.org/

[2] "Amazon Mechanical Turk" 2007. 12 Feb 2014. https://www.mturk.com/

[3] "Kaggle: Go from Big Data to Big Analytics" 2005. 12 Feb 2014. http://www.kaggle.com/

Wikipedia uses a wiki as its main system for content construction. Wikis were first proposed by Ward Cunningham in 1995 and allow users to edit contents and collaborate on the web more efficiently. MediaWiki, the wiki platform behind Wikipedia, is already widely used as a collaborative environment inside organizations. Important cases include Intellipedia, a deployment of the MediaWiki platform covering 16 U.S. Intelligence agencies, and Wiki Proteins, a collaborative environment for knowledge discovery and annotation (Mons et al. 2008).

Wikipedia relies on a simple but highly effective way to coordinate its curation process, and accounts and roles are in the base of this system. All users are allowed to edit Wikipedia contents. Administrators, however, have additional permissions in the system (Curry et al. 2010). Most of Wikis and CMS platforms target unstructured and semi-structured data content, allowing users to classify and interlink unstructured content.

6.5.1 Data Curation Platforms

- **Data Tamer:** This prototype aims to replace the current developer-centric extract-transform-load (ETL) process with automated data integration. The system uses a suit of algorithms to automatically map schemas and de-duplicate entities. However, human experts and crowds are leveraged to verify integration updates that are particularly difficult for algorithms.
- **ZenCrowd:** This system tries to address the problem of linking named entities in text with a knowledge base. ZenCrowd bridges the gap between automated and manual linking by improving the results of automated linking with humans. The prototype was demonstrated for linking named entities in news articles with entities in linked open data cloud.
- **CrowdDB:** This database system answers SQL queries that cannot be answered by a database management system or a search engine. As opposed to the exact operation in databases, CrowdDB allows fuzzy operations with the help of humans, for example, ranking items by relevance or comparing equivalence of images.
- **Qurk:** Although similar to CrowdDB, this system tries to improve costs and latency of human-powered sorts and joins. In this regard, Qurk applies techniques such as batching, filtering, and output agreement.
- **Wikipedia Bots:** Wikipedia runs scheduled algorithms to access quality of text articles, known as Bots. These bots also flag articles that require further review by experts. SuggestBot recommends flagged articles to a Wikipedia editor based on their profile.

6.6 Future Requirements and Emerging Trends for Big Data Curation

This section aims at providing a *roadmap* for data curation based on a *set of future requirements for data curation* and *emerging data curation approaches* for coping with the requirements. Both future requirements and the emerging approaches were collected by an extensive analysis of the state-of-the-art approaches.

6.6.1 Future Requirements for Big Data Curation

The list of future requirements was compiled by selecting and categorizing the most recurrent demands in a state-of-the-art survey and which emerged in domain expert interviews as a fundamental direction for the future of data curation. Each requirement is categorized according to the following attributes (Table 6.1):

- **Core Requirement Dimensions:** Consists of the main categories needed to address the requirement. The dimensions are *technical, social, incentive, methodological, standardization, economic,* and *policy.*
- **Impact-level:** Consists of the impact of the requirement for the data curation field. By its construction, only requirements above a certain impact threshold are listed. Possible values are medium, medium-high, high, very high.
- **Affected areas:** Lists the areas which are most impacted by the requirement. Possible values are science, government, industry sectors (financial, health, media and entertainment, telco, manufacturing), and environmental.
- **Priority:** Covers the level of priority that is associated with the requirement. Possible values are: short-term (<3 years), medium-term (3–7 years), and consolidation (>7 years).
- **Core Actors:** Covers the main actors that should be responsible for addressing the core requirement. Core actors are government, industry, academia, non-governmental organizations, and user communities.

6.6.2 Emerging Paradigms for Big Data Curation

In the state-of-the-art analysis, key social, technical, and methodological approaches emerged for addressing the future requirements. In this section, these emerging approaches are described as well as their coverage in relation to the category of requirements. Emerging approaches are defined as approaches that have a limited adoption. These approaches are summarized in Table 6.2.

Table. 6.1 Future requirements for data curation

Requirement category	Requirement	Core requirement dimension	Impact-level	Affected areas	Priority	Core actors
Incentives creation	Creation of incentives mechanisms for the maintenance and publication of curated datasets	Economic, social, policy	Very high	Science, government, environmental, financial, health	Short-term	Government
Economic models	Definition of models for the data economy	Economic, policy	Very high	All sectors	Short-term	Government, industry
Social engagement mechanisms	Understanding of social engagement mechanisms	Social, technical	Medium	Science, government, environmental	Long-term	Academia, NGOs, industry
Curation at scale	Reduction of the cost associated with the data curation task (scalability)	Technical, social, economic	Very high	All sectors	Medium-term	Academia, industry, user communities
Human-data interaction	Improvement of the human–data interaction aspects. Enabling domain experts and casual users to query, explore, transform, and curate data	Technical	Very high	All sectors	Long-term	Academia, industry
Trust	Inclusion of trustworthiness mechanisms in data curation	Technical	High	All sectors	Short-term	Academia, industry
Standardization and interoperability	Integration and interoperability between data curation platforms/standardization	Technical, social, policy, methodological	Very high	All sectors	Short-term	User communities, industry, academia
Curation models	Investigation of theoretical and domain-specific models for data curation	Technical, methodological	Medium-high	All sectors	Long-term	Academia
Unstructured-structured integration	Better integration between unstructured and structured data and tools	Technical	Medium	Science, media, health, financial, government	Long-term	Academia, industry

Table 6.2 Emerging approaches for addressing the future requirements

Requirement category	Emerging approach	Adoption/status	Exemplar use case
Incentives creation and social engagement mechanisms	Open and interoperable data policies	Early-stage/Limited adoption	Data.gov.uk
	Better recognition of the data curation role	Lacking adoption/ Despite the exemplar use cases, the data curator role is still not recognized	Chemspider, Wikipedia, Protein Data Bank
	Attribution and recognition of data and infrastructure contributions	Standards emerging/ Adoption missing	Altmetrics (Priem et al. 2010), ORCID
	Better understanding of social engagement mechanisms	Early-stage	GalaxyZoo (Forston et al. 2011), Foldit (Khatib et al. 2011)
Economic models	Pre-competitive partnerships	Seminal use cases	Pistoia Alliance (Barnes et al. 2009)
	Public–private partnerships	Seminal use cases	Geoconnections (Harper 2012)
	Quantification of the economic impact of data	Seminal use cases	Technopolis Group (2011) ("Data centres: their use, value and impact")
Curation at scale	Human computation and Crowdsourcing services	Industry-level adoption/ Services are available but there is space for market specialization	CrowdFlower, Amazon Mechanical Turk
	Evidence-based measurement models of uncertainty over data	Research stage	IBM Watson (Ferrucci et al. 2010)
	Programming by demonstration, induction of data transformation workflows	Research stage/Fundamental research areas are developed. Lack of applied research in a workflow and data curation context	Tuchinda et al. (2007), Tuchinda (2011)
	Curation at source	Existing use cases both in academic projects and industry	The New York Times
	General-purpose data curation pipelines	Available Infrastructure	OpenRefine, Karma, Scientific Workflow management systems
	Algorithmic validation/annotation	Early stage	Wikipedia, Chemspider
Human–data interaction	Focus ease of interactivity	Seminal tools available	OpenRefine
	Natural language interfaces, schema-agnostic queries	Research stage	IBM Watson (Ferrucci et al. 2010), Treo (Freitas and Curry 2014)

(continued)

Table 6.2 (continued)

Requirement category	Emerging approach	Adoption/status	Exemplar use case
Trust	Capture of data curation decisions	Standards are in place, instrumentation of applications needed	OpenPhacts
	Fine-grained permission management models and tools	Coarse-grained infrastructure available.	Qin and Atluri (2003), Ryutov et al. (2009), Kirrane et al. (2013), Rodriguez-Doncel et al. (2013)
Standardization and interoperability	Standardized data model	Standards are available	RDF(S), OWL
	Reuse of vocabularies	Technologies for supporting vocabulary reuse is needed	Linked Open Data Web (Berners-Lee 2009)
	Better integration and communication between tools	Low	N/A
	Interoperable provenance representation	Standard in place/Standard adoption is still missing	W3C PROV
Curation models	Definition of minimum information models for data curation	Low adoption	MIRIAM (Laibe and Le Novère 2007)
	Nanopublications	Emerging concept	Mons and Velterop (2009), Groth et al. (2010)
	Investigation of theoretical principles and domain-specific models for data curation	Emerging concept	Pearl and Bareinboim (2011)
Unstructured-structured integration	NLP Pipelines	Tools are available, adoption is low	IBM Watson (Ferrucci et al. 2010)
	Entity recognition and alignment	Tools are available, adoption is low	DBpedia Spotlight (Mendes et al. 2011), IBM Watson (Ferrucci et al. 2010)

6.6.2.1 Social Incentives and Engagement Mechanisms

Open and Interoperable Data Policies The demand for high-quality data is the driver of the evolution of data curation platforms. The effort to produce and maintain high-quality data needs to be supported by a solid incentives system, which at this point in time is not fully in place. High-quality open data can be one of the drivers of societal impact by supporting more efficient and reproducible science (eScience) (Norris 2007), and more transparent and efficient governments (eGovernment) (Shadbolt et al. 2012). These sectors play the *innovators* and *early adopters* roles in the *data curation technology adoption lifecycle* and are the main drivers of innovation in data curation tools and methods. Funding agencies and policy makers have a fundamental role in this process and should direct and support scientists and government officials to make available their data products in an interoperable way. The demand for high quality and interoperable data can drive the evolution of data curation methods and tools.

Attribution and Recognition of Data and Infrastructure Contributions From the eScience perspective, scientific and editorial committees of prestigious publications have the power to change the methodological landscape of scholarly communication, by emphasizing reproducibility in the review process and by requiring publications to be supported by high quality data when applicable. From the scientist perspective, publications supported by data can facilitate reproducibility and avoid rework and as a consequence increase scientific efficiency and impact of the scientific products. Additionally, as data becomes more prevalent as a primary scientific product it becomes a citable resource. Mechanisms such as ORCID (Thomson Reuters Technical Report 2013) and Altmetrics (Priem et al. 2010) already provide the supporting elements for identifying, attributing, and quantifying impact outputs such as datasets and software. The recognition of data and software contributions in academic evaluation systems is a critical element for driving high-quality scientific data.

Better Recognition of the Data Curation Role The cost of publishing high-quality data is not negligible and should be an explicit part of the estimated costs of a project with a data deliverable. Additionally, the methodological impact of data curation requires that the role of the data curator be better recognized across the scientific and publishing pipeline. Some organizations and projects have already a clear definition of different data curator roles. Examples are Wikipedia, New York Times (Curry et al. 2010), and Chemspider (Pence and Williams 2010). The reader is referred to the case studies to understand the activities of different data curation roles.

Better Understanding of Social Engagement Mechanisms While part of the incentives structure may be triggered by public policies, or by direct financial gain, others may emerge from the direct benefits of being part of a project that is meaningful for a user community. Projects such as Wikipedia, GalaxyZoo (Forston et al. 2011), or FoldIt (Khatib et al. 2011) have collected large bases of volunteer data curators exploring different sets of incentive mechanisms, which can be based on visibility and social or professional status, social impact, meaningfulness, or fun. The understanding of these principles and the development of the mechanisms behind the engagement of large user bases is an important issue for amplifying data curation efforts.

6.6.2.2 Economic Models

Emerging economic models can provide the financial basis to support the generation and maintenance of high-quality data and the associated data curation
infrastructures.

Pre-competitive Partnerships for Data Curation A *pre-competitive collaboration* scheme is one economic model in which a consortium of organizations, which
are typically competitors, collaborate in parts of the Research & Development
(R&D) process which does not impact on their commercial competitive advantage.
This allows partners to share the *costs* and *risks* associated with parts of the R&D
process. One case of this model is the Pistoia Alliance (Barnes et al. 2009), which is
a precompetitive alliance of life science companies, vendors, publishers, and
academic groups that aims to lower barriers to innovation by improving the
interoperability of R&D business processes. The Pistoia Alliance was founded by
pharmaceutical companies such as AstraZeneca, GSK, Pfizer, and Novartis, and
examples of shared resources include data and data infrastructure tools.

Public-Private Data Partnerships for Curation Another emerging economic
model for data curation are *public–private partnerships* (PPP), in which private
companies and the public sector collaborate towards a mutual benefit partnership.
In a PPP the risks, costs, and benefits are shared among the partners, which have
non-competing, complementary interests over the data. Geospatial data and its high
impact for both the public (environmental, administration) and private (natural
resources companies) sectors is one of the early cases of PPPs. GeoConnections
Canada is an example of a PPP initiative launched in 1999, with the objective of
developing the Canadian Geospatial Data Infrastructure (CGDI) and publishing
geospatial information on the web (Harper 2012; Data Curation Interview: Joe
Sewash 2014). GeoConnections has been developed on a collaborative model
involving the participation of federal, provincial, and territorial agencies, and the
private and academic sectors.

Quantification of the Economic Impact of Data The development of approaches
to quantify the economic impact, value creation, and associated costs behind data
resources is a fundamental element for justifying private and public investments in
data infrastructures. One exemplar case of value quantification is the JISC study
"Data centres: their use, value and impact" (Technopolis Group 2011), which
provides a quantitative account of the value creation process of eight data centres.
The creation of quantitative financial measures can provide the required evidence to
support data infrastructure investments both public and private, creating sustainable
business models grounded on data assets, expanding the existing data economy.

6.6.2.3 Curation at Scale

Human Computation and Crowdsourcing Services Crowdsourcing platforms are rapidly evolving but there is still a major opportunity for *market differentiation* and *growth*. CrowdFlower, for example, is evolving in the direction of *providing better APIs*, supporting *better integration with external systems*.

Within crowdsourcing platforms, people show variability in the quality of work they produce, as well as the amount of time they take for the same work. Additionally, the accuracy and latency of human processors is not uniform over time. Therefore, appropriate methods are required to route tasks to the right person at the right time (Hassan et al. 2012). Furthermore combining work by different people on the same task might also help in improving the quality of work (Law and von Ahn 2009). Recruitment of suitable humans for computation is a major challenge of human computation.

Today, these platforms are mostly restricted to tasks that can be delegated to a paid generic audience. Possible future differentiation avenues include: (1) support for highly specialized domain experts, (2) more flexibility in the selection of demographic profiles, (3) creation of longer term (more persistent) relationships with teams of workers, (4) creation of a major general purpose open crowdsourcing service platform for voluntary work, and (5) using historical data to provide more productivity and automation for data curators (Kittur et al. 2007).

Instrumenting Popular Applications for Data Curation In most cases data curation is performed with common office applications: regular spreadsheets, text editors, and email (Data Curation Interview: James Cheney 2014). These tools are an intrinsic part of existing data curation infrastructures and users are familiarized with them. These tools, however, lack some of the functionalities which are fundamental for data curation: (1) capture and representation of user actions; (2) annotation mechanisms/vocabulary reuse; (3) ability to handle large-scale data; (4) better search capabilities; and (5) integration with multiple data sources.

Extending applications with large user bases for data curation provides an opportunity for a low barrier penetration of data curation functionalities into more ad hoc data curation infrastructures. This allows wiring fundamental data curation processes into existing routine activities without a major disruption of the user working process (Data Curation Interview: Carole Goble 2014).

General-Purpose Data Curation Pipelines While the adaptation and instrumentation of regular tools can provide a low-cost generic data curation solution, many projects will demand the use of tools designed from the start to support more sophisticated data curation activities. The development of *general-purpose data curation frameworks* that integrate core data curation functionalities into a large-scale data curation platform is a fundamental element for organizations that do large-scale data curation. Platforms such as Open Refine[4] and Karma (Gil

---

[4] http://openrefine.org/

et al. 2011) provide examples of emerging data curation frameworks, with a focus on data transformation and integration. Differently from Extract Transform Load (ETL) frameworks, data curation platforms provide a better support for ad hoc, dynamic, manual, less frequent (long tail), and less scripted data transformations and integration. ETL pipelines can be seen as concentrating recurrent activities that become more formalized into a scripted process. General-purpose data curation platforms should target domain experts, trying to provide tools that are usable for people outside the computer science/information technology background.

Algorithmic Validation/Annotation Another major direction for reducing the cost of data curation is related to the automation of data curation activities. Algorithms are becoming more intelligent with advances in machine learning and artificial intelligence. It is expected that machine intelligence will be able to validate, repair, and annotate data within seconds, which might take hours for humans to perform (Kong et al. 2011). In effect, humans will be involved as required, e.g. for defining curation rules, validating hard instances, or providing data for training algorithms (Hassan et al. 2012).

The simplest form of automation consists of scripting curation activities that are recurrent, creating specialized curation agents. This approach is used, for example, in Wikipedia (Wiki Bots) for article cleaning and detecting vandalism. Another automation process consists of providing an algorithmic approach for the validation or annotation of the data against reference standards (Data Curation Interview: Antony Williams 2014). This would contribute to a "likesonomy" where both humans and algorithms could provide further evidence in favour or against data (Data Curation Interview: Antony Williams 2014). These approaches provide a way to automate more recurrent parts of the curation tasks and can be implemented today in any curation pipeline (there are no major technological barriers). However, the construction of these algorithmic or reference bases has a high cost effort (in terms of time consumption and expertise), since they depend on an explicit formalization of the algorithm or the reference criteria (rules).

Data Curation Automation More sophisticated automation approaches that could alleviate the need for the explicit formalization of curation activities will play a fundamental role in reducing the cost of data curation. There is significant potential for the application of machine learning in the data curation field. Two research areas that can impact data curation automation are:

- **Curating by Demonstration (CbD)/Induction of Data Curation Workflows:** Programming by example [or programming by demonstration (PbD)] (Cypher 1993; Flener and Schmid 2008; Lieberman 2001) is a set of end user development approaches in which user actions on concrete instances are generalized into a program. PbD can be used to allow distribution and amplification of the system development tasks by allowing users to become programmers. Despite being a traditional research area, and with research on PbD data integration (Tuchinda et al. 2007, 2011), PbD methods have not been extensively applied into data curation systems.

- **Evidence-based Measurement Models of Uncertainty over Data:** The quantification and estimation of generic and domain-specific models of uncertainty from distributed and heterogeneous evidence bases can provide the basis for the decision on what should be delegated or validated by humans and what can be delegated to algorithmic approaches. IBM Watson is an example of a system that uses at its centre a statistical model to determine the probability of an answer being correct (Ferrucci et al. 2010). Uncertainty models can also be used to route tasks according to the level of expertise, minimizing the cost and maximizing the quality of data curation.

6.6.2.4 Human–Data Interaction

Interactivity and Ease of Curation Actions Data interaction approaches that facilitate data transformation and access are fundamental for expanding the spectrum of data curators' profiles. There are still major barriers for interacting with structured data and the process of querying, analysing, and modifying data inside databases is in most cases mediated by IT professionals or domain-specific applications. Supporting domain experts and casual users in querying, navigating, analysing, and transforming structured data is a fundamental functionality in data curation platforms.

According to Carole Goble "from a big data perspective, the challenges are around finding the slices, views or ways into the dataset that enables you to find the bits that need to be edited, changed" (Data Curation Interview: Carole Goble 2014). Therefore, appropriate summarization and visualization of data is important not only from the usage perspective but also from the maintenance perspective (Hey and Trefethen 2004). Specifically, for the collaborative methods of data cleaning, it is fundamental to enable the discovery of anomalies in both structured and unstructured data. Additionally, making data management activities more mobile and interactive is required as mobile devices overtake desktops. The following technologies provide direction towards better interaction:

- **Data-Driven Documents[5] (D3.js):** D3.js is library for displaying interactive graphs in web documents. This library adheres to open web standard such as HTML5, SVG, and CSS, to enable powerful visualizations with open source licensing.
- **Tableau[6]:** This software allows users to visualize multiple dimensions of relational databases. Furthermore it enables visualization of unstructured data through third-party adapters. Tableau has received a lot of attention due to its ease of use and free access public plan.

---

[5] http://d3js.org/

[6] http://www.tableausoftware.com/public/

- **Open Refine**[7]: This open source application allows users to clean and transform data from a variety of formats such as CSV, XML, RDF, JSON, etc. Open Refine is particularly useful for finding outliers in data and checking the distribution of values in columns through facets. It allows data reconciliation with external data sources such as Freebase and OpenCorporates.[8]

Structured query languages such as SQL are the default approach for interacting with databases, together with graphical user interfaces that are developed as a façade over structured query languages. The query language syntax and the need to understand the schema of the database are not appropriate for domain experts to interact and explore the data. Querying progressively more complex structured databases and dataspaces will demand different approaches suitable for different tasks and different levels of expertise (Franklin et al. 2005). New approaches for interacting with structured data have evolved from the early research stage and can provide the basis for new suites of tools that can facilitate the interaction between user and data. Examples are keyword search, visual query interfaces, and natural language query interfaces over databases (Franklin et al. 2005; Freitas et al. 2012a, b; Kaufmann and Bernstein 2007). Flexible approaches for database querying depend on the ability of the approach to interpret the user query intent, matching it with the elements in the database. These approaches are ultimately dependent on the creation of semantic models that support semantic approximation (Freitas et al. 2011). Despite going beyond the proof-of-concept stage, these functionalities and approaches have not migrated to commercial-level applications.

6.6.2.5 Trust

Provenance Management As data reuse grows, the consumer of third-party data needs to have mechanisms in place to verify the trustworthiness and the quality of the data. Some of the data quality attributes can be evident by the data itself, while others depend on an understanding of the broader context behind the data, i.e. the provenance of the data, the processes, artefacts, and actors behind the data creation.

Capturing and representing the context in which the data was generated and transformed and making it available for data consumers is a major requirement for data curation for datasets targeted towards third-party consumers. Provenance standards such as W3C PROV[9] provide the grounding for the interoperable representation of the data. However, data curation applications still need to be instrumented to capture provenance. Provenance can be used to explicitly capture and represent the curation decisions that are made (Data Curation Interview: Paul Groth 2014). However, there is still a relatively low adoption on provenance

---

[7] https://github.com/OpenRefine/OpenRefine/wiki

[8] https://www.opencorporates.com

[9] http://www.w3.org/TR/prov-primer/

capture and management in data applications. Additionally, manually evaluating trust and quality from provenance data can be a time-consuming process. The representation of provenance needs to be complemented by automated approaches to derive trust and assess data quality from provenance metadata, under the context of a specific application.

Fine-Grained Permission Management Models and Tools Allowing large groups of users to collaborate demands the creation of fine-grained permission/rights associated with curation roles. Most systems today have a coarse-grained permission system, where system stewards oversee general contributors. While this mechanism can fully address the requirements of some projects, there is a clear demand for more fine-grained permission systems, where permissions can be defined at a data item level (Qin and Atluri 2003; Ryutov et al. 2009) and can be assigned in a distributed way. In order to support this fine-grained control, the investigation and development of automated methods for permissions inference and propagation (Kirrane et al. 2013), as well as low-effort distributed permission assignment mechanisms, is of primary importance. Analogously, similar methods can be applied to a fine-grained control of digital rights (Rodrıguez-Doncel et al. 2013).

6.6.2.6   Standardization and Interoperability

Standardized Data Model and Vocabularies for Data Reuse A large part of the data curation effort consists of integrating and repurposing data created under different contexts. In many cases this integration can involve hundreds of data sources. Data model standards such as the Resource Description Framework (RDF)[10] facilitate data integration at the data model level. The use of Universal Resource Identifiers (URIs) in the identification of data entities works as a web-scale open foreign key, which promotes the reuse of identifiers across different datasets, facilitating a distributed data integration process.

The creation of terminologies and vocabularies is a critical methodological step in a data curation project. Projects such as the New York Times (NYT) Index (Curry et al. 2010) or the Protein Data Bank (PDB) (Bernstein et al. 1977) prioritize the creation and evolution of a vocabulary that can serve to represent and annotate the data domain. In the case of PDB, the vocabulary expresses the representation needs of a community. The use of shared vocabularies is part of the vision of the linked data web (Berners-Lee 2009) and it is one methodological tool that can be used to facilitate semantic interoperability. While the creation of a vocabulary is more related to a methodological dimension, semantic search, schema mapping, or ontology alignment approaches (Shvaiko and Euzenat 2005; Freitas et al. 2012a, b) are central for reducing the burden of manual vocabulary mapping on the end user side, reducing the burden for terminological reuse (Freitas et al. 2012a, b).

---

[10] http://www.w3.org/TR/rdf11-primer/

Improved Integration and Communication between Curation Tools Data is created and curated in different contexts and using different tools (which are specialized to satisfy different data curation needs). For example, a user may analyse possible data inconsistencies with a visualization tool, do schema mapping with a different tool, and then correct the data using a crowdsourcing platform. The ability to move the data seamlessly between different tools and capture user curation decisions and data transformations across different platforms is fundamental to support more sophisticated data curation operations that may demand highly specialized tools to make the final result trustworthy (Data Curation Interview: Paul Groth 2014; Data Curation Interview: James Cheney 2014). The creation of standardized data models and vocabularies (such as W3C PROV) addresses part of the problem. However, data curation applications need to be adapted to capture and manage provenance and to provide better adoption over existing standards.

6.6.2.7   Data Curation Models

Minimum Information Models for Data Curation Despite recent efforts in the recognition and understanding behind the field of data curation (Palmer et al. 2013; Lord et al. 2004), the processes behind it still need to be better formalized. The adoption of methods such as minimum information models (La Novere et al. 2005) and their materialization in tools is one example of methodological improvement that can provide a minimum quality standard for data curators. In eScience, MIRIAM (minimum information required in the annotation of models) (Laibe and Le Novère 2007) is an example of a community-level effort to standardize the annotation and curation processes of quantitative models of biological systems.

Curating Nanopublications, Coping with the Long Tail of Science With the increase in the amount of scholarly communication, it is increasingly difficult to find, connect, and curate scientific statements (Mons and Velterop 2009; Groth et al. 2010). Nanopublications are core scientific statements with associated contexts (Groth et al. 2010), which aim at providing a synthetic mechanism for scientific communication. Nanopublications are still an emerging paradigm, which may provide a way for the distributed creation of semi-structured data in both scientific and non-scientific domains.

Investigation of Theoretical Principles and Domain-Specific Models Models for data curation should evolve from the ground practice into a more abstract description. The advancement of automated data curation algorithms will depend on the definition of theoretical models and on the investigation of the principles behind data curation (Buneman et al. 2008). Understanding the causal mechanisms behind workflows (Cheney 2010) and the generalization conditions behind data transportability (Pearl and Bareinboim 2011) are examples of theoretical models that can impact data curation, guiding users towards the generation and representation of data that can be reused in broader contexts.

6.6.2.8 Unstructured and Structured Data Integration

Entity Recognition and Linking Most of the information on the web and in organizations is available as unstructured data (text, videos, etc.). The process of making sense of information available as unstructured data is time-consuming: differently from structured data, unstructured data cannot be directly compared, aggregated, and operated. At the same time, unstructured data holds most of the information of the *long tail of data variety* (Fig. 6.2).

Extracting structured information from unstructured data is a fundamental step for making the long tail of data analysable and interpretable. Part of the problem can be addressed by information extraction approaches (e.g. relation extraction, entity recognition, and ontology extraction) (Freitas et al. 2012a, b; Schutz and Buitelaar 2005; Han et al. 2011; Data Curation Interview: Helen Lippell 2014). These tools extract information from text and can be used to automatically build semi-structured knowledge from text. There are information extraction frameworks that are mature to certain classes of information extraction problems, but their adoption remains limited to early adopters (Curry et al. 2010; Data Curation Interview: Helen Lippell 2014).

Use of Open Data to Integrate Structured and Unstructured Data Another recent shift in this area is the availability of large-scale structured data resources, in particular open data, which is supporting information extraction. For example, entities in open datasets such as DBpedia (Auer et al. 2007) and Freebase (Bollacker et al. 2008) can be used to identify named entities (people, places, and organizations) in texts, which can be used to categorize and organize text contents. Open data in this scenario works as a common-sense knowledge base for entities and can be extended with domain-specific entities inside organizational environments. Named entity recognition and linking tools such as DBpedia Spotlight (Mendes et al. 2011) can be used to link structured and unstructured data.

Complementarily, unstructured data can be used to provide a more comprehensive description for structured data, improving content accessibility and semantics. *Distributional semantic models*, semantic models that are built from large-scale collections (Freitas et al. 2012a, b), can be applied to structured databases (Freitas and Curry 2014) and are examples of approaches that can be used to enrich the semantics of the data.

Natural Language Processing Pipelines The Natural Language Processing (NLP) community has mature approaches and tools that can be directly applied to projects that deal with unstructured data. Open source projects such as Apache UIMA[11] facilitate the integration of NLP functionalities into other systems. Additionally, strong industry use cases such as IBM Watson (Ferrucci et al. 2010), Thomson Reuters, The New York Times (Curry et al. 2010), and the Press

---

[11] http://uima.apache.org/

Association (Data Curation Interview: Hellen Lippell) are shifting the perception of NLP techniques from the academic to the industrial field.

6.7   Sectors Case Studies for Big Data Curation

In this section, case studies are discussed that cover different data curation processes over different domains. The purpose behind the case studies is to capture the different workflows that have been adopted or designed in order to deal with data curation in the big data context.

6.7.1   Health and Life Sciences

6.7.1.1   ChemSpider

ChemSpider[12] is a search engine that provides free access to the structure-centric chemical community. It has been designed to aggregate and index chemical structures and their associated information into a single searchable repository. ChemSpider contains tens of millions of chemical compounds with associated data and is serving as a data provider to websites and software tools. Available since 2007, ChemSpider has collated over 300 data sources from chemical vendors, government databases, private laboratories, and individuals. Used by chemists for identifier conversion and predictions, ChemSpider datasets are also heavily leveraged by chemical vendors and pharmaceutical companies as pre-competitive resources for experimental and clinical trial investigation.

Data curation in ChemSpider consists of the manual annotation and correction of data (Pence and Williams 2010). This may include changes to the chemical structures of a compound, addition or deletion of identifiers, associating links between a chemical compound, its related data sources, etc. ChemSpider supports two different ways for curators to help in curating data at ChemSpider:

- Post comments on a record in order to highlight the need for appropriate action by a master curator.
- As a registered member with curation rights, directly curate the data or remove erroneous data.

ChemSpider adopts a meritocratic model for their curation activities. *Normal curators* are responsible for deposition, which is checked, and verified by *master curators*. Normal curators in turn can be invited to become masters after some qualifying period of contribution. The platform has a blended human and

---

[12] http://www.chemspider.com

computer-based curation process. Robotic curation uses algorithms for error correction and data validation at deposition time.

ChemSpider uses a mixture of computational approaches to perform certain levels of data validation. They have built their own chemical data validation tool, which is called CVSP (chemical validation and standardization platform). CVSP helps chemists to check chemicals to determine whether or not they are validly represented, or if there are any data quality issues so that they can flag those quality issues easily and efficiently.

Using the open community model, ChemSpider distributes its curation activity across its community using crowdsourcing to accommodate massive growth rates and quality issues. They use a wiki-like approach for people to interact with the data, so that they can annotate it, validate it, curate it, flag it, and delete it. ChemSpider is in the process of implementing an automated recognition system that will measure the contribution effort of curators through the data validation and engagement process. The contribution metrics can be publicly viewable and accessible through a central profile for the data curator.

6.7.1.2   Protein Data Bank

The Research Collaboratory for Structural Bioinformatics Protein Data Bank[13] (RCSB PDB) is a group dedicated to improve the understanding of the functions of biological systems through the study of 3D structure of biological macromolecules. The PDB has had over 300 million dataset downloads.

A significant amount of the curation process at PDB consists of providing standardized vocabulary for describing the relationships between biological entities, varying from organ tissue to the description of the molecular structure. The use of standardized vocabularies helps with the nomenclature used to describe protein and small molecule names and their descriptors present in the structure entry. The data curation process covers the identification and correction of inconsistencies over the 3D protein structure and experimental data. In order to implement a global hierarchical governance approach to the data curation workflow, PDB staff review and annotate each submitted entry before robotic curation checks for plausibility as part of the data deposition, processing, and distribution. The data curation effort is distributed across their sister sites.

Robotic curation automates the data validation and verification. Human curators contribute to the definition of rules for the detection of inconsistencies. The curation process is also propagated retrospectively, where errors found in the data are corrected retrospectively to the archives. Up-to-date versions of the datasets are released on a weekly basis to keep all sources consistent with the current standards and to ensure good data curation quality.

---

[13] http://www.pdb.org

6.7.1.3 FoldIt

Foldit (Good and Su 2011) is a popular example of a human computation applied to
a complex problem, i.e. finding patterns of protein folding. The developers of Foldit
have used gamification to enable human computation. Through these games people
can predict protein structure that might help in targeting drugs at particular disease.
Current computer algorithms are unable to deal with the exponentially high number
of possible protein structures. To overcome this problem, Foldit uses competitive
protein folding to generate the best proteins (Eiben et al. 2012).

6.7.2 Media and Entertainment

6.7.2.1 Press Association

Press Association (PA) is the national news agency for the UK and Ireland and a
leading multimedia content provider across web, mobile, broadcast, and print. For
the last 145 years, PA has been providing feeds (text, data, photos, and videos) to
major UK media outlets as well as corporate customers and the public sector.

The objective of data curation at Press Association is to select the most relevant
information for its customers, classifying, enriching, and distributing it in ways that
can be readily consumed. The curation process at Press Association employs a large
number of curators in the content classification process, working over a large
number of data sources. A curator inside PA is an analyst who collects, aggregates,
classifies, normalizes, and analyses the raw information coming from different data
sources. Since the nature of the information analysed is typically high volume and
near real time, data curation is a big challenge inside the company and the use of
automated tools plays an important role in this process. In the curation process,
automatic tools provide a first level triage and classification, which is further refined
by the intervention of human curators as shown in Fig. 6.3.

The data curation process starts with an article submitted to a platform which
uses a set of linguistic extraction rules over unstructured text to automatically
derive tags for the article, enriching it with machine readable structured data. A
data curator then selects the terms that better describe the contents and inserts new
tags if necessary. The tags enrich the original text with the general category of the
analysed contents, while also providing a description of specific entities (places,
people, events, facts) that are present in the text. The metadata manager then
reviews the classification and the content is published online.

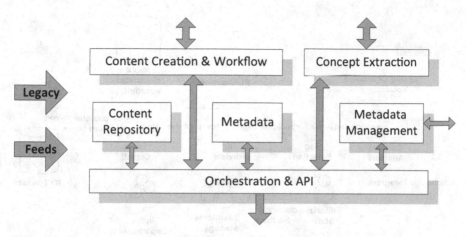

Fig. 6.3 Press Association content and metadata pattern workflow

6.7.2.2   The New York Times

The New York Times (NYT) is the largest metropolitan and the third largest newspaper in the United States. The company has a long history of the curation of its articles in its 100-year-old curated repository (NYT Index).

The New York Times' curation pipeline (see Fig. 6.4) starts with an article getting out of the newsroom. The first level curation consists of the content classification process done by the editorial staff, which consists of several hundred journalists. Using a web application, a member of the editorial staff submits the new article through a rule-based information extraction system (in this case, SAS Teragram[14]). Teragram uses a set of linguistic extraction rules, which are created by the taxonomy managers based on a subset of the controlled vocabulary used by the Index Department. Teragram suggests tags based on the index vocabulary that can potentially describe the content of the article (Curry et al. 2010). The member of the editorial staff then selects the terms that better describe the contents and inserts new tags if necessary.

Taxonomy managers review the classification and the content is published online, providing continuous feedback into the classification process. In a later stage, the article receives a second level curation by the index department, which appends additional tags and a summary of the article to the stored resource.

6.7.3   Retail

6.7.3.1   eBay

eBay is one of the most popular online marketplaces that caters for millions of products and customers. eBay has employed human computation to solve two

---

[14] SAS Teragram http://www.teragram.com

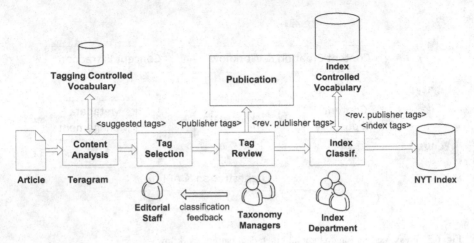

Fig. 6.4 The New York Times article classification curation workflow

important issues of data quality: managing product taxonomies and finding identifiers in product descriptions. Crowdsourced workers help eBay in improving the
speed and quality of product classification algorithms at lower costs.

6.7.3.2 Unilever

Unilever is one of the world's largest manufacturers of consumer goods, with global
operations. Unilever utilized crowdsourced human computation within their marketing strategy for new products. Human computation was used to gather sufficient
data about customer feedback and to analyse public sentiment of social media.
Initially Unilever developed a set of machine-learning algorithms to conduct an
analysis sentiment of customers across their product range. However, these sentiment analysis algorithms were unable to account for regional and cultural differences between target populations. Therefore, Unilever effectively improved the
accuracy of sentiment analysis algorithms with crowdsourcing, by verifying the
output algorithms and gathering feedback from an online crowdsourcing platform,
i.e. Crowdflower.

6.8   Conclusions

With the growth in the number of data sources and of decentralized content
generation, ensuring data quality becomes a fundamental issue for data management environments in the big data era. The evolution of data curation methods and
tools is a cornerstone element for ensuring data quality at the scale of big data.
    Based on the evidence collected by an extensive investigation that included a
comprehensive literature analysis, survey, interviews with data curation experts,

questionnaires, and case studies, the future requirements and emerging trends for data curation were identified. The analysis can provide to data curators, technical managers, and researchers an up-to-date view of the challenges, approaches, and opportunities for data curation in the big data era.

References

Ashley, K. (2014). Data curation interview. Expert interview series for the EU-project BIG (318062; ICT-2011.4.4). http://big-project.eu/text-interviews

Auer, S., Bizer, C., Kobilarov, G., Lehmann, J., Cyganiak, R., & Ives, Z. (2007). DBpedia: A nucleus for a web of open data. In *Proceedings of the 6th International The Semantic Web and 2nd Asian Conference on Asian Semantic Web Conference* (pp. 722–735).

Barnes, M. R., Harland, L., Foord, S. M., Hall, M. D., Dix, I., Thomas, S., et al. (2009). Lowering industry firewalls: Pre-competitive informatics initiatives in drug discovery. *Nature Reviews Drug Discovery, 8*(9), 701–708.

Berners-Lee, T. (2009). Linked data design issues. http://www.w3.org/DesignIssues/LinkedData.html

Bernstein, F. C., Koetzle, T. F., Williams, G. J., Meyer, E. F., Jr., Brice, M. D., & Rodgers, J. R. (1977). The Protein Data Bank: A computer-based archival file for macromolecular structures. *Journal of Molecular Biology, 112*(3), 535–542.

Bollacker, K., Evans, C., Paritosh, P., Sturge, T., & Taylor, J. (2008). Freebase: A collaboratively created graph database for structuring human knowledge. In *Proceedings of the ACM SIGMOD International Conference on Management of Data* (pp. 1247–1250). New York, NY.

Brodie, M. L., & Liu, J. T. (2010). The power and limits of relational technology in the age of information ecosystems. *On the Move Federated Conferences.*

Buneman, P., Cheney, J., Tan, W., & Vansummeren, S. (2008). Curated databases. In *Proceedings of the Twenty-Seventh ACM SIGMOD-SIGACT-SIGART Symposium on Principles of Database Systems.*

Cheney, J. (2010). Causality and the semantics of provenance. *arXiv preprint arXiv:1004.3241.*

Cheney, J. (2014). Data curation interview. Expert interview series for the EU-project BIG (318062; ICT-2011.4.4). http://big-project.eu/text-interviews

Cragin, M., Heidorn, P., Palmer, C. L., & Smith, L. C. (2007). *An educational program on data curation, ALA science & technology section conference.*

CrowdFlower. (2012). *Crowdsourcing: Utilizing the cloud-based workforce* (Whitepaper).

Curry, E., & Freitas, A. (2014). *Coping with the long tail of data variety.* Athens: European Data Forum.

Curry, E., Freitas, A., & O'Riáin, S. (2010). The role of community-driven data curation for enterprise. In D. Wood (Ed.), *Linking enterprise data* (pp. 25–47). Boston, MA: Springer US.

Cypher, A. (1993). *Watch what i do: Programming by demonstration*. Cambridge, MA: MIT Press.

Doan, A., Ramakrishnan, R., & Halevy, A. (2011). Crowdsourcing systems on the world-wide web. *Communications of the ACM, 54*(4), 86–96.

Eiben, C. B., et al. (2012). Increased Diels-Alderase activity through backbone remodeling guided by Foldit players. *Nature Biotechnology, 30*, 190–192.

Ferrucci, D., Brown, E., Chu-Carroll, J., Fan, J., Gondek, D., Kalyanpur, A. A., et al. (2010). Building Watson: An overview of the DeepQA project. *AI Magazine, 31*(3), 59–79.

Flener, P., & Schmid, U. (2008). An introduction to inductive programming. *Artificial Intelligence Review, 29*, 45–62.

Fortson, L., Masters, K., Nichol, R., Borne, K., Edmondson, E., & Lintott, C., et al. (2011). *Galaxy Zoo: Morphological classification and citizen science, machine learning and mining for astronomy*. Chapman & Hall.

Franklin, M., Halevy, A., & Maier, D. (2005). From databases to dataspaces: A new abstraction for information management. *ACM SIGMOD Record, 34*(4), 27–33.

Freitas, A., Carvalho, D., Pereira da Silva, J. C., O'Riain, S., & Curry, E. (2012a). A semantic best-effort approach for extracting structured discourse graphs from Wikipedia. In *Proceedings of the 1st Workshop on the Web of Linked Entities (WoLE 2012) at the 11th International Semantic Web Conference (ISWC)*.

Freitas, A., & Curry, E. (2014). Natural language queries over heterogeneous linked data graphs: A distributional-compositional semantics approach. In *Proceedings of the 19th International Conference on Intelligent User Interfaces (IUI)*, Haifa.

Freitas, A., Curry, E., Oliveira, J. G., & O'Riain, S. (2012b). Querying heterogeneous datasets on the linked data web: Challenges, approaches and trends. *IEEE Internet Computing, 16*(1), 24–33.

Freitas, A., Oliveira, J. G., O'Riain, S., Curry, E., & Pereira da Silva, J. C. (2011). Querying Linked data using semantic relatedness: A vocabulary independent approach. In *Proceedings of the 16th International Conference on Applications of Natural Language to Information Systems (NLDB)*.

Gartner. (2007). 'Dirty Data' is a Business Problem, Not an IT Problem, says Gartner, Press release.

Gil, Y., Szekely, P., Villamizar, S., Harmon, T. C., Ratnakar, V., Gupta, S., et al. (2011). Mind your metadata: Exploiting semantics for configuration, adaptation, and provenance in scientific workflows. In *Proceedings of the 10th International Semantic Web Conference (ISWC)*.

Goble, C. (2014). Data curation interview. Expert interview series for the EU-project BIG (318062; ICT-2011.4.4). http://big-project.eu/text-interviews

Good, B. M., & Su, A. I. (2011). Games with a scientific purpose. *Genome Biology, 12*(12), 135.

Groth, P., Gibson, A., & Velterop, J. (2010). The anatomy of a nanopublication. *Information Services and Use, 30*, 1–2. 51–56.

Groth, P. (2014). Data curation interview. Expert interview series for the EU-project BIG (318062; ICT-2011.4.4). http://big-project.eu/text-interviews

Han, X., Sun, L., & Zhao, J. (2011). Collective entity linking in web text: A graph-based method. In *Proceedings of the 34th International ACM SIGIR Conference on Research and Development in Information Retrieval*.

Harper, D. (2012). *GeoConnections and the Canadian Geospatial Data Infrastructure (CGDI): An SDI Success Story, Global Geospatial Conference*.

Hassan, U. U., O'Riain, S., & Curry, E. (2012). Towards expertise modelling for routing data cleaning tasks within a community of knowledge workers. In *Proceedings of the 17th International Conference on Information Quality*.

Hedges, M., & Blanke, T. (2012). Sheer curation for experimental data and provenance. In *Proceedings of the 12th ACM/IEEE-CS Joint Conference on Digital Libraries* (405–406).

Hey, T., & Trefethen, A. E. (2004). UK e-science programme: Next generation grid applications. *International Journal of High Performance Computing Applications, 18*(3), 285–291.

Howe, D., Costanzo, M., Fey, P., Gojobori, T., Hannick, L., Hide, W., & Yon Rhee, S. (2008). Big data: The future of biocuration. *Nature, 455*(7209), 47–50.

Ipeirotis, P. G. (2010). Analyzing the amazon mechanical turk marketplace. *XRDS: Crossroads, The ACM Magazine for Students, 17*(2), 16–21.

Kaggle. (2005). *Go from big data to big analytics.* http://www.kaggle.com/

Kaufmann, E., & Bernstein, A. (2007). How useful are natural language interfaces to the semantic web for casual end-users? In *Proceedings of the 6th International The Semantic Web Conference* (pp. 281–294).

Khatib, F., DiMaio, F., Foldit Contenders Group, Foldit Void Crushers Group, Cooper, S., Kazmierczyk, M. et al. (2011). Crystal structure of a monomeric retroviral protease solved by protein folding game players. *Nature Structural and Molecular Biology, 18*, 1175–1177.

Kirrane, S., Abdelrahman, A., Mileo, S., & Decker, S. (2013). Secure manipulation of linked data. In *Proceedings of the 12th International Semantic Web Conference.*

Kittur, A., Chi, E., Pendleton, B. A., Suh, B., & Mytkowicz, T. (2007). Power of the few vs. wisdom of the crowd: Wikipedia and the rise of the bourgeoisie. *World Wide Web, 1*(2), 19.

Knight, S. A., & Burn, J. (2005). Developing a framework for assessing information quality on the World Wide Web. *Informing Science, 8*, 159–172.

Kong, N., Hanrahan, B., Weksteen, T., Convertino, G., & Chi, E. H. (2011). VisualWikiCurator: Human and machine intelligence for organizing wiki content. In *Proceedings of the 16th International Conference on Intelligent User Interfaces* (pp. 367–370).

La Novere, N., Finney, A., Hucka, M., Bhalla, U. S., Campagne, F., Collado-Vides, J., et al. (2005). Minimum information requested in the annotation of biochemical models (MIRIAM). *Nature Biotechnology, 23*(12), 1509–1515.

Laibe, C., & Le Novère, N. (2007). MIRIAM resources: Tools to generate and resolve robust cross-references in Systems Biology. *BMC Systems Biology, 1*, 58.

Law, E., & von Ahn, L. (2009). Input-agreement: A new mechanism for collecting data using human computation games. In *Proceedings of the SIGCHI Conference on Human Factors in Computing Systems* (vol. 4, pp. 1197–1206).

Law, E., & von Ahn, L. (2011). Human computation. *Synthesis Lectures on Artificial Intelligence and Machine Learning, 5*, 1–121.

Lieberman, H. (2001). *Your wish is my command: Programming By example.* San Francisco, CA: Morgan Kaufmann.

Lippell, H. (2014). Data curation interview. Expert interview series for the EU-project BIG (318062; ICT-2011.4.4). http://big-project.eu/text-interviews

Lord, P., Macdonald, A., Lyon, L., & Giaretta, D. (2004, September). From data deluge to data curation. In *Proceedings of the UK e-science all hands meeting* (pp. 371–357).

Lynch, N. (2014). Data curation interview. Expert interview series for the EU-project BIG (318062; ICT-2011.4.4). http://big-project.eu/text-interviews

Mendes, P. N., Jakob, M., García-Silva, A., & Bizer, C. (2011, September). DBpedia spotlight: Shedding light on the web of documents. In *Proceedings of the 7th International Conference on Semantic Systems* (pp. 1–8). New York: ACM.

Mons, B., Ashburner, M., Chichester, C., van Mulligen, E., Weeber, M., den Dunnen, J., et al. (2008). Calling on a million minds for community annotation in WikiProteins. *Genome Biology, 9*(5), R89.

Mons, B., & Velterop, J. (2009). *Nano-Publication in the e-science era, International Semantic Web Conference.*

Morris, H. D., & Vesset, D. (2005). *Managing Master Data for Business Performance Management: The Issues and Hyperion's Solution, Technical Report.*

Norris, R. P. (2007). How to make the dream come true: The astronomers' data manifesto. *Data Science Journal, 6*, S116–S124.

Palmer, C. L., et al. (2013). *Foundations of Data Curation: The Pedagogy and Practice of "Purposeful Work" with Research Data.*

Pearl, J., & Bareinboim, E. (2011). Transportability of causal and statistical relations: A formal approach. In *Proceedings of the 25th National Conference on Artificial Intelligence (AAAI)*.

Pence, H. E., & Williams, A. (2010). ChemSpider: An online chemical information resource. *Journal of Chemical Education, 87*(11), 1123–1124.

Priem, J., Taraborelli, D., Groth, P., & Neylon, C. (2010). Altmetrics: A manifesto. http:// altmetrics.org/manifesto/

Qin, L., & Atluri, V. (2003). Concept-level access control for the Semantic Web. In *Proceedings of the ACM Workshop on XML Security – XMLSEC '03*. ACM Press.

Rodrıguez-Doncel, V., Gomez-Perez, A., & Mihindukulasooriya, N. (2013). Rights declaration in Linked Data. In *Proceedings of the Fourth International Workshop on Consuming Linked Data, COLD 2013*, Sydney, Australia, October 22, 2013.

Rowe, N. (2012). *The state of master data management, building the foundation for a better enterprise*. Aberdeen Group.

Ryutov, T., Kichkaylo, T., & Neches, R. (2009). Access control policies for semantic networks. In *2009 I.E. International Symposium on Policies for Distributed Systems and Networks* (pp. 150–157).

Schutz, A., & Buitelaar, P. (2005). RelExt: A tool for relation extraction from text in ontology extension. In *Proceedings of the 4th International Semantic Web Conference*.

Sewash, J. (2014). Data curation interview. Expert interview series for the EU-project BIG (318062; ICT-2011.4.4). http://big-project.eu/text-interviews

Shadbolt, N., O'Hara, K., Berners-Lee, T., Gibbins, N., Glaser, H., Hall, W., et al. (2012). Linked open government data: Lessons from Data.gov.uk. *IEEE Intelligent Systems, 27*(3), Spring Issue, 16–24.

Shvaiko, P., & Euzenat, J. (2005). A survey of schema-based matching approaches. *Journal on Data Semantics, IV*, 146–171.

Sheth, A. (1999). Changing focus on interoperability in information systems: From System, Syntax, Structure to Semantics. *Interoperating Geographic Information Systems The Springer International Series in Engineering and Computer Science* (vol. 495, pp. 5–29).

Surowiecki, J. (2005). *The wisdom of crowds*. New York: Random House LLC.

Technopolis Group. (2011). *Data centres: Their use, value and impact* (JISC Report).

Thomson Reuters Technical Report, ORCID: The importance of proper identification and attribution across the scientific literature ecosystem. (2013).

Tuchinda, R., Knoblock, C. A., & Szekely, P. (2011). Building Mashups by demonstration. *ACM Transactions on the Web (TWEB), 5*(3), Art. 16.

Tuchinda, R., Szekely, P., & Knoblock, C. A. (2007). Building data integration queries by demonstration. In *Proceedings of the International Conference on Intelligent User Interface*.

Wang, R., & Strong, D. (1996). Beyond accuracy: What data quality means to data consumers. *Journal of Management Information Systems, 12*(4), 5–33.

Williams, A. (2014). Data curation interview. Expert interview series for the EU-project BIG (318062; ICT-2011.4.4). http://big-project.eu/text-interviews

Chapter 7
Big Data Storage

Martin Strohbach, Jörg Daubert, Herman Ravkin, and Mario Lischka

7.1 Introduction

This chapter provides an overview of big data storage technologies which served as
an input towards the creation of a cross-sectorial roadmap for the development of
big data technologies in a range of high-impact application domains. Rather than
elaborating on concrete individual technologies, this chapter provides a broad
overview of data storage technologies so that the reader may get a high level
understanding about the capabilities of individual technologies and areas that
require further research. Consequently, the social and economic impacts are
described, and selected case studies illustrating the use of big data storage technologies are provided. The full results of the analysis on big data storage can be found
in Curry et al. (2014).

The position of big data storage within the overall big data value chain can be
seen in Fig. 7.1. Big data storage is concerned with storing and managing data in a
scalable way, satisfying the needs of applications that require access to the data.
The ideal big data storage system would allow storage of a virtually unlimited
amount of data, cope both with high rates of random write and read access, flexibly
and efficiently deal with a range of different data models, support both structured
and unstructured data, and for privacy reasons, only work on encrypted data.

M. Strohbach (✉) • J. Daubert
AGT International, Hilpertstr, 35, 64295 Darmstadt, Germany
e-mail: MStrohbach@agtinternational.com; jdaubert@agtinternational.com

H. Ravkin
Department of Industrial Engineering, Tel-Aviv University, Ramat-Aviv, Tel-Aviv 69978,
Israel
e-mail: Herman.Ravkin@gmail.com

M. Lischka
acentrix GmbH, Erika-Mann-Strasse 69, 80636 Munich, Germany
e-mail: m.lischka@acentrix.de

© The Author(s) 2016
J.M. Cavanillas et al. (eds.), *New Horizons for a Data-Driven Economy*,
DOI 10.1007/978-3-319-21569-3_7

Big Data Value Chain

Data Acquisition	Data Analysis	Data Curation	Data Storage	Data Usage
• Structured data • Unstructured data • Event processing • Sensor networks • Protocols • Real-time • Data streams • Multimodality	• Stream mining • Semantic analysis • Machine learning • Information extraction • Linked Data • Data discovery • 'Whole world' semantics • Ecosystems • Community data analysis • Cross-sectorial data analysis	• Data Quality • Trust / Provenance • Annotation • Data validation • Human-Data Interaction • Top-down/Bottom-up • Community / Crowd • Human Computation • Curation at scale • Incentivisation • Automation • Interoperability	• In-Memory DBs • NoSQL DBs • NewSQL DBs • Cloud storage • Query Interfaces • Scalability and Performance • Data Models • Consistency, Availability, Partition-tolerance • Security and Privacy • Standardization	• Decision support • Prediction • In-use analytics • Simulation • Exploration • Visualisation • Modeling • Control • Domain-specific usage

Fig. 7.1 Data storage in the big data value chain

Obviously, all these needs cannot be fully satisfied. But over recent years many new storage systems have emerged that at least partly address these challenges.[1]

This chapter provides an overview of big data storage technologies and identifies some areas where further research is required. *Big data storage technologies* are referred to as storage technologies that in some way specifically address the volume, velocity, or variety challenge and do *not* fall in the category of relational database systems. This does not mean that relational database systems do not address these challenges, but alternative storage technologies such as columnar stores and clever combinations of different storage systems, e.g. using the Hadoop Distributed File System (HDFS), are often more efficient and less expensive (Marz and Warren 2014).

Big data storage systems typically address the volume challenge by making use of distributed, shared nothing architectures. This allows addressing increased storage requirements by scaling out to new nodes providing computational power and storage. New machines can seamlessly be added to a storage cluster and the storage system takes care of distributing the data between individual nodes transparently.

Storage solutions also need to cope with the velocity and variety of data. Velocity is important in the sense of query latencies, i.e. how long does it take to get a reply for a query? This is particularly important in the face of high rates of incoming data. For instance, random write access to a database can slow down query performance considerably if it needs to provide transactional guarantees. In contrast, variety relates to the level of effort that is required to integrate and work with data that originates from a large number of different sources. For instance, graph databases are suitable storage systems to address these challenges.

---

[1] See for instance the map of 451 Research available at https://451research.com/state-of-the-database-landscape

Section 7.2 summarizes key insights and Sect. 7.3 illustrates the social and economic impact of data storage. Section 7.4 presents the current state-of-the-art including storage technologies and solutions for security and privacy. Section 7.5 includes future requirements and emerging trends for data storage that will play an important role for unlocking the value hidden in large datasets. Section 7.6 presents three selected case studies, and the chapter is concluded in Sect. 7.7.

7.2 Key Insights for Big Data Storage

As a result of the analysis of current and future data storage technologies, a number of insights were gained relating to data storage technologies. It became apparent that big data storage has become a commodity business and that scalable storage technologies have reached an enterprise-grade level that can manage virtually unbounded volumes of data. Evidence is provided by the widespread use of Hadoop-based solutions offered by vendors such as Cloudera (2014a), Hortonworks (2014), and MapR (2014) as well as various NoSQL[2] database vendors, in particular those that use in-memory and columnar storage technologies. Compared to traditional relational database management systems that rely on row-based storage and expensive caching strategies, these novel big data storage technologies offer better scalability at lower operational complexity and costs.

Despite these advances that improve the performance, scalability, and usability of storage technologies, there is still significant untapped potential for big data storage technologies, both for using and further developing the technologies:

- **Potential to Transform Society and Businesses across Sectors:** Big data storage technologies are a key enabler for advanced analytics that have the potential to transform society and the way key business decisions are made. This is of particular importance in traditionally non-IT-based sectors such as energy. While these sectors face non-technical issues such as the lack of skilled big data experts and regulatory barriers, novel data storage technologies have the potential to enable new value-generating analytics in and across various industrial sectors.
- **Lack of Standards Is a Major Barrier:** The history of NoSQL is based on solving specific technological challenges which lead to a range of different storage technologies. The large range of choices coupled with the lack of standards for querying the data makes it harder to exchange data stores as it may tie application specific code to a certain storage solution.
- **Open Scalability Challenges in Graph-Based Data Stores:** Processing data based on graph data structures is beneficial in an increasing amount of applications. It allows better capture of semantics and complex relationships with other

---

[2] NoSQL is typically referred to as "Not only SQL".

pieces of information coming from a large variety of different data sources, and has the potential to improve the overall value that can be generated by analysing the data. While graph databases are increasingly used for this purpose, it remains hard to efficiently distribute graph-based data structure across computing nodes.

• **Privacy and Security Is Lagging Behind:** Although there are several projects and solutions that address privacy and security, the protection of individuals and securing their data lags behind the technological advances of data storage systems. Considerable research is required to better understand how data can be misused, how it needs to be protected and integrated in big data storage solutions.

7.3   Social and Economic Impact of Big Data Storage

As emerging big data technologies and their use in different sectors show, the capability to store, manage, and analyse large amounts of heterogeneous data hints towards the emergence of a data-driven society and economy with huge transformational potential (Manyika et al. 2011). Enterprises can now store and analyse more data at a lower cost while at the same time enhancing their analytical capabilities. While companies such as Google, Twitter, and Facebook are established players for which data constitutes the key asset, other sectors also tend to become more data driven. For instance, the health sector is an excellent example that illustrates how society can expect better health services by better integration and analysis of health-related data (iQuartic 2014).

Many other sectors are heavily impacted by the maturity and cost-effectiveness of technologies that are able to handle big datasets. For instance, in the media sector the analysis of social media has the potential to transform journalism by summarizing news created by a large amount of individuals. In the transport sector, the consolidated data management integration of transport systems has the potential to enable personalized multimodal transportation, increasing the experience of travellers within a city and at the same time helping decision-makers to better manage urban traffic. In all of these areas, NoSQL storage technologies prove a key enabler to efficiently analyse large amounts of data and create additional business value.

On a cross-sectorial level, the move towards a data-driven economy can be seen by the emergence of data platforms such as datamarket.com (Gislason 2013), infochimp.com, and open data initiatives of the European Union such as opendata.europa.eu and other national portals (e.g. data.gov, data.gov.uk, data.gov.sg) (Ahmadi Zeleti et al. 2014). Technology vendors are supporting the move towards a data-driven economy as can be seen by the positioning of their products and services. For instance, Cloudera is offering a product called the *enterprise data hub* (Cloudera 2014b), an extended Hadoop ecosystem that is positioned as a data management and analysis integration point for the whole company.

Further to the benefits described above, there are also threats to big data storage technologies that must be addressed to avoid any negative impact. This relates for instance to the challenge of protecting the data of individuals and reducing the energy consumption of data centres (Koomey 2008).

7.4 Big Data Storage State-of-the-Art

This section provides an overview of the current state-of-the-art in big data storage technologies. Section 7.4.1 describes the storage technologies, and Sect. 7.4.2 presents technologies related to secure and privacy-preserving data storage.

7.4.1 Data Storage Technologies

During the last decade, the need to deal with the data explosion (Turner et al. 2014) and the hardware shift from *scale-up* to *scale-out* approaches led to an explosion of new big data storage systems that shifted away from traditional relational database models. These approaches typically sacrifice properties such as data consistency in order to maintain fast query responses with increasing amounts of data. Big data stores are used in similar ways as traditional relational database management systems, e.g. for online transactional processing (OLTP) solutions and data warehouses over structured or semi-structured data. Particular strengths are in handling unstructured and semi-structured data at large scale.

This section assesses the current state-of-the-art in data store technologies that are capable of handling large amounts of data, and identifies data store related trends. Following are differing types of storage systems:

- **Distributed File Systems:** File systems such as the Hadoop File System (HDFS) (Shvachko et al. 2010) offer the capability to store large amounts of unstructured data in a reliable way on commodity hardware. Although there are file systems with better performance, HDFS is an integral part of the Hadoop framework (White 2012) and has already reached the level of a de-facto standard. It has been designed for large data files and is well suited for quickly ingesting data and bulk processing.
- **NoSQL Databases:** Probably the most important family of big data storage technologies are NoSQL database management systems. NoSQL databases use data models from outside the relational world that do not necessarily adhere to the transactional properties of atomicity, consistency, isolation, and durability (ACID).
- **NewSQL Databases:** A modern form of relational databases that aim for comparable scalability as NoSQL databases while maintaining the transactional guarantees made by traditional database systems.
- **Big Data Querying Platforms:** Technologies that provide query facades in front of big data stores such as distributed file systems or NoSQL databases. The

main concern is providing a high-level interface, e.g. via SQL[3] like query languages and achieving low query latencies.

7.4.1.1 NoSQL Databases

NoSQL databases are designed for scalability, often by sacrificing consistency. Compared to relational databases, they often use low-level, non-standardized query interfaces, which make them more difficult to integrate in existing applications that expect an SQL interface. The lack of standard interfaces makes it harder to switch vendors. NoSQL databases can be distinguished by the data models they use.

- **Key-Value Stores:** Key-value stores allow storage of data in a schema-less way. Data objects can be completely unstructured or structured and are accessed by a single key. As no schema is used, it is not even necessary that data objects share the same structure.
- **Columnar Stores:** According to Wikipedia "A column-oriented DBMS is a database management system (DBMS) that stores data tables as sections of columns of data rather than as rows of data, like most relational DBMSs" (Wikipedia 2013). Such databases are typically sparse, distributed, and persistent multi-dimensional sorted maps in which data is indexed by a triple of a row key, column key, and a timestamp. The value is represented as an uninterrupted string data type. Data is accessed by column families, i.e. a set of related column keys that effectively compress the sparse data in the columns. Column families are created before data can be stored and their number is expected to be small. In contrast, the number of columns is unlimited. In principle columnar stores are less suitable when all columns need to be accessed. However in practice this is rarely the case, leading to superior performance of columnar stores.
- **Document Databases:** In contrast to the values in a key-value store, documents are structured. However, there is no requirement for a common schema that all documents must adhere to as in the case for records in relational databases. Thus document databases are referred to as storing semi-structured data. Similar to key-value stores, documents can be queried using a unique key. However, it is possible to access documents by querying their internal structure, such as requesting all documents that contain a field with a specified value. The capability of the query interface is typically dependent on the encoding format used by the databases. Common encodings include XML or JSON.
- **Graph Databases:** Graph databases, such as Neo4J (2015), store data in graph structures making them suitable for storing highly associative data such as social network graphs. A particular flavour of graph databases are triple stores such as AllegroGraph (Franz 2015) and Virtuoso (Erling 2009) that are specifically

---

[3] Here and throughout this chapter SQL refers to the Standard Query Language as defined in the ISO/IEC Standard 9075-1:2011.

designed to store RDF triples. However, existing triple store technologies are not yet suitable for storing truly large datasets efficiently.

While in general NoSQL data stores scale better than relational databases, scalability decreases with increased complexity of the data model used by the data store. This particularly applies to graph databases that support applications that are both write and read intensive. One approach to optimize read access is to partition the graph into sub-graphs that are minimally connected between each other and to distribute these sub-graphs between computational nodes. However, as new edges are added to a graph the connectivity between sub-graphs may increase considerably. This may lead to higher query latencies due to increased networks traffic and non-local computations. Efficient *sharding schemes* must therefore carefully consider the overhead required for dynamically re-distributing graph data.

7.4.1.2 NewSQL Databases

NewSQL databases are a modern form of relational databases that aim for comparable scalability with NoSQL databases while maintaining the transactional guarantees made by traditional database systems. According to Venkatesh and Nirmala (2012) they have the following characteristics:

- SQL is the primary mechanism for application interaction
- ACID support for transactions
- A non-locking concurrency control mechanism
- An architecture providing much higher per-node performance
- A scale-out, shared-nothing architecture, capable of running on a large number of nodes without suffering bottlenecks

The expectation is that NewSQL systems are about 50 times faster than traditional OLTP RDBMS. For example, VoltDB (2014) scales linearly in the case of non-complex (single-partition) queries and provides ACID support. It scales for dozens of nodes where each node is restricted to the size of the main memory.

7.4.1.3 Big Data Query Platforms

Big data query platforms provide query facades on top of underlying big data stores that simplify querying the underlying data stores. They typically offer an SQL-like query interface for accessing the data, but differ in their approach and performance.

Hive (Thusoo et al. 2009) provides an abstraction on top of the Hadoop Distributed File System (HDFS) that allows structured files to be queried by an SQL-like query language. Hive executes the queries by translating queries in MapReduce jobs. As a consequence, Hive queries have a high latency even for small datasets. Benefits of Hive include the SQL-like query interface and the flexibility to evolve schemas easily. This is possible as the schema is stored independently from the data and the data is only validated at query time. This approach is referred to as schema-on-read compared to the schema-on-write approach of SQL databases. Changing the schema is therefore a comparatively cheap operation. The Hadoop columnar store HBase is also supported by Hive.

In contrast to Hive, Impala (Russel 2013) is designed for executing queries with low latencies. It re-uses the same metadata and SQL-like user interface as Hive but uses its own distributed query engine that can achieve lower latencies. It also supports HDFS and HBase as underlying data stores.

Spark SQL (Shenker et al. 2013) is another low latency query façade that supports the Hive interface. The project claims that "it can execute Hive QL queries up to 100 times faster than Hive without any modification to the existing data or queries" (Shenker et al. 2013). This is achieved by executing the queries using the Spark framework (Zaharia et al. 2010) rather than Hadoop's MapReduce framework.

Finally, Drill is an open source implementation of Google's Dremel (Melnik et al. 2002) that similar to Impala is designed as a scalable, interactive ad-hoc query system for nested data. Drill provides its own SQL-like query language DrQL that is compatible with Dremel, but is designed to support other query languages such as the Mongo Query Language. In contrast to Hive and Impala, it supports a range of schema-less data sources, such as HDFS, HBase, Cassandra, MongoDB, and SQL databases.

7.4.1.4 Cloud Storage

As cloud computing grows in popularity, its influence on big data grows as well. While Amazon, Microsoft, and Google build on their own cloud platforms, other companies including IBM, HP, Dell, Cisco, Rackspace, etc., build their proposal around OpenStack, an open source platform for building cloud systems (OpenStack 2014).

According to IDC (Grady 2013), by 2020 40 % of the digital universe "will be 'touched' by cloud computing", and "perhaps as much as 15 % will be maintained in a cloud".

Cloud in general, and particularly cloud storage, can be used by both enterprises and end users. For end users, storing their data in the cloud enables access from everywhere and from every device in a reliable way. In addition, end users can use cloud storage as a simple solution for online backup of their desktop data. Similarly for enterprises, cloud storage provides flexible access from multiple locations and quick and easy scale capacity (Grady 2013) as well as cheaper storage prices and better support based on economies of scale (CloudDrive 2013) with cost effectiveness especially high in an environment where enterprise storage needs are changing over time up and down.

Technically cloud storage solutions can be distinguished between object and block storage. Object storage "is a generic term that describes an approach to addressing and manipulating discrete units of storage called objects" (Margaret

Rouse 2014a). In contrast, block storage data is stored in volumes also referred to as blocks. According to Margaret Rouse (2014b), "each block acts as an individual hard drive" and enables random access to bits and pieces of data thus working well with applications such as databases.

In addition to object and block storage, major platforms provide support for relational and non-relational database-based storage as well as in-memory storage and queue storage. In cloud storage, there are significant differences that need to be taken into account in the application-planning phase:

- As cloud storage is a service, applications using this storage have less control and may experience decreased performance as a result of networking. These performance differences need to be taken into account during design and implementation stages.
- Security is one of the main concerns related to public clouds. As a result the Amazon CTO predicts that in five years all data in the cloud will be encrypted by default (Vogels 2013).
- Feature rich clouds like AWS supports calibration of latency, redundancy, and throughput levels for data access, thus allowing users to find the right trade-off between cost and quality.

Another important issue when considering cloud storage is the supported consistency model (and associated scalability, availability, partition tolerance, and latency). While Amazon's Simple Storage Service (S3) supports eventual consistency, Microsoft Azure blob storage supports strong consistency and at the same time high availability and partition tolerance. Microsoft uses two layers: (1) a stream layer "which provides high availability in the face of network partitioning and other failures", and (2) a partition layer which "provides strong consistency guarantees" (Calder et al. 2011).

7.4.2 Privacy and Security

Privacy and security are well-recognized challenges in big data. The CSA Big Data Working Group published a list of *Top 10 Big Data Security and Privacy Challenges* (Mora et al. 2012). The following are five of those challenges that are vitally important for big data storage.

7.4.2.1 Security Best Practices for Non-relational Data Stores

The security threats for NoSQL databases are similar to traditional RDBMS and therefore the same best practices should be applied (Winder 2012). However, many security measures that are implemented by default within traditional RDBMS are missing in NoSQL databases (Okman et al. 2011). Such measures would include encryption of sensitive data, sandboxing of processes, input validation, and strong user authentication.

Some NoSQL suppliers recommend the use of databases in a trusted environment with no additional security or authentication measures in place. However, this approach is hardly reasonable when moving big data storage to the cloud.

Security of NoSQL databases is getting more attention by security researchers and hackers, and security will further improve as the market matures. For example, there are initiatives to provide access control capabilities for NoSQL databases based on Kerberos authentication modules (Winder 2012).

7.4.2.2 Secure Data Storage and Transaction Logs

Particular security challenges for data storage arise due to the distribution of data. With auto-tiering, operators give away control of data storage to algorithms in order to reduce costs. Data whereabouts, tier movements, and changes have to be accounted for by transaction log.

Auto-tiering strategies have to be carefully designed to prevent sensitive data being moved to less secure and thus cheaper tiers; monitoring and logging mechanisms should be in place in order to have a clear view on data storage and data movement in auto-tiering solutions (Mora et al. 2012).

Proxy re-encryption schemes (Blaze et al. 2006) can be applied to multi-tier storage and data sharing in order to ensure seamless confidentiality and authenticity (Shucheng et al. 2010). However, performance has to be improved for big data applications. Transaction logs for multi-tier operations systems are still missing.

7.4.2.3 Cryptographically Enforced Access Control and Secure Communication

Today, data is often stored unencrypted, and access control solely depends on a gate-like enforcement. However, data should only be accessible by authorized entities by the guarantees of cryptography—likewise in storage as well as in transmission. For these purposes, new cryptographic mechanisms are required that provide the required functionalities in an efficient and scalable way.

While cloud storage providers are starting to offer encryption, cryptographic key material should be generated and stored at the client and never handed over to the cloud provider. Some products add this functionality to the application layer of big data storage, e.g., *zNcrypt*, *Protegrity Big Data Protection for Hadoop*, and the *Intel Distribution for Apache Hadoop* (now part of *Cloudera*).

Attribute-based encryption (Goyal et al. 2006) is a promising technology to integrate cryptography with access control for big data storage (Kamara and Lauter 2010; Lee et al. 2013; Li et al. 2013).

7.4.2.4 Security and Privacy Challenges for Granular Access Control

Diversity of data is a major challenge due to equally diverse security requirements, e.g., legal restrictions, privacy policies, and other corporate policies. Fine-grained access control mechanisms are needed to assure compliance with these requirements.

Major big data components use Kerberos (Miller et al. 1987) in conjunction with token-based authentication, and Access Control Lists (ACL) based upon users and jobs. However, more fine-grained mechanism, for instance Attribute-Based Access Control (ABAC) and eXtensible Access Control Markup Language (XACLM), are required to model the vast diversity of data origins and analytical usages.

7.4.2.5 Data Provenance

Integrity and history of data objects within value chains is crucial. Traditional provenance governs mostly ownership and usage. With big data however, the complexity of provenance metadata will increase (Glavic 2014).

Initial efforts have been made to integrate provenance into the big data ecosystem (Ikeda et al. 2011; Sherif et al. 2013); however, secure provenance requires guarantees of integrity and confidentiality of provenance data in all forms of big data storage and remains an open challenge. Furthermore, the analysis of very large provenance graphs is computationally intensive and requires fast algorithms.

7.4.2.6 Privacy Challenges in Big Data Storage

Researchers have shown (Acquisti and Gross 2009) that big data analysis of publicly available information can be exploited to guess the social security number of a person. Some products selectively encrypt data fields to create reversible anonymity, depending on the access privileges.

Anonymizing and de-identifying data may be insufficient as the huge amount of data may allow for re-identification. A roundtable discussion (Bollier and Firestone 2010) advocated *transparency on the handling of data and algorithms* as well as a *new deal on big data* (Wu and Guo 2013) to empower the end user as the owner of the data. Both options not only involve organization transparency, but also technical tooling such as *Security & Privacy by Design* and the results of the EEXCESS EU FP7 project (Hasan et al. 2013).

7.5   Future Requirements and Emerging Paradigms for Big Data Storage

This section provides an overview of future requirements and emerging trends.

7.5.1   Future Requirements for Big Data Storage

Three key areas have been identified that can be expected to govern future big data storage technologies. This includes standardization of query interfaces, increasing support for data security, protection of users' privacy, and the support of semantic data models.

7.5.1.1   Standardized Query Interfaces

In the medium to long-term NoSQL databases would greatly benefit from standardized query interfaces, similar to SQL for relational systems. Currently no standards exist for the individual NoSQL storage types beyond de-facto standard APIs for graph databases (Blueprints 2014) and the SPARQL data manipulation language (Aranda et al. 2013) supported by triplestore's vendors. Other NoSQL databases usually provide their own declarative language or API, and standardization for these declarative languages is missing.

While for some database categories (key/value, document, etc.) declarative language standardization is still missing, there are efforts discussing standardization needs. For instance the ISO/IEC JTC Study Group on big data has recently recommended that existing ISO/IEC standards committee should further investigate the "definition of standard interfaces to support non-relational data stores" (Lee et al. 2014).

The definition of standardized interfaces would enable the creation of a data virtualization layer that would provide an abstraction of heterogeneous data storage systems as they are commonly used in big data use cases. Some requirements of a data virtualization layer have been discussed online in an Infoworld blog article (Kobielus 2013).

7.5.1.2   Security and Privacy

Interviews were conducted with consultants and end users of big data storage who have responsibility for security and privacy, to gain their personal views and insights. Based upon these interviews and the gaps identified in Sect. 7.4.2, several future requirements for security and privacy in big data storage were identified.

Data Commons and Social Norms   Data stored in large quantities will be subject to sharing as well as derivative work in order to maximize big data benefits. Today, users are not aware how big data processes their data (transparency), and it is not clear how big data users can share and obtain data efficiently. Furthermore, legal constraints with respect to privacy and copyright in big data are currently not completely clear within the EU. For instance, big data allows novel analytics based upon aggregated data from manifold sources. How does this approach affect private information? How can rules and regulations for remixing and derivative works be applied to big data? Such uncertainty may lead to a disadvantage of the EU compared to the USA.

Data Privacy   Big data storage must comply with EU privacy regulations such as Directive 95/46/EC when personal information is being stored. Today, heterogeneous implementations of this directive render the storage of personal information in big data difficult. The General Data Protection Regulation (GDRP)—first proposed in 2012—is an on-going effort to harmonize data protection among EU member states. The GDRP is expected to influence future requirements for big data storage. As of 2014, the GDRP is subject to negotiations that make it difficult to estimate the final rules and start of enforcement. For instance, the 2013 draft version allows *data subjects* (persons) to request data controllers to delete personal data, which is often not sufficiently considered by big data storage solutions.

Data Tracing and Provenance   Tracing and provenance of data is becoming more and more important in big data storage for two reasons: (1) users want to understand where data comes from, if the data is correct and trustworthy, and what happens to their results and (2) big data storage will become subject to compliance rules as big data enters critical business processes and value chains. Therefore, big data storage has to maintain provenance metadata, provide provenance along the data processing chain, and offer user-friendly ways to understand and trace the usage of data.

Sandboxing and Virtualization   Sandboxing and virtualization of big data analytics becomes more important in addition to access control. According to economies of scale, big data analytics benefit from resource sharing. However, security breaches of shared analytical components lead to compromised cryptographic access keys and full storage access. Thus, jobs in big data analytics must be sandboxed to prevent an escalation of security breaches and therefore unauthorized access to storage.

7.5.1.3   Semantic Data Models

The multitude of heterogeneous data sources increases development costs, as applications require knowledge about individual data formats of each individual source. An emerging trend is the semantic web and in particular the semantic sensor web that tries to address this challenge. A multitude of research projects are concerned with all levels of semantic modelling and computation. As detailed in this book, the need for semantic annotations has for instance been identified for the health sector. The requirement for data storage is therefore to support the large-scale storage and management of semantic data models. In particular trade-offs between expressivity and efficient storage and querying need to be further explored.

7.5.2 Emerging Paradigms for Big Data Storage

There are several new paradigms emerging for the storage of large and complex datasets. These new paradigms include, among others, the increased use of NoSQL databases, convergence with analytics frameworks, and managing data in a central data hub.

7.5.2.1 Increased Use of NoSQL Databases

NoSQL databases, most notably graph databases and columnar stores, are increasingly used as a replacement or complement to existing relational systems.

For instance, the requirement of using semantic data models and cross linking data with many different data and information sources strongly drives the need to be able to store and analyse large amounts of data using graph-based models. However, this requires overcoming the limitation of current graph-based systems as described above. For instance, Jim Webber states "Graph technologies are going to be incredibly important" (Webber 2013). In another interview, Ricardo Baeza-Yates, VP of Research for Europe and Latin America at Yahoo!, also states the importance of handling large-scale graph data (Baeza-Yates 2013). The Microsoft research project Trinity achieved a significant breakthrough in this area. Trinity is an in-memory data storage and distributed processing platform. By building on its very fast graph traversal capabilities, Microsoft researchers introduced a new approach to cope with graph queries. Other projects include Google's knowledge graph and Facebook's graph search that demonstrate the increasing relevance and growing maturity of graph technologies.

7.5.2.2 In-Memory and Column-Oriented Designs

Many modern high-performance NoSQL databases are based on columnar designs. The main advantage is that in most practical applications only a few columns are needed to access the data. Consequently storing data in columns allows faster access. In addition, column-oriented databases often do not support the expensive join operations from the relational world. Instead, a common approach is to use a single wide column table that stores the data based on a fully denormalized schema.

According to Michael Stonebraker "SQL vendors will all move to column stores, because they are wildly faster than row stores" (Stonebraker 2012a).

High-performance in-memory databases such as SAP HANA typically combine in-memory techniques with column-based designs. In contrast to relational systems that cache data in-memory, in-memory databases can use techniques such as anti-caching (DeBrabant et al. 2013). Harizopoulos et al. have shown that the most time for executing a query is spent on administrative tasks such as buffer management and locking (Harizopoulos et al. 2008).

7.5.2.3 Convergence with Analytics Frameworks

During the course of the project many scenarios have been identified that call for better analysis of available data to improve operations in various sectors. Technically, this means an increased need for complex analytics that goes beyond simple aggregations and statistics. Stonebraker points out that the need for complex analytics will strongly impact existing data storage solutions (Stonebraker 2012b).

As use case specific analytics are one of the most crucial components that are creating actual business value, it becomes increasingly important to scale up these analytics satisfying performance requirements, but also to reduce the overall development complexity and cost. Figure 7.2 shows some differences between using separate systems for data management and analytics versus integrated analytical databases.

7.5.2.4 The Data Hub

A central data hub that integrates all data in an enterprise is a paradigm that considers managing all company data as a whole, rather than in different, isolated databases managed by different organizational units. The benefit of a central data hub is that data can be analysed as a whole, linking various datasets owned by the company thus leading to deeper insights.

Typical technical implementations are based on a Hadoop-based system that may use HDFS or HBase (Apache 2014) to store an integrated master dataset. On one hand, this master dataset can be used as ground truth and backup for existing data management systems, but it also provides the basis for advanced analytics that combine previously isolated datasets.

Companies such as Cloudera use this paradigm to market their Hadoop distribution (Cloudera 2014b). Many use cases of enterprise data hub exist already. A case study in the financial sector is described in the next section.

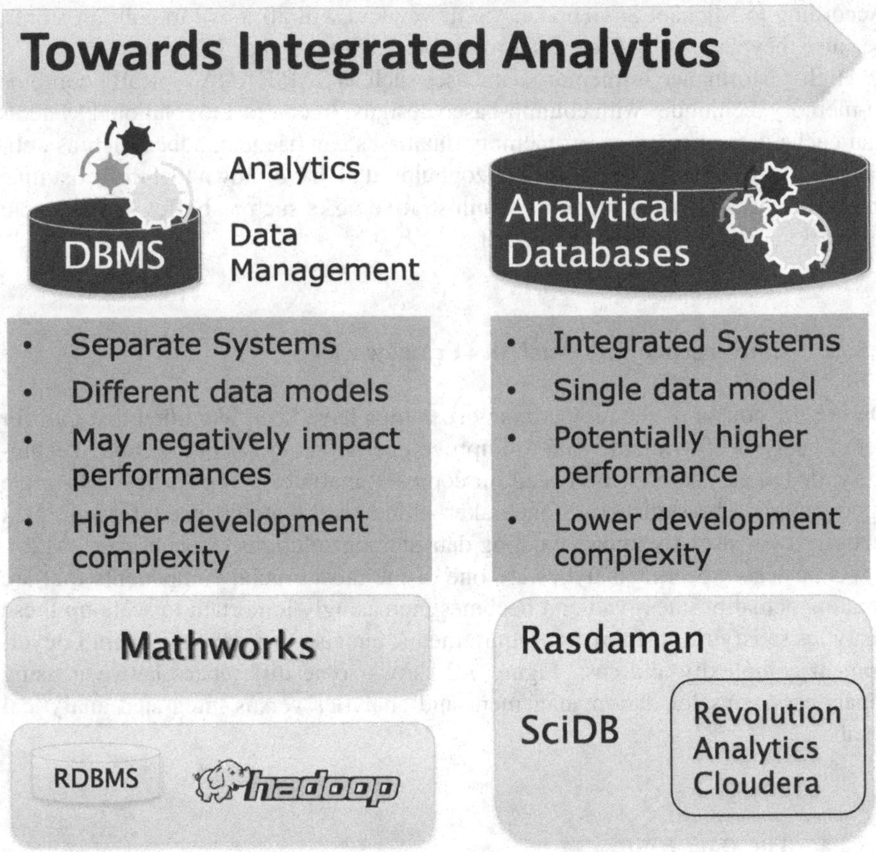

Fig. 7.2 Paradigm shift from pure data storage systems to integrated analytical databases

7.6 Sector Case Studies for Big Data Storage

In this section three selected use cases are described that illustrate the potential and need for future storage technologies. The health use case illustrates how social media based analytics is enabled by NoSQL storage technologies. The second use case from the financial sector illustrates the emerging paradigm of a centralized data hub. The last use case from the energy sector illustrates the benefits of managing fine-grained Internet of Things (IoT) data for advanced analytics. An overview of the key characteristics of the use case can be found in Table 7.1. More case studies are presented in Curry et al. (2014).

Table 7.1 Key characteristics of selected big data storage case studies

Case study	Sector	Volume	Storage technologies	Key requirements
Treato: Social media based medication intelligence	Health	>150 TB	HBase	Cost-efficiency, scalability limitations of relational DBs
Centralized data hub	Finance	Between several petabytes and over 150 PB	Hadoop/ HDFS	Building more accurate models, scale of data, suitability for unstructured data
Smart grid	Energy	Tens of TB per day	Hadoop	Data volume, operational challenges

7.6.1 Health Sector: Social Media-Based Medication Intelligence

Treato is an Israeli company that specializes in mining user-generated content from blogs and forums in order to provide brand intelligence services to pharmaceutical companies. As Treato is analysing the social web, it falls into the "classical" category of analysing large amounts of unstructured data, an application area that often asks for big data storage solutions. Treato's service as a use case demonstrates the value of using big data storage technologies. The information is based on a case study published by Cloudera (2012), the company that provided the Hadoop distribution Treato has been using.

While building its prototype, Treato discovered "that side effects could be identified through social media long before pharmaceutical companies or the Food & Drug Administration (FDA) issued warnings about them. For example, when looking at discussions about Singulair, an asthma medication, Treato found that almost half of UGC discussed mental disorders; the side effect would have been identifiable four years before the official warning came out." (Cloudera 2012).

Treato initially faced two major challenges: First, it needed to develop the analytical capabilities to analyse patient's colloquial language and map that into a medical terminology suitable for delivering insights to its customers. Second, it was necessary to analyse large amounts of data sources as fast as possible in order to provide accurate information in real time.

The first challenge, developing the analytics, has been addressed initially with a non-Hadoop system based on a relational database. With that system Treato was facing the limitation that it could only handle "data collection from dozens of websites and could only process a couple of million posts per day" (Cloudera 2012). Thus, Treato was looking for a cost-efficient analytics platform that could fulfil the following key requirements:

1. Reliable and scalable storage
2. Reliable and scalable processing infrastructure
3. Search engine capabilities for retrieving posts with high availability
4. Scalable real-time store for retrieving statistics with high availability

As a result Treato decided on a Hadoop-based system that uses HBase to store the list of URLs to be fetched. The posts available at these URLs are analysed by using natural language processing in conjunction with their proprietary ontology. In addition "each individual post is indexed, statistics are calculated, and HBase tables are updated" (Cloudera 2012).

According to the case study report, the Hadoop-based solution stores more than 150 TB of data including 1.1 billion online posts from thousands of websites including about more than 11,000 medications and more than 13,000 conditions. Treato is able to process 150–200 million user posts per day.

For Treato, the impact of the Hadoop-based storage and processing infrastructure is that they obtain a scalable, reliable, and cost-effective system that may even create insights that would not have been possible without this infrastructure. The case study claims that with Hadoop, Treato improved execution time at least by a factor of six. This allowed Treato to respond to a customer request about a new medication within one day.

7.6.2 Finance Sector: Centralized Data Hub

As mapped out in the description of the sectorial roadmaps (Lobillo et al. 2013), the financial sector is facing challenges with respect to increasing data volumes and a variety of new data sources such as social media. Here use cases are described for the financial sector based on a Cloudera solution brief (Cloudera 2013).

Financial products are increasingly digitalized including online banking and trading. As online and mobile access simplifies access to financial products, there is an increased level of activity leading to even more data. The potential of big data in this scenario is to use all available data for building accurate models that can help the financial sector to better manage financial risks. According to the solution brief, companies have access to several petabytes of data. According to Larry Feinsmith, managing director of JPMorgan Chase, his company is storing over 150 petabytes online and use Hadoop for fraud detection (Cloudera 2013).

Secondly, new data sources add to both the volume and variety of available data. In particular, unstructured data from weblogs, social media, blogs, and other news feeds can help in customer relationship management, risk management, and maybe even algorithmic trading (Lobillo et al. 2013). Pulling all the data together in a centralized data hub enables more detailed analytics that can provide a competitive edge. However traditional systems cannot keep up with the scale, costs, and cumbersome integration of traditional extract, transform, load (ETL) processes using fixed data schemes, nor are they able to handle unstructured data. Big data storage systems however scale extremely well and can process both structured and unstructured data.

7.6.3 Energy: Device Level Metering

In the energy sector, smart grid and smart meter management is an area that promises both high economic and environmental benefits. As depicted in Fig. 7.3, the introduction of renewable energies such as photovoltaic systems deployed on houses can cause grid instabilities. Currently grid operators have little knowledge about the last mile to energy consumers. Thus they are not able to appropriately react to instabilities caused at the very edges of the grid network. By analysing smart meter data sampled at second intervals, short-term forecasting of energy demands and managing the demand of devices such as heating and electrical cars becomes possible, thus stabilizing the grid. If deployed in millions of households the data volumes can reach petabyte scale, thus greatly benefiting from new storage technologies. Table 7.2 shows the data volume only for the raw data collected for one day.

The Peer Energy Cloud (PEC) project (2014) is a public funded project that has demonstrated how smart meter data can be analysed and used for trading energy in the local neighbourhood, thus increasing the overall stability of the power grid. Moreover, it has successfully shown that by collecting more fine granular data, i.e. monitoring energy consumption of individual devices in the household, the accuracy of predicting the energy consumption of households can be significantly improved (Ziekow et al. 2013). As the data volumes increase it becomes

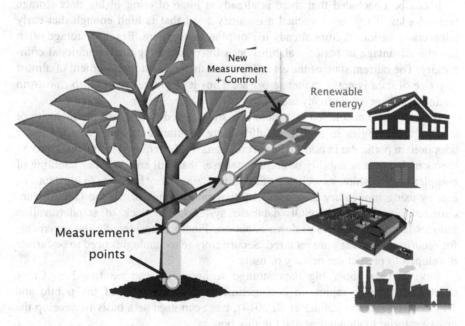

Fig. 7.3 Introduction of renewable energy at consumer sites changes the topology of the energy grid and requires new measurement points at the leaves of the grid

Table 7.2 Calculation of the amount of data sampled by smart meters

Sampling rate	1 Hz
Record size	50 Bytes
Raw data per day and household	4.1 MB
Raw data per day for 10 Mio customers	~39 TB

increasingly difficult to handle the data with legacy relational databases (Strohbach et al. 2011).

7.7 Conclusions

The chapter contains an overview of current big data storage technologies as well as emerging paradigms and future requirements. The overview specifically included technologies and approaches related to privacy and security. Rather than focusing on detailed descriptions of individual technologies a broad overview was provided, and technical aspects that have an impact on creating value from large amounts of data highlighted. The social and economic impact of big data storage technologies was described, and three selected case studies in three different sectors were detailed, which illustrate the need for easy to use scalable technologies.

It can be concluded that there is already a huge offering of big data storage technologies. They have reached a maturity level that is high enough that early adopters in various sectors already use or plan to use them. Big data storage often has the advantage of better scalability at a lower price tag and operational complexity. The current state of the art reflects that the efficient management of almost any size of data is not a challenge per se. Thus it has huge potential to transform business and society in many areas.

It can also be concluded that there is a strong need to increase the maturity of storage technologies so that they fulfil future requirements and lead to a wider adoption, in particular in non-IT-based companies. The required technical improvements include the scalability of graph databases that will enable better handling of complex relationships, as well as further minimizing query latencies to big datasets, e.g. by using in-memory databases. Another major roadblock is the lack of standardized interfaces to NoSQL database systems. The lack of standardization reduces flexibility and slows down adoption. Finally, considerable improvements for security and privacy are required. Secure storage technologies need to be further developed to protect the privacy of users.

More details about big data storage technologies can be found in Curry et al. (2014). This report, in conjunction with the analysis of the public and 10 industrial sectors (Zillner et al. 2014), has been used as a basis to develop the cross-sectorial roadmap described in this book.

References

Acquisti, A., & Gross, R. (2009). Predicting social security numbers from public data. *Proceedings of the National Academy of Sciences, 106*(27), 10975–10980.

Ahmadi Zeleti, F., Ojo, A., & Curry, E. (2014). Business models for the open data industry: Characterization and analysis of emerging models. In *15th Annual International Conference on Digital Government Research* (dg.o 2014) (pp. 215–226). ACM.

Apache. (2014). Apache HBase Project Website. http://hbase.apache.org. Accessed Nov 21, 2014.

Aranda, C. B., Corby, O., Das, S., Feigenbaum, L., Gearon, P., Glimm, B., et al. (2013). SPARQL 1.1 overview. In *W3C Recommendation*.

Baeza-Yates, R. (2013). BIG Interview by John Dominque.

Blaze, M., Bleumer, G., & Strauss, M. (2006). Divertible protocols and atomic proxy cryptography. In *Proceedings of Eurocrypt* (pp. 127–144).

Blueprints. (2014). Blueprints Project Homepage. https://github.com/tinkerpop/blueprints/wiki. Accessed Feb 4, 2015.

Bollier, D., & Firestone, C. M. (2010). *The promise and peril of big data*. Washington, DC: Aspen Institute, Communications and Society Program.

Calder, B., Wang, J., Ogus, A., Nilakantan, N., Skjolvsvold, A., McKelvie, S. et al. (2011). Windows azure storage: a highly available cloud storage service with strong consistency. In: *Proceedings of the Twenty-Third ACM Symposium on Operating Systems Principles* (143–157). New York, NY: ACM.

CloudDrive. (2013). Advantages of cloud data storage. http://www.clouddrive.com.au/download/www.clouddrive.com.au-WhitePaper.pdf. Accessed Nov 20, 2013.

Cloudera. (2012). Treato Customer Case Study. https://www.cloudera.com/content/dam/cloudera/Resources/PDF/casestudy/Cloudera_Customer_Treato_Case_Study.pdf

Cloudera. (2013). *Identifying fraud, managing risk and improving compliance in financial services.*

Cloudera. (2014a). Cloudera Company Web page. www.cloudera.com. Accessed May 6, 2015.

Cloudera. (2014b). Rethink data. http://www.cloudera.com/content/cloudera/en/new/. Accessed Feb 4, 2014.

Curry, E., Ngonga, A., Domingue, J., Freitas, A., Strohbach, M., Becker, T., et al. (2014). D2.2.2. Final version of the technical white paper. Public deliverable of the EU-Project BIG (318062; ICT-2011.4.4).

DeBrabant, J., Pavlo, A., Tu, S., Stonebraker, M., & Zdonik, S. (2013). Anti-caching: a new approach to database management system architecture. In *Proceedings of the VLDB Endowment* (pp 1942–1953).

Erling, O. (2009). Virtuoso, a Hybrid RDBMS/Graph Column Store. In: Virtuoso Open-Source Wiki. http://virtuoso.openlinksw.com/dataspace/doc/dav/wiki/Main/VOSArticleVirtuosoAHybridRDBMSGraphColumnStore. Accessed Feb 6, 2015.

Franz. (2015). Allegrograph product web page. http://franz.com/agraph/allegrograph/. Accessed Feb 6, 2015.

Gislason, H. (2013). BIG Interview by John Dominque.

Glavic, B. (2014). Big data provenance: Challenges and implications for benchmarking. In T. Rabl, M. Poess, C. Baru, & H.-A. Jacobsen (Eds.), *Specifying big data benchmarks* (pp. 72–80). Berlin: Springer.

Goyal, V., Pandey, O., Sahai, A., & Waters, B. (2006). Attribute-based encryption for fine-grained access control of encrypted data. In *Proceedings of the 13th ACM Conference on Computer and Communications Security* (pp. 89–98).

Grady, J. (2013). *Is enterprise cloud storage a good fit for your business?* http://www.1cloudroad.com/is-enterprise-cloud-storage-a-good-fit-for-your-business

Harizopoulos, S., Abadi, D. J., Madden, S., & Stonebraker, M. (2008). OLTP through the looking glass, and what we found there. In *Proceedings of the 2008 ACM SIGMOD International Conference on Management data (SIGMOD '08).*

Hasan, O., Habegger, B., Brunie, L., Bennani, N., & Damiani, E. (2013). A discussion of privacy challenges in user profiling with big data techniques: The EEXCESS use case. *IEEE International Congress on Big Data* (pp. 25–30).

Hortonworks. (2014). Hortonworks Company Web Page. http://hortonworks.com/. Accessed Feb 6, 2015.

Ikeda, R., Park, H., & Widom, J. (2011). Provenance for generalized map and reduce workflows. In *Biennial Conference on Innovative. Data Systems Research* (pp. 273–283).

iQuartic. (2014). iQuartic pioneers use of Hadoop with Electronic Health Records (EHRs/EMRs). In: iQuartic Blog. http://www.iquartic.com/blog/. Accessed Feb 7, 2014.

Kamara, S., & Lauter, K. (2010). Cryptographic cloud storage. In *Financial Cryptography and Data Security* (pp. 136–149).

Kobielus, J. (2013) Big Data needs data virtualization. In: InfoWorld Webpage. http://www.infoworld.com/article/2611579/big-data/big-data-needs-data-virtualization.html. Accessed Nov 18, 2014.

Koomey, J. G. (2008). Worldwide electricity used in data centers. *Environmental Research Letters, 3*, 034008. doi:10.1088/1748-9326/3/3/034008.

Lee, C.-C., Chung, P.-S., & Hwang, M.-S. (2013). A survey on attribute-based encryption schemes of access. *International Journal of Network Security, 15*, 231–240.

Lee, K., Manning, S., Melton, J., Boyd, D., Grady, N., & Levin, O. (2014). Final SGBD report to JTC1, ISO/IEC JTC1 SGBD document no. N0095.

Li, M., Yu, S., Zheng, Y., Ren, K., Lou, W., et al. (2013). Scalable and secure sharing of personal health records in cloud computing using attribute-based encryption. *IEEE Transactions on Parallel and Distributed Systems, 24*, 131–143.

Lobillo, F., Puente, M. A., Lippell, H., Zillner, S., Bretschneider, C., Oberkampf, H., et al. (2013). BIG deliverable D2.4.1 – First draft of sector's roadmaps.

Manyika, J., Chui, M., Brown, B., Bughin, J., Dobbs, R., Roxburgh, C., et al. (2011). *Big data: The next frontier for innovation, competition, and productivity.* Sydney: McKinsey Global Institute. http://www.mckinsey.com/insights/business_technology/big_data_the_next_frontier_for_innovation.

MapR. (2014). MapR Company Website. https://www.mapr.com/. Accessed Feb 6, 2014.

Margaret Rouse. (2014a). *Object Storage.* http://searchstorage.techtarget.com/definition/object-storage. Accessed Nov 20, 2014.

Margaret Rouse. (2014b). *Block Storage.* http://searchstorage.techtarget.com/definition/block-storage. Accessed Feb 4, 2014.

Marz, N., & Warren, J. (2014). A new paradigm for Big Data. In N. Marz & J. Warren (Eds.), *Big Data: Principles and best practices of scalable real-time data systems.* Shelter Island, NY: Manning Publications.

Melnik, S., Garcia-Molina, H., & Rahm, E. (2002). Similarity flooding: A versatile graph matching algorithm and its application to schema matching. In *Proceedings of the 18th International Conference Data Engineering.* IEEE Computer Society (pp. 117–128).

Miller, S. P., Neuman, B. C., Schiller, J. I., & Saltzer, J. H. (1987, December 21). *Section E.2.1: Kerberos authentication and authorization system.* MIT Project Athena, Cambridge, MA.

Mora, A. C., Chen, Y., Fuchs, A., Lane, A., Lu, R., Manadhata, P. et al. (2012). *Top Ten Big Data Security and Privacy Challenges.* Cloud Security Alliance (CSA).

Neo4j. (2015). Neo4j Company Website. http://neo4j.com/. Accessed Feb 6, 2015.

Okman, L., Gal-Oz, N., Gonen, Y., et al. (2011). Security issues in nosql databases. In *2011 I.E. 10th International Conference on Trust, Security and Privacy in Computing and Communications (TrustCom)* (pp. 541–547).

OpenStack. (2014). OpenStack Website. http://www.openstack.org. Accessed Feb 3, 2014.

PEC. (2014). Peer Energy Cloud Project Website. http://www.peerenergycloud.de/. Accessed Feb 6, 2015.

Russel, J. (2013). *Cloudera Impala.* O#Reilly Media

Shenker, S., Stoica, I., Zaharia, M., & Xin, R. (2013). Shark: SQL and rich analytics at scale. In *Proceedings of the 2013 ACM SIGMOD International Conference on Management of Data* (pp. 13–24).

Sherif, A., Sohan, R., & Hopper, A. (2013). HadoopProv: Towards provenance as a first class citizen in MapReduce. In *Proceedings of the 5th USENIX Workshop on the Theory and Practice of Provenance.*

Shucheng, Y., Wang, C., Ren, K., & Lou, W. (2010). Achieving secure, scalable, and fine-grained data access control in cloud computing. *INFOCOM* (pp. 1–9).

Shvachko, K. H. K., Radia, S., & Chansler, R. (2010). The Hadoop distributed file system. In *IEEE 26th Symposium on Mass Storage Systems and Technologies* (pp. 1–10).

Stonebraker, M. (2012a) What Does "Big Data" Mean? In: BLOG@ACM. http://cacm.acm.org/blogs/blog-cacm/155468-what-does-big-data-mean/fulltext. Accessed Feb 5, 2015.

Stonebraker, M. (2012b). What Does "Big Data" Mean? (Part 2). In: BLOG@ACM. http://cacm.acm.org/blogs/blog-cacm/156102-what-does-big-data-mean-part-2/fulltext. Accessed Apr 25, 2013.

Strohbach, M., Ziekow, H., Gazis, V., & Akiva, N. (2011). Towards a big data analytics framework for IoT and smart city applications. In F. Xhafa & P. Papajorgji (Eds.), *Modeling and processing for next generation big data technologies with applications* (pp. 257–282). Berlin: Springer.

Thusoo, A., Sarma, J., Jain, N., Shao, Z., Chakka, P., Anthony, S., et al. (2009). Hive – a warehousing solution over a map-reduce framework. *Statistics and Operations Research Transactions, 2,* 1626–1629.

Turner, V., Gantz, J. F., Reinsel, D., & Minton, S. (2014). *The digital universe of opportunities: Rich data and the increasing value of the internet of things.* Framingham, MA: International Data Corporation (IDC). http://idcdocserv.com/1678. Accessed Aug 19, 2015.

Venkatesh, P., & Nirmala, S. (2012). NewSQL – The new way to handle big data. In: Blog. http://www.opensourceforu.com/2012/01/newsql-handle-big-data/. Accessed Nov 18, 2014.

Vogels, W. (2013). Day 2 Keynote. AWS reInvent.

VoltDB. (2014). VoltDB Company Website. http://www.voltdb.com. Accessed Nov 21, 2014.

Webber, J. (2013). BIG Interview by John Dominque.

White, T. (2012). *Hadoop: The Definitive Guide.* O'Reilly.

Wikipedia. (2013). *Column-oriented DBMS.* http://en.wikipedia.org/wiki/Column-oriented_DBMS. Accessed Apr 25, 2013.

Winder, D. (2012). Securing NoSQL applications: Best practises for big data security. *Computer Weekly.*

Wu, C., & Guo, Y. (2013). Enhanced user data privacy with pay-by-data model. In *Proceeding of 2013 I.E. International Conference on Big Data* (pp. 53–57).

Zaharia, M., Chowdhury, M., Franklin, M. J., Shenker, S., & Stoica, I. (2010). Spark: Cluster computing with working sets. In *HotCloud'10 Proceedings of the 2nd USENIX Conference on Hot Topics in Cloud Computing* (p. 10).

Ziekow, H., Goebel, C., Struker, J., & Jacobsen, H.-A. (2013). The potential of smart home sensors in forecasting household electricity demand. In *Smart Grid Communications (SmartGridComm), 2013 I.E. International Conferences* (pp. 229–234).

Zillner, S., Neururer, S., Munne, R., Prieto, E., Strohbach, M., van Kasteren, T., et al. (2014). D2.3.2. Final Version of the Sectorial Requisites. Public Deliverable of the EU-Project BIG (318062; ICT-2011.4.4).

Chapter 8
Big Data Usage

Tilman Becker

8.1 Introduction

One of the core business tasks of advanced data usage is the support of business decisions. Data usage is a wide field that is addressed in this chapter by viewing data usage from various perspectives, including the underlying technology stacks, trends in various sectors, the impact on business models, and requirements on human–computer interaction.

The full life-cycle of information is covered in this book, with previous chapters covering data acquisition, storage, analysis, and curation. The position of big data usage within the overall big data value chain can be seen in Fig. 8.1. Data usage covers the business goals that need access to such data, its analyses, and the tools needed to integrate the analyses in business decision-making.

The process of decision-making includes reporting, exploration of data (browsing and lookup), and exploratory search (finding correlations, comparisons, what-if scenarios, etc.). The business value of such information logistics is twofold: (1) control over the value chain and (2) transparency of the value chain. The former is generally independent from big data; the latter, however, provides opportunities and requirements for data markets and services.

Big data influences the validity of data-driven decision-making in the future. Influencing factors are (1) the time range for decisions/recommendations, from short term to long term and (2) the various databases (in a non-technical sense) from past, historical data to current and up-to-date data.

New data-driven applications will strongly influence the development of new markets. A potential blocker of such developments is always the need for new

T. Becker (✉)
German Research Centre for Artificial Intelligence (DFKI), Stuhlsatzenhausweg 3, 66123
Saarbrücken, Germany
e-mail: tilman.becker@dfki.de

© The Author(s) 2016   143
J.M. Cavanillas et al. (eds.), *New Horizons for a Data-Driven Economy*,
DOI 10.1007/978-3-319-21569-3_8

Big Data Value Chain

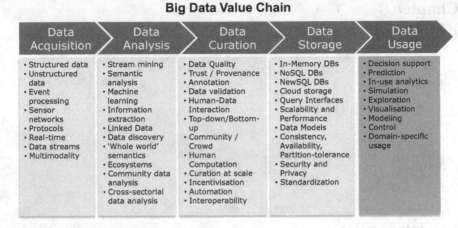

Fig. 8.1 Data usage in the big data value chain

partner networks (combination of currently separate capabilities), business processes, and markets.

A special area of use cases for big data is the manufacturing, transportation, and logistics sector. These sectors are undergoing a transformational change as part of an industry-wide trend, called "Industry 4.0", which originates in the digitization and interlinking of products, production facilities, and transportation infrastructure as part of the developing "Internet of Things". Data usage has a profound impact in these sectors, e.g. applications of predictive analysis in maintenance are leading to new business models as the manufacturers of machinery are in the best position to provide big data-based maintenance. The emergence of cyber-physical systems (CPS) for production, transportation, logistics, and other sectors brings new challenges for simulation and planning, for monitoring, control, and interaction (by experts and non-experts) with machinery or data usage applications.

On a larger scale, new services and a new service infrastructure is required. Under the title "smart data" and smart data services, requirements for data and also service markets are formulated. Besides the technology infrastructure for the interaction and collaboration of services from multiple sources, there are legal and regulatory issues that need to be addressed. A suitable service infrastructure is also an opportunity for SMEs to take part in big data usage scenarios by offering specific services, e.g., through data usage service marketplaces.

Access to data usage is given through specific tools and in turn through query and scripting languages that typically depend on the underlying data stores, their execution engines, APIs, and programming models. In Sect. 8.5.1, different technology stacks and some of the trade-offs involved are discussed. Section 8.5.2 presents general aspects of decision support, followed by a discussion of specific access to analysis results through visualization and new explorative interfaces. Human–computer interaction will play a growing role in decision support since many cases cannot rely on pre-existing models of correlation. In such cases, user interfaces (e.g. in data visualization for visual analytics) must support an exploration of the data and their potential connections. Emerging trends and future requirements are presented in Sect. 8.6 with special emphasis on Industry 4.0 and the emerging need for smart data and smart services.

8.2 Key Insights for Big Data Usage

The key insights for big data usage identified are as follows:

Predictive Analytics A prime example for the application of predictive analytics is in predictive maintenance based on sensor and context data to predict deviations from standard maintenance intervals. Where data points to a stable system, maintenance intervals can be extended, leading to lower maintenance costs. Where data points to problems before reaching a scheduled maintenance, savings can be even higher if a breakdown, repair cost, and downtimes can be avoided. Information sources go beyond sensor data and tend to include environmental and context data, including usage information (e.g. high load) of the machinery. As predictive analysis depends on new sensors and data processing infrastructure, large manufacturers are switching their business model and investing in new infrastructure themselves (realizing scale effects on the way) and leasing machinery to their customers.

Industry 4.0 A growing trend in manufacturing is the employment of cyber-physical systems. It brings about an evolution of old manufacturing processes, on the one hand making available a massive amount of sensor and other data and on the other hand bringing the need to connect all available data through communication networks and usage scenarios that reap the potential benefits. Industry 4.0 stands for the entry of IT into the manufacturing industry and brings with it a number of challenges for IT support. This includes services for diverse tasks such as planning and simulation, monitoring and control, interactive use of machinery, logistics and enterprise resource planning (ERP), predictive analysis, and eventually prescriptive analysis where decision processes can be automatically controlled by data analysis.

Smart Data and Service Integration When further developing the scenario for Industry 4.0 above, services that solve the tasks at hand come into focus. To enable the application of smart services to deal with the big data usage problems, there are technical and organizational matters. Data protection and privacy issues, regulatory issues, and new legal challenges (e.g. with respect to ownership issues for derived data) must all be addressed.

On a technical level, there are multiple dimensions along which the interaction of services must be enabled: on a hardware level from individual machines, to facilities, to networks; on a conceptual level from intelligent devices to intelligent systems and decisions; on an infrastructure level from IaaS to PaaS and SaaS to new services for big data usage and even to business processes and knowledge as a service.

Interactive Exploration When working with large volumes of data in large variety, the underlying models for functional relations are oftentimes missing. This means data analysts have a greater need for exploring datasets and analyses. This is addressed through visual analytics and new and dynamic ways of data visualization, but new user interfaces with new capabilities for the exploration of data are needed. Integrated data usage environments provide support, e.g., through history mechanisms and the ability to compare different analyses, different parameter settings, and competing models.

8.3   Social and Economic Impact for Big Data Usage

One of the most important impacts of big data usage scenarios is the discovery of new relations and dependencies in the data that lead, on the surface, to economic opportunities and more efficiency. On a deeper level, big data usage can provide a better understanding of these dependencies, making the system more transparent and supporting economic as well as social decision-making processes (Manyika et al. 2011). Wherever data is publicly available, social decision-making is supported; where relevant data is available on an individual-level, personal decision-making is supported. The potential for transparency through big data usage comes with a number of requirements: (1) regulations and agreements on data access, ownership, protection, and privacy, (2) demands on data quality (e.g. on the completeness, accuracy, and timeliness of data), and (3) access to the raw data as well as access to appropriate tools or services for big data usage.

Transparency thus has an economic and social and personal dimension. Where the requirements listed above can be met, decisions become transparent and can be made in a more objective, reproducible manner, where the decision processes are open to involve further players.

The current economic drivers of big data usage are large companies with access to complete infrastructures. These include sectors like advertising at Internet companies and sensor data from large infrastructures (e.g. smart grids or smart cities) or for complex machinery (e.g. airplane engines). In the latter examples, there is a trend towards even closer integration of data usage at large companies as the big data capabilities remain with the manufactures (and not the customers), e.g. when engines are only rented and the big data infrastructure is owned and managed by the manufacturers.

There is a growing requirement for standards and accessible markets for data as well as for services to manage, analyse, and exploit further uses of data. Where such requirements are met, opportunities are created for SMEs to participate in more complex use cases for big data usage. Section 8.5.2.1 discusses these requirements for smart data and corresponding smart data services.

8.4 Big Data Usage State-of-the-Art

This section provides an overview of the current state of the art in big data usage, addressing briefly the main aspects of the technology stacks employed and the subfields of decision support, predictive analysis, simulation, exploration, visualization, and more technical aspects of data stream processing. Future requirements and emerging trends related to big data usage will be addressed in Sect. 8.6.

8.4.1 Big Data Usage Technology Stacks

Big data applications rely on the complete data value chain that is covered in the BIG project, starting at data acquisition, including curation, storage, analysis, and being joined for data usage. On the technology side, a big data usage application relies on a whole stack of technologies that cover the range from data stores and their access to processing execution engines that are used by query interfaces and languages.

It should be stressed that the complete big data technology stack can be seen as much broader, i.e., encompassing the hardware infrastructure, such as storage systems, servers, datacentre networking infrastructure, corresponding data organization and management software, as well as a whole range of services ranging from consulting and outsourcing to support and training on the business side as well as the technology side.

Actual user access to data usage is given through specific tools and in turn through query and scripting languages that typically depend on the underlying data stores, their execution engines, APIs, and programming models. Some examples include SQL for classical relational database management systems (RDBMS), Dremel and Sawzall for Google's file system (GFS), and MapReduce, Hive, Pig, and Jaql for Hadoop-based approaches, Scope for Microsoft's Dryad and CosmosFS, and many other offerings, e.g. Stratosphere's[1] Meteor/Sopremo and ASTERIX's AQL/Algebricks.

Analytics tools that are relevant for data usage include SystemT (IBM, for data mining and information extraction) and Matlab (U. Auckland and Mathworks, resp. for mathematical and statistical analysis), tools for business intelligence and analytics (SAS Analytics (SAS), Vertica (HP), SPSS (IBM)), tools for search and indexing (Lucene and Solr (Apache)), and specific tools for visualization (Tableau, Tableau Software). Each of these tools has its specific area of application and covers different aspects of big data.

The tools for big data usage support business activities that can be grouped into three categories: lookup, learning, and investigating. The boundaries are sometimes fuzzy and learning and investigating might be grouped as examples of exploratory search. Decision support needs access to data in many ways, and as big data more

---

[1] Stratosphere is further developed in the Apache Flink project.

often allows the detection of previously unknown correlations, data access must be more often from interfaces that enable exploratory search and not mere access to predefined reports.

8.4.1.1 Trade-Offs in Big Data Usage Technologies

An in-depth case study analysis of a complete big data application was performed to determine the decisions involved in weighing the advantages and disadvantages of the various available components of a big data technology stack. Figure 8.2 shows the infrastructure used for Google's YouTube Data Warehouse (YTDW) as detailed in Chattopadhyay (2011). Some of the core lessons learned by the YouTube team include an acceptable trade-off in functionality when giving priority to low-latency queries. This justified the decision to stick with the ([Dremel tool (for querying large datasets) that has acceptable drawbacks in expressive power (when compared to SQL-based tools), yet provides low-latency results and scales to what Google considers "medium" scales. Note, however, that Google is using "trillions of rows in seconds", and running on "thousands of CPUs and petabytes of data", processing "quadrillions of records per month". While Google regards this as medium scale, this might be sufficient for many applications that are clearly in the realms of big data. Table 8.1 shows a comparison of various data usage technology components used in the YTDW, where latency refers to the time the systems need to answer request; scalability to the ease of using ever larger datasets; SQL refers to the (often preferred) ability to use SQL (or similar) queries; and power refers to the expressive power of search queries.

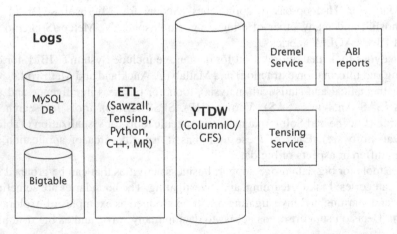

Fig. 8.2 The YouTube Data Warehouse (YTDW) infrastructure. Derived from Chattopadhyay (2011)

Table 8.1 Comparison of data usage technologies used in YTDW. Source: Chattopadhyay (2011)

	Sawzall	Tenzing	Dremel
Latency	High	Medium	Low
Scalability	High	High	Medium
SQL	None	High	Medium
Power	High	Medium	Low

8.4.2 Decision Support

Current decision support systems—as far as they rely on static reports—use these techniques but do not allow sufficient dynamic usage to reap the full potential of exploratory search. However, in increasing order of complexity, these groups encompass the following business goals:

- **Lookup:** On the lowest level of complexity, data is merely retrieved for various purposes. These include fact retrieval and searches for known items, e.g. for verification purposes. Additional functionalities include navigation through datasets and transactions.
- **Learning:** On the next level, these functionalities can support knowledge acquisition and interpretation of data, enabling comprehension. Supporting functionalities include comparison, aggregation, and integration of data. Additional components might support social functions for data exchange. Examples for learning include simple searches for a particular item (knowledge acquisition), e.g. a celebrity and their use in advertising (retail). A big data search application would be expected to find all related data and present an integrated view.
- **Investigation:** On the highest level of decision support systems, data can be analysed, accreted, and synthesized. This includes tool support for exclusion, negation, and evaluation. At this level of analysis, true discoveries are supported and the tools influence planning and forecasting. Higher levels of investigation (discovery) will attempt to find important correlations, say the influence of seasons and/or weather on sales of specific products at specific events. More examples, in particular of big data usage for high-level strategic business decisions, are given in Sect. 8.6 on future requirements.

At an even higher level, these functionalities might be (partially) automated to provide predictive and even normative analyses. The latter refers to automatically derived and implemented decisions based on the results of automatic (or manual) analysis. However, such functions are beyond the scope of typical decision support systems and are more likely to be included in complex event processing (CEP) environments where the low latency of automated decision is weighed higher than the additional safety of a human-in-the-loop that is provided by *decision support systems*.

8.4.3 Predictive Analysis

A prime example of predictive analysis is predictive maintenance based on big data usage. Maintenance intervals are typically determined as a balance between a costly, high frequency of maintenance and an equally costly danger of failure before maintenance. Depending on the application scenario, safety issues often mandate frequent maintenance, e.g., in the aerospace industry. However, in other cases the cost of machine failures is not catastrophic and determining maintenance intervals becomes a purely economic exercise.

The assumption underlying predictive analysis is that given sufficient sensor information from a specific machine and a sufficiently large database of sensor and failure data from this machine or the general machine type, the specific time to failure of the machine can be predicted more accurately. This approach promises to lower costs due to:

- *Longer maintenance intervals* as "unnecessary" interruptions of production (or employment) can be avoided when the regular time for maintenance is reached. A predictive model allows for an extension of the maintenance interval, based on current sensor data.
- *Lower number of failures* as the number of failures occurring earlier than scheduled maintenance can be reduced based on sensor data and predictive maintenance calling for earlier maintenance work.
- *Lower costs for failures* as potential failures can be predicted by predictive maintenance with a certain advance warning time, allowing for scheduling maintenance/exchange work, lowering outage times.

8.4.3.1 New Business Model

The application of predictive analytics requires the availability of sensor data for a specific machine (where "machine" is used as a fairly generic term) as well as a comprehensive dataset of sensor data combined with failure data.

Equipping existing machinery with additional sensors, adding communication pathways from sensors to the predictive maintenance services, etc., can be a costly proposition. Based on experiencing reluctance from their customers in such investments, a number of companies (mainly manufacturers of machines) have developed new business models addressing these issues.

Prime examples are GE wind turbines and Rolls Royce airplane engines. Rolls Royce engines are increasingly offered for rent, with full-service contracts including maintenance, allowing the manufacturer to lift the benefits from applying predictive maintenance. By correlating the operational context with engine sensor data, failures can be predicted early, reducing (the costs of) replacements, allowing for planned maintenance rather than just scheduled maintenance. GE OnPoint solutions offer similar service packages that are sold in conjunction with GE engines.[2]

8.4.4 Exploration

Exploring big datasets and the corresponding analytics results can be distributed across multiple sources and formats (e.g. new portals, travel blogs, social networks, web services, etc.). To answer complex questions—e.g. "Which astronauts have been on the moon?", "Where is the next Italian restaurant with high ratings?", "Which sights should I visit in what order?"—users have to start multiple requests to multiple, heterogeneous sources and media. Finally, the results have to be combined manually.

Support for the human trial-and-error approach can add value by providing intelligent methods for automatic information extraction and aggregation to answer complex questions. Such methods can transform the data analysis process to become explorative and iterative. In a first phase, relevant data is identified and then a second learning phase context is added for such data. A third exploration phase allows various operations for deriving decisions from the data or transforming and enriching the data.

Given the new complexity of data and data analysis available for exploration, there are a number of emerging trends in explorative interfaces that are discussed in Sect. 8.5.2.4 on complex exploration.

8.4.5 Iterative Analysis

An efficient, parallel processing of iterative data streams brings a number of technical challenges. Iterative data analysis processes typically compute analysis results in a sequence of steps. In every step, a new intermediate result or state is computed and updated. Given the high volumes in big data applications, computations are executed in parallel, distributing, storing, and managing the state efficiently across multiple machines. Many algorithms need a high number of iterations to compute the final results, requiring low latency iterations to minimize overall response times. However, in some applications, the computational effort is reduced significantly between the first and the last iterations. Batch-based systems such as Map/Reduce (Dean and Ghemawat 2008) and Spark (Apache 2014) repeat all computations in every iteration even when the (partial) results do not change.

---

[2] See http://www.aviationpros.com/press_release/11239012/tui-orders-additional-genx-powered-boeing-787s

Truly iterative dataflow systems like Stratosphere (Stratosphere 2014) of specialized graph systems like GraphLab (Low et al. 2012) and Google Pregel (Malewicz et al. 2010) exploit such properties and reduce the computational cost in every iteration.

Future requirements on technologies and their applications in big data usage are described in Sect. 8.5.1.3, covering aspects of pipelines versus materialization and error tolerance.

8.4.6   Visualization

Visualizing the results of an analysis including a presentation of trends and other predictions by adequate visualization tools is an important aspect of big data usage. The selection of relevant parameters, subsets, and features is a crucial element of data mining and machine learning with many cycles needed for testing various settings. As the settings are evaluated on the basis of the presented analysis results, a high-quality visualization allows for a fast and precise evaluation of the quality of results, e.g., in validating the predictive quality of a model by comparing the results against a test dataset. Without supportive visualization, this can be a costly and slow process, making visualization an important factor in data analysis.

For using the results of data analytics in later steps of a data usage scenario, for example, allowing data scientists and business decision-makers to draw conclusions from the analysis, a well-selected visual presentation can be crucial for making large result sets manageable and effective. Depending on the complexity of the visualizations, they can be computationally costly and hinder interactive usage of the visualization.

However, explorative search in analytics results is essential for many cases of big data usage. In some cases, the results of a big data analysis will be applied only to a single instance, say an airplane engine. In many cases, though, the analysis dataset will be as complex as the underlying data, reaching the limits of classical statistical visualization techniques and requiring interactive exploration and analysis (Spence 2006; Ward et al. 2010). In Shneiderman's seminal work on visualization (Shneiderman 1996), he identifies seven types of tasks: overview, zoom, filter, details-on-demand, relate, history, and extract.

Yet another area of visualization applies to data models that are used in many machine-learning algorithms and differ from traditional data mining and reporting applications. Where such data models are used for classification, clustering, recommendations, and predictions, their quality is tested with well-understood datasets. Visualization supports such validation and the configuration of the models and their parameters.

Finally, the sheer size of datasets is a continuous challenge for visualization tools that is driven by technological advances in GPUs, displays, and the slow adoption of immersive visualization environments such as caves, VR, and AR. These aspects are covered in the fields of scientific and information visualization.

The following section elaborates the application of visualization for big data usage, known as visual analytics. Section 8.5.1.4 presents a number of research challenges related to visualization in general.

8.4.6.1   Visual Analytics

A definition of visual analytics, taken from Keim et al. (2010) recalls first mentions of the term in 2004. More recently, the term is used in a wider context, describing a new multidisciplinary field that combines various research areas including visualisation, human–computer interaction, data analysis, data management, geo-spatial and temporal data processing, spatial decision support and statistics.

The "Vs" of big data affect visual analytics in a number of ways. The **volume** of big data creates the need to visualize high dimensional data and their analyses and to display multiple data types such as linked graphs. In many cases interactive visualization and analysis environments are needed that include dynamically linked visualizations. Data **velocity** and the dynamic nature of big data calls for correspondingly dynamic visualizations that are updated much more often than previous, static reporting tools. Data **variety** presents new challenges for cockpits and dashboards.

The main new aspects and trends are:

- Interactivity, visual queries, (visual) exploration, multi-modal interaction (touchscreen, input devices, AR/VR)
- Animations
- User adaptivity (personalization)
- Semi-automation and alerting, CEP (complex event processing), and BRE (business rule engines)
- Large variety in data types, including graphs, animations, microcharts (Tufte), gauges (cockpit-like)
- Spatiotemporal datasets and big data applications addressing geographic information systems (GIS)
- Near real-time visualization. Sectors finance industry (trading), manufacturing (dashboards), oil/gas—CEP, BAM (business activity monitoring)
- Data granularity varies widely
- Semantics

Use cases for visual analytics include multiple sectors, e.g. marketing, manufacturing, healthcare, media, energy, transportation (see also the use cases in Sect. 8.6), but also additional market segments such as software engineering.

A special case of visual analytics that is spearheaded by the US intelligence community is visualization for cyber security. Due to the nature of this market segment, details can be difficult to obtain; however there are publications available, e.g. the VizSec conferences.[3]

8.5   Future Requirements and Emerging Trends for Big Data Usage

This section provides an overview of future requirements and emerging trends that resulted from the task force's research.

8.5.1   Future Requirements for Big Data Usage

As big data usage is becoming more important, there are issues on the underlying assumptions that become more important. The key issue is a necessary validation of the underlying data. The following quote as attributed to Ronald Coase, winner of the Nobel Prize in economics in 1991, put it as a joke alluding to the inquisition: "If you torture the data long enough, it [they] will confess to anything".

On a more serious note there are some common misconceptions in big data usage:

1. Ignoring modelling and instead relying on correlation rather than an understanding of causation.
2. The assumption that with enough—or even all (see next point)—data available, no models are needed (Anderson 2008).
3. Sample bias. Implicit in big data is the expectation that *all* data will (eventually) be sampled. This is rarely ever true; data acquisition depends on technical, economical, and social influences that create sample bias.
4. Overestimation of accuracy of analysis: it is easy to ignore false positives.

To address these issues, the following future requirements will gain importance:

1. Include more modelling, resort to simulations, and correct (see next point) for sample bias.
2. Understand the data sources and the sample bias that is introduced by the context of data acquisition. Create a model of the real, total dataset to correct for sample bias.
3. Data and analysis transparency: If the data and the applied analyses are known, it is possible to judge what the (statistical) chances are that correlations are not

---

[3] http://www.vizsec.org

only "statistically significant" but also that the number of tested, possible correlations is not big enough to make the finding of some correlation almost inevitable.

With these general caveats as background, the key areas that are expected to govern the future of big data usage have been identified:

- Data quality in big data usage
- Tool performance
- Strategic business decisions
- Human resources, big data specific positions

The last point is exemplified by a report on the UK job market in big data (e-skills 2013) where demand is growing strongly. In particular, the increasing number of administrators sought shows that big data is growing from experimental status to a core business unit.

8.5.1.1 Specific Requirements

Some general trends are already identifiable and can be grouped into the following requirements:

- Use of big data for marketing purposes
- Detect abnormal events of incoming data in real time
- Use of big data to improve efficiency (and effectiveness) in core operations
  - Realizing savings during operations through real-time data availability, more fine-grained data, and automated processing
  - Better data basis for planning of operational details and new business processes
  - Transparency for internal and external (customers) purposes
- Customization, situation adaptivity, context-awareness, and personalization
- Integration with additional datasets
  - Open data
  - Data obtained through sharing and data marketplaces
- Data quality issues where data is not curated or provided under pressure, e.g., to acquire an account in a social network where the intended usage is anonymous
- Privacy and confidentiality issues, data access control
- Interfaces
  - Interactive and flexible, ad hoc analyses to provide situation-adaptive and context-aware reactions, e.g. recommendations
  - Suitable interfaces to provide access to big data usage in non-office environments, e.g. mobile situations, factory floors, etc.
  - Tools for visualization, query building, etc.

- Discrepancy between the technical know-how necessary to execute data analysis (technical staff) and usage in business decisions (by non-technical staff)
- Need for tools that enable early adoption. As the developments in industry are perceived to be accelerating, the head start from early adoption is also perceived as being of growing importance and a growing competitive advantage.

8.5.1.2 Industry 4.0

For applications of big data in areas such as manufacturing, energy, transportation, and even health, wherever intelligent machines are involved in the business process, there is a need for aligning hardware technology (i.e. machines and sensors) with software technology (i.e. the data representation, communication, storage, analysis, and control of the machinery). Future developments in embedded systems that are developing into "cyber-physical systems" will need to synchronize the joint development of hardware (computing, sensing, and networking) and software (data formats, operating systems, and analysis and control systems).

Industrial suppliers are beginning to address these issues. GE software identifies "However well-developed industrial technology may be, these short-term and long-term imperatives cannot be realized using today's technology alone. The software and hardware in today's industrial machines are very interdependent and closely coupled, making it hard to upgrade software without upgrading hardware, and vice versa" (Chauhan 2013).

On the one hand this adds a new dependency to big data usage, namely the dependency on hardware systems and their development and restrictions. On the other hand, it opens new opportunities to address more integrated systems with big data usage applications at the core of supporting business decisions.

8.5.1.3 Iterative Data Streams

There are two prominent areas of requirements for efficient and robust implementations of big data usage that relate to the underlying architectures and technologies in distributed, low-latency processing of large datasets and large data streams.

- **Pipelining and materialization:** High data rates pose a special challenge for data stream processing. The underlying architectures are based on a pipeline approach where processed data can be handed to the next processing step with very low delay to avoid pipeline congestion. In cases where such algorithms do not exist, data is collected and stored before being processed. Such approaches are called "materialization". Low latency for queries can typically only be realized in pipelining approaches.
- **Error tolerance:** Fault tolerance and error minimization are an important challenge for pipelining systems. Failures in compute nodes are common and

can cause parts of the analysis result to be lost. Parallel systems must be designed in a robust way to overcome such faults without failing. A common approach are continuous *check points* at which intermediate results are saved, allowing the reconstruction of a previous state in case of an error. Saving data at checkpoints is easy to implement, yet results in high execution costs due to the synchronization needs and storage costs when saving to persistent storage. New alternative algorithms use optimistic approaches that can recreate valid states allowing the continuation of computing. Such approaches add costs only in cases of errors but are applicable only in restricted cases.

8.5.1.4 Visualization

There are a number of future trends that need to be addressed in the area of visualization and visual analytics in the medium to far future, for example (Keim et al. 2010):

- Visual perception and cognitive aspects
- "Design" (visual arts)
- Data quality, missing data, data provenance
- Multi-party collaboration, e.g., in emergency scenarios
- Mass-market, end user visual analytics

In addition, Markl et al. (2013) compiled a long list of research questions from which the following are of particular importance to data usage and visualization:

- How can visualization support the process of constructing data models for prediction and classification?
- Which visualization technologies can support an analyst in explorative analysis?
- How can audio and video (animations) be automatically collected and generated for visual analytics?
- How can meta-information such as semantics, data quality, and provenance be included into the visualization process?

8.5.2 Emerging Paradigms for Big Data Usage

A number of emerging paradigms for big data usage have been identified that fall into two categories. The first category encompasses all aspects of integration of big data usage into larger business processes and the evolution towards a new trend called "smart data". The second trend is much more local and concerns the interface tools for working with big data. New exploration tools will allow data scientists and analysts in general to access more data more quickly and support decision-making by finding trends and correlations in the dataset that can be grounded in models of the underlying business processes.

There are a number of technology trends that are emerging (e.g. in-memory databases) that allow for a sufficiently fast analysis to enable explorative data analysis and decision support. At the same time, new services are developing, providing data analytics, integration, and transformation of big data to organizational knowledge.

As in all new digital markets, the development is driven in part by start-ups that fill new technology niches; however, the dominance of big players is particularly important as they have much easier access to big data. The transfer of technology to SMEs is faster than in previous digital revolutions; however, appropriate business cases for SMEs are not easy to design in isolation and typically involve the integration into larger networks or markets.

8.5.2.1   Smart Data

The concept of smart data is defined as the effective application of big data that is successful in bringing measurable benefits and has a clear meaning (semantics), measurable data quality, and security (including data privacy standards).[4]

Smart data scenarios are thus a natural extension of big data usage in any economically viable context. These can be new business models that are made possible by innovative applications of data analysis, or improving the efficiency/ profitability of existing business models. The latter are easy to start with as data is available and, as it is embedded in existing business processes, already has an assigned meaning (semantics) and business structure. Thus, it is the added value of guaranteed data quality and existing metadata that can make big data usage become a case of smart data.

Beyond the technical challenges, the advent of smart data brings additional challenges:

1. Solving regulatory issues regarding data ownership and data privacy (Bitkom 2012).
2. Making data more accessible by structuring through the addition of metadata, allowing for the integration of separate data silos (Bertolucci 2013).
3. Lifting the benefits from already available open data and linked data sources. Their market potential is currently not fully realized (Groves et al. 2013).

The main potential of data usage, according to Lo (2012), is found in the optimization of business processes, improved risk management, and market-oriented product development. The purpose of enhanced big data usage as smart data is in solving social and economical challenges in many sectors, including energy, manufacturing, health, and media.

---

[4] This section reflects the introduction of smart data as stated in a broadly supported memorandum, available at http://smart-data.fzi.de/memorandum/

For SMEs, the focus is on the integration into larger value chains that allow multiple companies to collaborate to give SMEs access to the effects of scale that underlie the promise of big data usage. Developing such collaborations is enabled by smart data when the meaning of data is explicit, allowing for the combination of planning, control, production, and state information data beyond the limits of each partnering company.

Smart data creates requirements in four areas: semantics, data quality, data security and privacy, and metadata.

Semantics Understanding and having available the meaning of datasets enables important steps in smart data processing:

- Interoperability
- Intelligent processing
- Data integration
- Adaptive data analysis

Metadata As a means to encode and store the meaning (semantics) of data. Metadata can also be used to store further information about data quality, provenance, usage rights, etc. Currently there are many proposals but no established standards for metadata.

Data Quality The quality and provenance of data is one of the well-understood requirements for big data (related to one of the "Vs", i.e. "veracity").

Data Security and Privacy These separate, yet related, issues are particularly influenced by existing regulatory standards. Violations of data privacy laws can easily arise from processing of personal data, e.g. movement profiles, health data, etc. Although such data can be enormously beneficial, violations of data privacy laws carry severe punishments. Other than doing away with such regulations, methods for anonymization (ICO 2012) and pseudonymization (Gowing and Nickson 2010) can be developed and used to address these issues.

8.5.2.2 Big Data Usage in an Integrated and Service-Based Environment

The continuing integration of digital services (Internet of Services), smart digital products (Internet of things), and production environments (Internet of Things, Industry 4.0) includes the usage of big data in most integration steps. A recent study by General Electric examined the various dimensions of integration within the airline industry (Evans and Annunziata 2012). Smart products like a turbine are integrated into larger machines, and in the first example this is an airplane. Planes are in turn part of whole fleets that operate in a complex network of airports, maintenance hangars, etc. At each step, the current integration of the business processes is extended by big data integration. The benefits for optimization can be harvested at each level (assets, facility, fleets, and the entire network) and by integrating knowledge from data across all steps.

8.5.2.3 Service Integration

The infrastructure within which big data usage will be applied will adapt to this integration tendency. Hardware and software will be offered as services, all integrated to support big data usage. See Fig. 8.3 for a concrete picture of the stack of services that will provide the environment for "Beyond technical standards and protocols, new platforms that enable firms to build specific applications upon a shared framework/architecture [are necessary]", as foreseen by the GE study or the "There is also a need for on-going innovation in technologies and techniques that will help individuals and organisations to integrate, analyse, visualise, and consume the growing torrent of big data", as sketched by McKinsey's study (Manyika et al. 2011).

Figure 8.3 shows big data as part of a virtualized service infrastructure. At the bottom level, current hardware infrastructure will be virtualized with cloud computing technologies; hardware infrastructure as well as platforms will be provided as services. On top of this cloud-based infrastructure, software as a service (SaaS) and on top of this business processes as a service (BPaaS) can be built. In parallel, big data will be offered as a service and embedded as the precondition for knowledge services, e.g. the integration of semantic technologies for analysis of unstructured and aggregated data. Note that big data as a service may be seen as extending a layer between PaaS and SaaS.

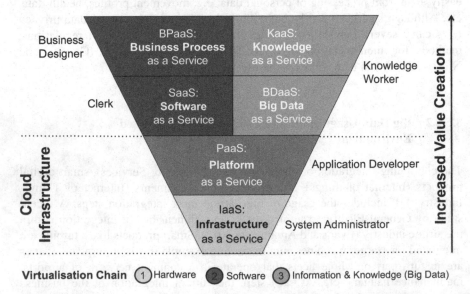

Fig. 8.3 Big data in the context of an extended service infrastructure. W. Wahlster (2013, Personal Communication)

This virtualization chain from hardware to software to information and knowledge also identifies the skills needed to maintain the infrastructure. Knowledge
workers or data scientists are needed to run big data and knowledge services.

8.5.2.4 Complex Exploration

Big data exploration tools support complex datasets and their analysis through a
multitude of new approaches, e.g. Sect. 8.5.1.4 on visualization. Current methods
for exploration of data and analysis results have a central shortcoming in that a user
can follow their exploration only selectively in one direction. If they enter a dead
end or otherwise unsatisfactory state, they have to backtrack to a previous state,
much as in depth-first search or hill-climbing algorithms. Emerging user interfaces
for parallel exploration (CITE) are more versatile and can be compared to best-first
or beam searches: the user can follow and compare multiple sequences of exploration at the same time.

Early instances of this approach have been developed under the name "subjunctive interfaces" (Lunzer and Hornbæk 2008) and applied to geographical datasets
(Javed et al. 2012) and as "parallel faceted browsing" (Buschbeck et al. 2013). The
latter approach assumes structured data but is applicable to all kinds of datasets,
including analysis results and CEP (complex event processing).

These complex exploration tools address an inherent danger in big data analysis
that arises when large datasets are automatically searched for correlations: an
increasing number of seemingly statistically significant correlations will be found
and need to be tested for underlying causations in a model or by expert human
analysis. Complex exploration can support the checking process by allowing a
parallel exploration of variations of a pattern and expected consequences of
assumed causation.

8.6   Sectors Case Studies for Big Data Usage

In this section an overview of case studies that demonstrate the actual and potential
value of big data usage is presented. More details can be found in Zillner
et al. (2013, 2014). The use cases selected here exemplify particular aspects that
are covered in those reports.

8.6.1   Healthcare: Clinical Decision Support

Description Clinical decision support (CDS) applications aim to enhance the
efficiency and quality of care operations by assisting clinicians and healthcare
professionals in their decision-making process. CDS applications enable context-

dependent information access by providing pre-diagnosis information, or by validating and correction of data. Thus, CDS systems support clinicians in informed decision-making, which again helps to reduce treatment errors as well as helps to improve efficiency.

By relying on big data technology, future clinical decisions support applications will become substantially more intelligent. An example use case is the pre-diagnosis of medical images, with treatment recommendations reflecting existing medical guidelines.

The core prerequisite is the comprehensive data integration and the very high level of data quality necessary for physicians to actually rely on automated decision support.

8.6.2 Public Sector: Monitoring and Supervision of Online Gambling Operators

Description This future scenario represents a clear need. The main goal involved is fraud detection that is hard to execute as the amount of data received in real time, on a daily and monthly basis, cannot be processed with standard database tools. Real-time data is received from gambling operators every five minutes. Currently, supervisors have to define the cases on which to apply offline analysis of selected data.

The core prerequisite is a need to explore data interactively, compare different models and parameter settings based on technology, e.g. complex event processing that allows the real-time analysis of such a dataset. This use case relates to the issues on visual analytics and exploration, and predictive analytics.

8.6.3 Telco, Media, and Entertainment: Dynamic Bandwidth Increase

Description The introduction of new Telco offerings (e.g. a new gaming application) can cause problems with bandwidth allocations. Such scenarios are of special importance to telecommunication providers, as more profit is made with data services than with voice services. In order to pinpoint the cause of bandwidth problems, transcripts of call-centre conversations can be mined to identify customers and games involved with timing information, putting into place infrastructure measures to dynamically change the provided bandwidth according to usage.

The core prerequisites are related to predictive analysis. If problems can be detected while they are building up, peaks can be avoided altogether. Where the decision support can be automated, this scenario can be extended to prescriptive analysis.

8.6.4 Manufacturing: Predictive Analysis

Description Where sensor data, contextual and environmental data, is available, possible failures of machinery can be predicted. The predictions are based on abnormal sensor values that correspond to functional models of failure. Furthermore, context information such as inferences on heavy or light usage depending on the tasks executed (taken, e.g. from an ERP system) and contributing information such as weather conditions, etc., can be taken into account.

The core prerequisites, besides classical requirements such as data integration from the various, partially unstructured, data sources, are transparent prediction models and sufficiently large datasets to enable the underlying machine-learning algorithms.

8.7 Conclusions

This chapter provides state of the art as well as future requirements and emerging trends of big data usage.

The major uses of big data applications are in decision support, in predictive analytics (e.g. for predictive maintenance), and in simulation and modelling. New trends are emerging in visualization (visual analytics) and new means of exploration and comparison of alternate and competing analyses.

A special area of use cases for big data is the manufacturing, transportation, and logistics sector with a new trend "Industry 4.0". The emergence of cyber-physical systems for production, transportation, logistics, and other sectors brings new challenges for simulation and planning, for monitoring, control, and interaction (by experts and non-experts) with machinery or big data usage applications. On a larger scale, new services and a new service infrastructure are required. Under the title "smart data" and smart data services, requirements for data and also service markets are formulated. Besides the technology infrastructure for the interaction and collaboration of services from multiple sources, there are legal and regulatory issues that need to be addressed. A suitable service infrastructure is also an opportunity for SMEs to take part in big data usage scenarios by offering specific services, e.g., through data service marketplaces.

References

Anderson, C. *The end of theory*. Wired, 16.07, 2008. Available at http://archive.wired.com/science/discoveries/magazine/16-07/pb_theory

Apache Spark. http://spark.apache.org/, (last retrieved April 2014).

Bertolucci, J. *IBM's Predictions: 6 Big Data Trends In 2014*, December 2013. Available at http://www.informationweek.com/big-data/big-data-analytics/ibms-predictions-6-big-data-trends-in-2014-/d/d-id/1113118

Bitkom. (Ed.). (2012). *Big Data im Praxiseinsatz – Szenarien, Beispiele, Effekte*. Available at http://www.bitkom.org/files/documents/BITKOM_LF_big_data_2012_online%281%29.pdf

Buschbeck, S., Jameson, A., Spirescu, A., Schneeberger, T., Troncy, R., & Khrouf, H., et al. (2013). Parallel faceted browsing. In *Extended Abstracts of CHI 2013, the Conference on Human Factors in Computing Systems (Interactivity Track)*.

Chattopadhyay, B. (Google), *Youtube Data Warehouse, Latest technologies behind Youtube, including Dremel and Tenzing*, XLDB 2011, Stanford.

Chauhan, N. (2013). *Modernizing machine-to-machine interactions: A platform for Igniting the Next Industrial Revolution, GE Software*. Available at http://www.gesoftware.com/sites/default/files/GE-Software-Modernizing-Machine-to-Machine-Interactions.pdf

Dean, J., & Ghemawat, S. (2008). MapReduce: Simplified data processing on large clusters. *Communications of the ACM, 51*(1), 107–113.

e-skills. (2013). *Big Data Analytics: An assessment of demand for labour and skills, 2012-2017*. e-skills, London. Available at http://www.e-skills.com/research/research-publications/big-data-analytics/

Evans, P. C., Annunziata, M. (2012). *Industrial internet: Pushing the boundaries of minds and machines*, GE, November 26, 2012.

Gowing, W., & Nickson, J. (2010) Pseudonymisation Technical White Paper, NHS connecting for health, March 2010.

Groves, P., Kayyali, B., Knott, D., & Van Kuiken, S. (2013). The 'big data' revolution in healthcare, January 2013. Available at http://www.mckinsey.com/insights/health_systems/~/media/7764A72F70184C8EA88D805092D72D58.ashx

ICO. (2012). *Anonymisation: Managing data protection risk code of practice*. Wilmslow: Information Commissioner's Office.

Javed, W., Ghani, S., & Elmqvist, N. (2012). PolyZoom: Multiscale and multifocus explora-tion in 2D visual spaces. In *Human factors in computing systems: CHI 2012 conference proceedings*. New York: ACM.

Keim, D., Kohlhammer, J., & Ellis, G. (eds.) (2010) *Mastering the information age: solving problems with visual analytics*. Eurographics Association.

Lo, S. (2012). *Big data facts and figures*, November 2012. Available at http://blogs.sap.com/innovation/big-data/big-data-facts-figures-02218

Low, Y., Bickson, D., Gonzalez, J., Guestrin, C., Kyrola, A., & Hellerstein, J. M. (2012). Distributed Graph-Lab: A framework for machine learning and data mining in the cloud. *Proceedings of the VLDB Endowment, 5*(8), 716–727.

Lunzer, A., & Hornbæk, K. (2008). Subjunctive interfaces: Extending applications to support parallel setup, viewing and control of alternative scenarios. *ACM Transactions on Computer-Human Interaction, 14*(4), 17.

Malewicz, G., Austern, M. H., Bik, A. J., Dehnert, J. C., Horn, I., Leiser, N., et al. (2010). Pregel: a system for large-scale graph processing. In *Proceedings of the 2010 ACM SIGMOD International Conference on Management of data*, ACM (pp. 135–146).

Manyika, J. et al. (2011). *Big data: The next frontier for innovation, competition, and productivity*. McKinsey & Company.

Markl, V., Hoeren, T., & Krcmar, H. (2013). Innovationspotenzialanalyse für die neuen Technologien für das Verwalten und Analysieren von großen Datenmengen, November 2013.

Shneiderman, B. (1996). The eyes have it: A task by data type taxonomy for information visualizations. In *Proceedings of Visual Languages*.

Spence, R. (2006). *Information visualization – design for interaction* (2nd ed.). Upper Saddle River, NJ: Prentice Hall.

Stratosphere Project. https://www.stratosphere.eu/, (last retrieved April 2014).

Ward, M., Grinstein, G. G., & Keim, D. (2010). *Interactive data visualization: Foundations, techniques, and applications*. Natick, MA: Taylor & Francis.

Zillner, S., Rusitschka, S., Munné, R., Lippell, H., Lobillo, F., Hussain, K., et al. (2013). *D2.3.1. First draft of the sectorial requisites*. Public Deliverable of the EU-Project BIG (318062; ICT-2011.4.4).

Zillner, S., Rusitschka, S., Munné, R., Strohbach, M., van Kasteren, T., Lippell, H., et al. (2014). *D2.3.2. Final version of the sectorial requisites*. Public Deliverable of the EU-Project BIG (318062; ICT-2011.4.4).

Part III
Usage and Exploitation of Big Data

Chapter 9
Big Data-Driven Innovation in Industrial Sectors

Sonja Zillner, Tilman Becker, Ricard Munné, Kazim Hussain, Sebnem Rusitschka, Helen Lippell, Edward Curry, and Adegboyega Ojo

9.1 Introduction

Regardless of what form it takes, data has the potential to tell stories, identify cost savings and efficiencies, new connections and opportunities, and enable improved understanding of the past to shape a better future (US Chamber of Commerce

S. Zillner (✉)
Corporate Technology, Siemens AG, Munich, Germany

School of International Business and Entrepreneurship, Steinbeis University, Berlin, Germany
e-mail: sonja.zillner@siemens.com

T. Becker
German Research Centre for Artificial Intelligence (DFKI), Stuhlsatzenhausweg 3, 66123
Saarbrücken, Germany
e-mail: tilman.becker@dfki.de

R. Munné
Atos Spain, S.A., Av. Diagonal, 200, 08018 Barcelona, Spain
e-mail: ricard.munne@atos.net

K. Hussain
Atos Spain, S.A., Albarracín 25 28037 Madrid, Spain
e-mail: kazim.hussain@atos.net

S. Rusitschka
Corporate Technology, Siemens AG, Munich, Germany
e-mail: sebnem.rusitschka@siemens.com

H. Lippell
Press Association, London, UK
e-mail: helen.lippell@pressassociation.com

E. Curry • A. Ojo
Insight Centre for Data Analytics, National University of Ireland Galway, Lower Dangan,
Galway, Ireland
e-mail: edward.curry@insight-centre.org; adegboyega.ojo@insight-centre.org

© The Author(s) 2016   169
J.M. Cavanillas et al. (eds.), *New Horizons for a Data-Driven Economy*,
DOI 10.1007/978-3-319-21569-3_9

Foundation 2014). Big data connotes the enormous volume of information including user-generated data from social media platforms (i.e. Internet data); machine, mobile, and GPS data as well as the Internet of Things (industrial and sensor data); business data including customer, inventory, and transactional data (enterprise data); datasets generated or collected by government agencies, as well as universities and non-profit organizations (public data) (US Chamber of Commerce Foundation 2014). For many businesses and governments in different parts of the world, techniques for processing and analysing these large volumes of data (big data) constitute an important resource for driving value creation, fostering new products, processes, and markets, as well as enabling the creation of new knowledge (OECD 2014). In 2013 alone, the data-driven economy added an estimated $67 billion in new value to the Australian economy, equivalent to 4.4 % of its gross domestic product or the whole of its retail sector (Stone and Wang 2014).

As a source of economic growth and development, big data constitutes an infrastructural resource that could be used in several ways to produce different products and services. It also enables creation of knowledge that is vital for controlling natural phenomenon, social systems, or organizational processes and supports complex decision-making (OECD 2014). In this vein, the international development community and the United Nations are seeking political support at the highest levels on harnessing data-driven innovations to support sustainable development, particularly under the new global Sustainable Development Goals (SDGs) (Independent Expert Advisory Group on Data Revolution 2014). Similarly, cities like Helsinki, Manchester, Amsterdam, Barcelona, and Chicago are leveraging big and open data from open sensor networks, public sector processes, and crowdsourced social data to improve mobility, foster co-creation of digital public services, and in general enable better city intelligence to support more effective city planning and development (Ojo et al. 2015).

At the same time, there is a growing understanding of the challenges associated with the exploitation of big data in society. These challenges range from paucity of requisite capacity (e.g. data literacy) to ethical dilemma in handling big data and how to incentivize the participation of other critical stakeholders in adopting and leveraging big data-driven innovation to tackle societal challenges (Hemerly 2013; Insight Centre for Data Analytics 2015).

This chapter describes what is involved in big data-driven innovation, provides examples of big data-driven innovations across different sectors, and synthesizes enabling factors and challenges associated with the development of a big data innovation ecosystem. The chapter closes by offering practical (policy) recommendations on how to develop viable big data innovation programs and initiatives.

9.2 Big Data-Driven Innovation

Innovation is an iterative process aimed at the creation of new products, processes, knowledge, or services by the use of new or even existing knowledge (Kusiak 2009). Data-driven innovation entails exploitation of any kind of data in the innovation process to create value (Stone and Wang 2014). The emerging trend of big data-driven innovation is leading to the development of data-driven goods and services and can enable data-driven planning, data-driven marketing, and data-driven operations across all industrial sectors and domains. From the economic perspective, data as a non-rivalrous good or commons such as oil serves an *infrastructural resource* (from a functional perspective) that could be exploited simultaneously by many users or actors for different competing or complementary ends. The demand for data in this sense according to the OECD (2014) is driven primarily by downstream productive activities that require data as an input and, in fact, a non-trivial capital. In addition, the same authors assert that data resources may be used as input into a wide variety of goods, including private, public, and social goods. In other words, big data potentially offers significant returns to scale and scope.

Big data-driven innovations are implicitly associated with a value chain model or more precisely a "virtual value chain" specifying how the data of interest will be gathered, organized, selected, transformed into products or services, and distributed (Rayport and Sviokla 1995; Piccoli 2012). Big data value chains as discussed in Chap. 3 are at the core of delivering data-driven innovation using big data technology. At the organizational level, at least two categories of strategic initiatives could result from big data-driven innovation and its underlying big data value chain. The first category of initiatives aims to make information available on aspects of organizational processes and services to enable improvements. In general, by instrumenting organizational operations, large amounts of data (i.e. big data) are generated that inform or drive required changes (Piccoli 2012). The second set of initiatives is external facing and involves exploitation of customer data such as search and user logs, transaction records, and other customer-generated contents to drive long-tail marketing, targeted and personalized recommendation, increased sale, and customer satisfaction. A popular example of this is Netflix's collaborative filtering algorithm to predict user movie ratings (Chen and Storey 2012). Yet another example is Google's use of users search behaviour to target advertising (US Chamber of Commerce Foundation 2014).

In the United States, hundreds of companies are utilizing open and big data (such as weather and GPS data) as key resources to generate value across different sectors including finance and investment, education, environment and weather, housing and real estate, and food and agriculture (US Chamber of Commerce Foundation 2014). The next section elaborates on a number of data-driven transformations across different sectors including telecommunication, healthcare, public sector, finance and insurance, media and entertainment, energy, and transport.

9.3 Transformation in Sectors

The BIG Project examined how big data technologies can enable business innovation and transformation within different sectors by gathering big data requirements from vertical industrial sectors, including health, public sector, finance, insurance, telecom, media, entertainment, manufacturing, retail, energy, and transport. There are a number of challenges that need to be addressed before big data-driven innovation is generally adopted. Big data can only succeed in driving innovation if a business puts a well-defined data strategy in place before it starts collecting and processing information. Obviously, investment in technology requires a strategy to use it according to commercial expectations; otherwise, it is better to keep current systems and procedures. Organizations within many sectors are now beginning to take the time to understand where this strategy should take them.

The full results of this analysis are available in Zillner et al. (2014). Part III of this book provides a concise summary of the key findings from a selected number of sectors. The remainder of this chapter provides an executive summary of the findings from each sector together with discussion and analysis.

9.3.1 Healthcare

Investigation of the healthcare sector in Chap. 10 revealed several developments, such as escalating healthcare costs, increased need for healthcare coverage, and shifts in provider reimbursement trends, which have triggered the demand for big data technology. In the sector the availability and access of health data is continuously improving, the required big data technology (such as advanced data integration and analytics technologies) are in place, and first-mover best-practice applications have demonstrated the potential of big data technology. However, the big data revolution in the healthcare domain is in a very early stage with the most potential for value creation and business development unclaimed as well as unexplored. Current roadblocks to big data-driven innovation are the established system incentives of the healthcare system that hinders collaboration and, thus, data sharing and exchange. The trend towards value-based healthcare delivery will foster the collaboration of stakeholders to enhance the value of the patient's treatment, and thus will significantly foster the need for big data applications.

9.3.2 Public Sector

The investigation of the public sector in Chap. 11 showed that the sector is facing some important challenges—the lack of productivity compared to other sectors, budgetary constraints, and other structural problems due to the aging population that will lead to an increasing demand for medical and social services, together with the foreseen lack of a young workforce in the future.

The public sector is increasingly aware of the potential value to be gained from big data-driven innovation via improvements in effectiveness and efficiency and with new analytical tools. Governments generate and collect vast quantities of data through their everyday activities, such as managing pensions and allowance payments, tax collection, etc. The main requirements, mostly non-technical, from the public sector are:

(i) *Interoperability:* An obstacle to exploit data assets due to the fragmentation of data ownership and the resulting data silos.
(ii) *Legislative support and political willingness:* The process of creating new legislation is often too slow to keep up with fast-moving technologies and business opportunities.
(iii) *Privacy and security issues:* The aggregation of data across administrative boundaries in a non-request-based manner is a real challenge.
(iv) *Big data skills:* Besides technical people, there is a lack of knowledge regarding the potential of big data in business-oriented people.

9.3.3 Finance and Insurance

As covered in Chap. 12 the finance and insurance sector is the clearest example of a data-driven industry. Big data represents a unique opportunity for most banking and financial services organizations to leverage their customer data to transform their business, realize new revenue opportunities, manage risk, and address customer loyalty. However, similarly to other emerging technologies, big data inevitably creates new challenges and data disruption for an industry already faced with governance, security, and regulatory requirements, as well as demands from the increasingly privacy-aware customer base.

At this moment not all finance companies are prepared to embrace big data, legacy information infrastructure, and organizational factors being the most significant barriers for its wide adoption in the sector. The deployment of big data solutions must be aligned with business objectives for a successful adoption of the technology to return the maximum business value.

9.3.4 Energy and Transport

Chapter 13 examines the sectors of energy and transport which from an infrastructure perspective, as well as from resource efficiency and quality of life perspectives, are very important for Europe. The high quality of the physical infrastructure and global competitiveness of the stakeholders needs to be maintained with respect to the digital transformation and big data-driven innovation.

The analysis of the available data sources in energy as well as their use cases in the different categories for big data value: operational efficiency, customer experience, and new business models make it clear that a mere utilization of existing big data technologies as employed by the online data businesses will not be sufficient. Domain- and device-specific adaptations are necessary for use in the cyber-physical systems of oil, gas, electrical, and transport. Innovation regarding privacy and confidentiality preserving data management and analysis is a primary concern of all energy and transport stakeholders that are dealing with customer data, be it business-to-consumer or business-to-business. Without satisfying the need for privacy and confidentiality, there will always be uncertainty around regulation and customer acceptance of new data-driven offering.

The increasing intelligence embedded in the infrastructures will enable the "in-field" analysis of the data to deliver "smart data". This seems to be necessary, since the analytics involved will require much more elaborate algorithms than for other sectors such as retail. Additionally, the stakes are very high since the optimization opportunities are within critical infrastructures.

9.3.5   Media and Entertainment

The media and entertainment industries have frequently been at the forefront of adopting new technologies. Chapter 14 details the key business problems that are driving media companies to look at big data-driven innovation as a way to reduce the costs of operating in an increasingly competitive landscape, and at the same time, the need to increase revenue from delivering content. It is no longer sufficient to publish a newspaper or broadcast a television programme—contemporary operators must drive value from their assets at every stage of the data lifecycle.

Media players are also more connected with their customers and competitors than ever before—thanks to the impact of disintermediation, content can be generated, shared, curated, and republished by literally anyone. This means that the ability of big data technologies to ingest and process many different data sources, and if required even in real-time, is a valuable asset companies are prepared to invest in.

As with the telecom industry, the legal and regulatory aspects of operating within Europe cannot be disregarded. As one example, it is critical that just because it is technically possible to accumulate vast amounts of detail about customers from their service usage, call centre interactions, social media updates, and so on, it does not mean that it is ethical to do so without being transparent about how the data will be used. Europe has much stronger data protection rules than the United States, meaning that individual privacy and global competitiveness will need to be balanced.

9.3.6 Telecommunication

The telecom sector seems to be convinced of the potential of big data technologies. The combination of benefits within marketing and offer management, customer relationship, service deployment, and operations can be summarized as the achievement of the operational excellence for telecom players.

There are a number of emerging big data telecom-specific commercial platforms available in the market that provide dashboards, reports to assist decision-making processes, and can be integrated with business support systems (BSS). Automatic actuation on the network as a result of the analysis is yet to come. Besides these platforms, Data as a Service (DaaS) is a trend some operators are following, which consists of providing companies and public sector organizations with analytical insights that enable third parties to become more effective.

Another very important factor within the sector is related to policy. The Connected Continent framework, aimed at benefiting customers and fostering the creation of the required infrastructure for Europe to become a connected community, at first sight, will most probably result in more strict regulations for telco players. A clear and stable framework is very important to foster investment in technology, including big data solutions.

9.3.7 Retail

The retail sector will be dependent on the collection of in-store data, product data, and customer data. To be successful in the future, retailers must have the ability to extract the right information out of huge data collections acquired in instrumented retail environments in real time. Existing business intelligence for retail analytics must be reorganized to understand customer behaviour and to be able to build more context-sensitive, consumer- and task-oriented recommendation tools for retailer-consumer dialog marketing.

9.3.8 Manufacturing

The core requirements in the manufacturing sector are the customization of products and production—"lot size one"—the integration of production in the larger product value chain, and the development of smart products.

The manufacturing industry is undergoing radical changes with the introduction of IT technology on a large scale. The developments under "Industry 4.0" include a growing number of sensors and connectivity in all aspects of the production process. Thus, data acquisition is concerned with making the already available data manageable, i.e., standardization and data integration are the biggest requirements. Data analysis is already applied in intra-mural applications and will be required for more integrated applications that cover complete logistics chains across factories in the production chain and even into the post-sale usage of (smart) products. Production planning needs to be supported by data-based simulation of these complete environments.

Complex and smart machinery, e.g., airplane engines, can benefit from big data-based predictive maintenance where sensor and context information is used with machine learning algorithms to avoid unnecessary maintenance and to schedule protective repairs when failures are predicted. Given the additional infrastructure costs, manufacturers are using new business models where machinery is leased and not sold; and in turn sensor data and services are owned and executed by the manufacturer and not the user of machinery. This leads to challenges in regulations and contracts concerning data ownership.

The European manufacturing sector can be both a market leader using big data in the context of Industry 4.0, and a leading market, where manufacturing big data is integrated in the larger product value chain and smart products can be put to use.

9.4   Discussion and Analysis

The analysis of the key findings across the sectors indicates that it is important to distinguish the technical from the business perspective. From a technological perspective, big data applications represent an evolutionary step. Big data technologies, such as decentralized networking and distributed computing for scalable data storage and scalable data analytics, semantic technologies and ontologies, machine learning, natural language processing, and other data mining techniques have been the focus of research projects for many years. Now these techniques are being combined and extended to address the technical challenge faced in the big data paradigm.

When analysed from the business perspective, it becomes clear that big data applications have a revolutionary—sometimes even disruptive—impact on the existing industrial business-as-usual practices. If thought through: new players emerge that are better suited to offer services based on mass data. Underlying business processes change fundamentally. For instance in the healthcare domain, big data technologies can be used to produce new insight about the effectiveness of treatments and this knowledge can be used to increase quality of care. However, in order to benefit from the value of these big data applications, the industry requires new reimbursement models that reward the quality instead of quantity of treatments. Similar changes are required in the energy industry: energy usage data from end users would have benefits for multiple stakeholders such as energy retailers, distribution network operators, and new players such as demand response providers and aggregators, energy efficiency service providers. But who is to invest in the technologies that would harvest the energy data in the first place? New participatory business value networks are required instead of static value chains.

Within all industries the 3 Vs of big data, volume, velocity, and variety, have been of relevance. In addition, industrial sectors that are already reviewing themselves in the light of the big data era add further Vs to reflect sectorial-specific aspects and to adapt the big data paradigm to their particular needs. Many of those extensions, such as data privacy, data quality, data confidentially, etc., address the challenge of data governance, while other extensions, such as value, address the fact that the potential business value of big data applications is yet unexplored and may not be well understood within the sector.

Within all industrial sectors it became clear that it was not the availability of technology, but the lack of business cases and business models that is hindering the implementation of big data. Usually, a business case needs to be clearly defined and convincing before investment is made in new applications. However, in the context of big data applications, the development of a concrete business case is a very challenging task. This is due to two reasons. First, as the impact of big data applications relies on the aggregation of not only one but also a large variety of heterogeneous data sources beyond organizational boundaries, the effective cooperation of multiple stakeholders with potentially diverging or at first orthogonal interests is required. Thus, the stakeholders' individual interests and constraints—which in addition are quite often moving targets—need to be reflected within the business case. Second, existing approaches for developing business models and business cases usually focus on single organizations and do not provide guidance for dynamic value networks of multiple stakeholders within a digital single market.

9.5 Conclusion and Recommendations

Data-driven innovation has the potential to impact all sectors of the economy. However to realize these, potential policymakers need to develop coherent policies for the use of data. This could be achieved by: (1) supporting education that focuses on data science skills, (2) removing the barriers to create a digital single market, (3) stimulating the necessary investment environment needed for big data technology, (4) making public data accessible through open data and removing data silos, (5) providing competitive technical infrastructure, and (6) promoting balanced legislation, and at the same time, policy must address issues such as privacy and security, ownership and transfer, and infrastructure and data civics (Hemerly 2013). In this vein, there are calls for a *magna carta* for data to address questions on how big data technologies could facilitate discrimination and marginalization; how to ensure that contracts between individuals and powerful big data companies or governments are fair; and where to situate the responsibility for the security of data (Insight Centre for Data Analytics 2015). In our opinion, further and sustainable progress in big data-driven innovation is contingent on actions by governments in collaboration with other major stakeholders in developing the right policy and regulatory environment based on empirical evidences from systematic research around some of the questions advanced above.

References

Chen, H., Chiang, R.H.L., & Storey, V. C. (2012). Business intelligence and analytics: From big data to big impact. In *MIS Quarterly, 36*(4), 1165–1188.

Hemerly, J. (2013). Public policy considerations for data-driven innovation. *Computer*, (June), 25–31.

Independent Expert Advisory Group on Data Revolution. (2014). *A world that counts – mobilizing the data revolution for sustainable development*. New York.

Insight Centre for Data Analytics. (2015). *Towards a Magna Carta for Data Insight Centre for Data Analytics White Paper*.

Kusiak, A. (2009). Innovation: A data-driven approach. *International Journal of Production Economics, 122*(1), 440–448. doi:10.1016/j.ijpe.2009.06.025.

OECD. (2014). *Data-driven Innovation for growth and well-being*.

Ojo, A., Curry, E., & Sanaz-Ahmadi, F. (2015). A tale of open data innovations in five smart cities. In *48th Annual Hawaii international conference on system sciences (HICSS-48)* (pp. 2326–2335). IEEE. doi:10.1109/HICSS.2015.280.

Piccoli, G. (2012). *Information systems for managers – text and cases* (2nd ed.). Wiley.

Rayport, J. F., & Sviokla, J. J. (1995). Exploiting the virtual value chain. *Harvard Business Review, 73*, 75–85. doi:10.1016/S0267-3649(00)88914-1.

Stone, D., & Wang, R. (2014). *Deciding with data – How data-driven innovation is fuelling Australia's economic growth*. PricewaterhouseCoopers (PwC). http://www.pwc.com.au/consulting/assets/publications/Data-drive-innovation-Sep14.pdf

US Chamber of Commerce Foundation. (2014). *The future of data-driven innovation*.

Zillner, S., Rusitschka, S., Munne, R., Lippell, H., Vilela, F. L., & Hussain, K., et al. (2014). *D2.3.2. Final version of the sectorial requisites*. Public Deliverable of the EU-Project BIG (318062; ICT-2011.4.4).

Chapter 10
Big Data in the Health Sector

Sonja Zillner and Sabrina Neururer

10.1 Introduction

Several developments in the healthcare sector, such as escalating healthcare costs, increased need for healthcare coverage, and shifts in provider reimbursement trends, trigger the demand for big data technologies in order to improve the overall efficiency and quality of care delivery. For instance, the McKinsey Company (2011) Study indicates a high financial impact of big data applications in the healthcare domain, of the order of a $300 billion value per year solely for the US. Similarly impressive numbers are provided by IBM: within the Executive Report of IBM Global Business Services (Korster and Seider 2010), the authors describe the healthcare system as highly inefficient, that is, approximately US$ 2.5 trillion is wasted annually and efficiency can be improved by 35 %. This is in comparison to other industries the largest opportunity for efficiency improvements. Moreover, major players are investing in the growth market of medicine for an aging population, for instance Google founded a new company Calico to tackle age-related health problems. In conclusion, *big data applications in healthcare have high future potential and opportunities.*

However, to the best of our knowledge, only a limited number of implemented big data based application scenarios can be found today. Although non-advanced

S. Zillner (✉)
Corporate Technology, Siemens AG, Munich, Germany

School of International Business and Entrepreneurship, Steinbeis University, Berlin, Germany
e-mail: sonja.zillner@siemens.com

S. Neururer
Department of Medical Statistics, Informatics and Health Economics, Innsbruck Medical University, Innsbruck, Austria

Semantic Technology Institute, University of Innsbruck, Innsbruck, Austria
e-mail: sabrina.neururer@i-med.ac.at

healthcare analytics applications—such as analytics for improved accounting, quality control, or clinical research—are available in a widespread manner, these applications do not make use of the potential of big data technologies. This is mainly due to the fact that health data cannot be easily accessed. High investment and effort is needed to enable efficient health data management and seamless health data access as the foundation for big data applications. As a consequence, convincing business cases are difficult to identify as the burden of the initial investment strongly reduces any profit expectations. In other words, one of the biggest challenges in the healthcare domain for the realization of big data applications is the fact that high investments, standards, and frameworks as well as new supporting technologies are needed in order to make health data available for subsequent big data analytics applications. Thus, the *efficient management and integration of health data is a key requirement* for big data applications in the healthcare domain that needs to be addressed.

The investigations (Zillner et al. 2014a, b) in this chapter found that the *highest impact of big data applications* in the healthcare domain is expected when it becomes possible to not only rely on one single, but various data sources such that different aspects from the various domains can be related. Therefore, the availability and integration of all related health data sources, such as clinical data, claims, cost and administrative data, pharmaceutical and research data, patient monitoring data, as well as the health data on the web, is of high relevance.

Health data is a form of "big data" not only because of the sheer volume but also for its complexity, diversity, and timeliness. Although large **volume** of structured data is already available today, the volume of unstructured data, such as biometric data, text reports, and medical images, will eclipse the whole data volume requirements. This is in close relation to the challenge of handling the high **variety** of health data, i.e. not only very heterogeneous data, such as images, structured reports, unstructured notes, etc., require new forms of (pre-) processing but also the semantics of its various domains, such as financial, administrative, research, patient or public health, needs to be reflected. The **value** of big data applications relies on the identification of convincing business cases. As the impact and success of healthcare business cases rely on the cooperation of multiple stakeholders with often diverging points of interests, they become challenging to identify.

10.2   Analysis of Industrial Needs in the Health Sector

The interviews and investigation in this section show that the high-level requirements of increased efficiency and quality of healthcare of today are often seen as opposing. The majority of high-quality health services rely on the analysis of larger amounts of data and content. This automatically leads to increased cost of care given that the means for automatic analysis of data, such as big data technologies, are still missing. However, with big data analytics, it becomes possible to segment the patients into groups and subsequently determine the differences between patient groups. Instead of asking the question "Is the treatment effective?", it becomes possible to answer the question "For which patient is this treatment effective?" This shift from average-based towards individualized healthcare bears the potential to significantly improve the overall quality of care in an efficient manner. Consequently, any information that could help to improve both the quality and the efficiency of healthcare at the same time was indicated as most relevant and useful.

High impact insights can only be realized if the data analytics is accomplished on heterogeneous datasets encompassing data from the clinical, administrative, financial, and public domain. This requires that the various stakeholders owning[1] the data are willing to share their data assets. However, there is a strong competition between the involved stakeholders of the healthcare industry. It is a competition for resources and the resources are limited. Each stakeholder is focused on their own financial interests, which often leads to sub-optimal treatment decisions. Consequently, the patient is currently the one who is suffering most. The interests and roles of the various stakeholder groups can be summarized as follows:

- **Patients** have interest in affordable, high quality, and broad coverage of healthcare. As of today, only very limited data about the patient's health conditions is available and patients have only very limited opportunities to actively engage in the process.
- **Hospital operators** are trying to optimize their income from medical treatments, i.e. they have a strong interest in improved efficiency of care, such as automated accounting routines, improved processes, or improved utilization of resources.
- **Clinicians and physicians** are interested in more automated and less labour-intensive routine processes, such as coding tasks, in order to have more time available for and with the patient. In addition, they are interested in accessing aggregated, analysed, and concisely presented health data that enables informed decision-making and high quality treatment decisions.
- **Payors**, such as governmental or private healthcare insurers. As of today, the majority of current reimbursement systems manage fee-for-service or Diagnose-related Group (DRG) based payments using simple IT-negotiation and data exchange processes between payors and healthcare providers and do not rely on data analytics. As payors are deciding which health services (i.e. which treatment, which diagnosis, or which preventative test) will be covered or not, their position and influence regarding the adoption of innovative treatments and practices is quite powerful. However, currently only limited and fragmented data about the effectiveness and value of health services is available; the reasons for treatment coverage often remain unclear and sometimes seem to be arbitrary.
- **Pharmaceuticals, life science, biotechnology, and clinical research:** Here the discovery of new knowledge is the main interest and focus. As of today, the

---

[1] The concept of data ownership influences how and by whom the data can be used. Thus, the term "ownership of data" is referred to both the possession of and responsibility for information, that is, the term "ownership of data" implies power as well as control.

various mentioned domains are mainly unconnected and accomplish their data analytics on single data sources. By integrating heterogeneous and distributed data sources, the impact of data analytic solutions is expected to increase significantly in the future.

- **Medical product providers** are interested in accessing and analysing clinical data in order to learn about their own products performance in comparison to competitors' products in order to increase revenue and/or improve the own market position.

To transform the current healthcare system into a preventative, pro-active, and value-based system, the seamless exchange and sharing of health data is needed. This again *requires effective cooperation between stakeholders*. However, today the healthcare setting is mainly determined by incentives that hinder cooperation. To foster the implementation and adaption of comprehensive big data applications in the healthcare sector, the underlying incentives and regulations defining the conditions and constraints under which the various stakeholders interact and cooperate need to be changed.

10.3 Potential Big Data Applications for Health

Analysis of the health sector (Zillner et al. 2014b) shows that several big data application scenarios exist that aim towards aligning the need of improved quality, which in general implies increased cost of care, with the need of improved efficiency of care. Common to all identified big data applications is the fact that they all require a means to semantically describe and align various heterogeneous data sources, means to ensure high data quality, means that address data privacy and security, as well as means for data analytics on integrated datasets.

For example, *Public Health Analytics* applications demonstrate the potential opportunities as well as associated technical requirements that are associated with big data technologies. Public health applications rely on the management of comprehensive and longitudinal health data from chronic (e.g. diabetes, congestive heart failure) or severe (e.g. cancer) diseases from the specific patient population in order to aggregate and analyse treatment and outcome data. Gained insights are very valuable as they help to reduce complications, slow disease progression, as well as improve treatment outcome. For instance, since 1970 Sweden is continuously investing in public health analytic initiatives leading to 90 registries that cover today 90 % of all Swedish patient data with selected characteristics (some cover even longitudinal data) (Soderland et al. 2012). A related study (PricewaterhouseCoopers (2009)) showed that Sweden has the best healthcare outcomes in Europe by average healthcare costs (9 % of the gross domestic product (GDP)). In order to achieve this, health data (which is stored in structured (e.g. lab reports) as well as unstructured data (e.g. medical reports, medical images)) need to be semantically enriched (*Semantic Data Enrichment*) in order to make the implicit semantics of health data understandable across the involved organizations and stakeholders. In addition, a common infrastructure with common standards allowing for seamless data sharing (*Data Sharing*) as well as for the physical integration of multiple data sources into one platform (*Data Integration*) are needed. In order to be compliant to the high data security and privacy requirements that are needed to protect the sensitive nature of longitudinal health data, common legal frameworks as well as technical means for data anonymization need to be in place (*Data Security and Privacy*). Moreover, in order to ensure the comparability of health datasets, processes ensuring high data quality through the standardized documentation as well as systematic analysis of health and outcome data of the specific patient population are required (*Data Quality*).

In terms of data handling, the other identified application scenarios yield very similar technical requirements. For instance, *Comparative Effectiveness Research* applications aim to compare the clinical and financial effectiveness of interventions in order to increase the efficiency and quality of clinical care services. To achieve this, large datasets encompassing clinical data (information about patient characteristics), financial data (cost data), and administrative data (treatments and services accomplished) are critically analysed in order to identify the clinically most effective, as well as most cost-effective treatments that work best for particular patients.

Clinical Operation Intelligence applications aim to identify waste in clinical processes in order to optimize them accordingly. By analysing medical procedures, performance opportunities, such as improved clinical processes, fine-tuning, and adaptation of clinical guidelines, can be realized. Other examples are *Clinical Decision Support (CDS)* applications seeking to enhance the efficiency and quality of care operations by assisting clinicians and healthcare professionals in their decision-making process by enabling context-dependent information access, by providing pre-diagnostic information or by validating and correcting the data provided. A further category of scenarios are applications addressing the *Secondary Usage of Health Data* that rely on the aggregation, analysis, and concise presentation of clinical, financial, administrative, as well as other related health data in order to discover new valuable knowledge, for instance, to identify trends, predict outcomes, or to influence patient care, drug development, and therapy choices. Finally, *Patient Engagement Applications* focus on establishing a platform/patient portal that fosters active patient engagement in healthcare processes. Any health apps that run on top of the patient platform rely on the integration of episodic health data from clinical settings as well as non-episodic data captured by devices to monitor health-related parameters, such as activity, diet, sleep, or weight.

10.4 Drivers and Constraints for Big Data in Health

The successful realization of big data in health has several drivers and constraints.

10.4.1 Drivers

The following **drivers** were identified for big data in the health sector:

- **Increased volume of electronic health data:** With the increasing adoption of electronic health record (EHR) technology (which is already the case in the USA), and the technological progress in the area of next generation sequencing and medical image segmentation, more and more health data will be available.
- **Need for improved operational efficiency:** To address greater patient volumes (aging population) and to reduce very high healthcare expenses, transparency of the operational efficiency is needed.
- **Value-based healthcare delivery:** Value-based healthcare relies on the alignment of treatment and financial success. In order to gain insights about the correlation between effectiveness and cost of treatments, data analytics solutions on integrated, heterogeneous, complex, and large sets of healthcare data are demanded.
- **US legislation:** The US Healthcare Reform, also known as Obamacare, fosters the implementation of EHR technologies as well as health data analytics. These have a significant impact on the international market for big health data applications.
- **Increased patient engagement:** Applications such as "PatientsLikeMe"[2] demonstrate the willingness of patients to actively engage in the healthcare process.
- **New incentives:** The current system incentives enforce "high number" instead of "high quality" of treatments. Although it is obvious that nobody wants to pay for treatments that are ineffective, this is still the case in many medical systems. In order to avoid low-quality reimbursements, the incentives of the medical systems need to be aligned with outcomes. Several initiatives, such as Accountable Care Organizations (ACO) (Centers for Medicare and Medicaid Services 2010), or Diagnose-related Groups (DRG) (Ma Ching-To Albert 1994), have been implemented in order to reward quality instead of quantity of treatments.

10.4.2 Constraints

The *constraints* for big data in the health sector can be summarized as follows:

- **Digitalization of health data:** Only a small percentage of health-related data is available in digital format.
- **Lack of standardized health data:** The seamless sharing of data requires that health data across hospitals and patients needs to be captured in a unified standardized way.

---

[2] http://www.patientslikeme.com/

- **Data silos:** Healthcare data is often stored in distributed data silos, which makes data analytics cumbersome and unstable.
- **Organizational silos:** Due to missing incentives, cooperation across different organizations, and sometimes even between departments within one organization, is rare and exceptional.
- **Data security and privacy:** Legal frameworks defining data access, security, and privacy issues and strategies are missing, hindering the sharing and exchange of data.
- **High investments:** The majority of big data applications in the healthcare sector rely on the availability of large-scale, high-quality, and longitudinal healthcare data. The collection and maintenance of such comprehensive data sources requires not only high investments, but also time (years) until the datasets are comprehensive enough to produce good analytical results.
- **Missing business cases and unclear business models:** Any innovative technology that is not aligned with a concrete business case, including associated responsibilities, is likely to fail. This is also true for big data solutions. Hence, the successful implementation of big data solutions requires transparency about: (a) who is paying for the solution, (b) who is benefiting from the solution, and (c) who is driving the solution. For instance, the implementation of data analytics solutions using clinical data requires high investments and resources to collect and store patient data, i.e. by means of an electronic health record (EHR) solution. Although it seems to be obvious how the involved stakeholder could benefit from the aggregated datasets, it remains unclear whether the stakeholder would be willing to pay for, or drive, such an implementation.

10.5   Available Health Data Resources

The healthcare system has several major pools of health data that are held by different stakeholders/parties:

- **Clinical data**, which is owned by the provider (such as hospitals, care centres, physicians, etc.) and encompasses any information stored within the classical hospital information systems or EHR, such as medical records, medical images, lab results, genetic data, etc.
- **Claims, cost, and administrative data**, which is owned by the provider and the payors and encompasses any datasets relevant for reimbursement issues, such as utilization of care, cost estimates, claims, etc.
- **Research data**, which is owned by the pharmaceutical companies, research labs/academia, and government and encompasses clinical trials, clinical studies, population and disease data, etc.
- **Patient monitoring data**, which is owned by patients or monitoring device producers and encompasses any information related to patient behaviours and preferences.

- **Health data on the web:** websites such as "PatientsLikeMe" are getting more and more popular. By voluntarily sharing data about rare diseases or remarkable experiences with common diseases, their communities and users are generating large sets of health data with valuable content.

The improvement of quality of care can be addressed if the various dimensions of health data are incorporated in the automated health data analysis. The data dimensions encompass (a) the clinical data describing the health status and history of a patient, (b) the administrative and clinical process data, (c) the knowledge about diseases as well as related (analysed) population data, and (d) the knowledge about changes. If the data analysis is restricted to only one data dimension, for example, the administrative and financial data, it will be possible to improve the already established management and reimbursement processes; however it will not be possible to identify new standards for individualized treatments. Hence, the highest clinical impact of big data approaches for the healthcare domain can be achieved if data from the four dimensions are aggregated, compared, and related.

As each data pool is held by different stakeholders/parties, the data in the health domain is highly fragmented. However, the integration of the various heterogeneous datasets is an important prerequisite of big health data applications and requires the effective involvement and interplay of the various stakeholders. Therefore, adequate system incentives, which support the seamless sharing and exchange of health data, are needed.

10.6 Health Sector Requirements

The Healthcare Sectorial Forum was able to identify and name several requirements, which need to be addressed by big data application in the healthcare domain. In the following, non-technical and technical requirements will be distinguished between.

10.6.1 Non-technical Requirements

Business-related requirements are called non-technical requirements and embrace important prerequisites and needs for big health data application, such as the need for high investments, value-based system incentives, or multi-stakeholder business cases.

Need for High Investments Due to the large-scale nature of big health data, the development and maintenance of big data application in the healthcare domain as well as the datasets themselves require high investments. Big health data applications mainly rely on large-scale, high quality, and often longitudinal healthcare data, which require several years of data gathering to establish comprehensive sets of data that can be analysed to produce accurate and insightful results. Such high investments can rarely be defrayed by one single party but needs to engage multiple stakeholders, which leads directly to the next non-technical requirement.

Multi-stakeholder Business Cases Due to the high investment needs described above, it is often essential that several different stakeholders cooperate in order to cover the investment costs. Here the interests of the stakeholders often diverge. Another important issue is that the main beneficiaries of a solution are often not the ones that are able or willing to finance a complete solution (e.g. patients). Nevertheless, even though it is often apparent how involved stakeholders could benefit from a certain big data solution with aggregated datasets of high quality, it often remains unclear whether those stakeholders are able or willing to drive or pay for such a solution.

Need for Value-Based System Incentives In order to increase the effectiveness of medical treatments, it is necessary to avoid low-quality reimbursements. This means that the current situation of high-number treatments instead of high-quality treatments needs to be improved. Since nobody wishes to pay for ineffective treatments, the incentives of health systems need to be well aligned with outcomes (e.g. performance-based financing and reimbursement systems) and, in addition, the cooperation between stakeholders needs to be rewarded.

10.6.2 Technical Requirements

Technical requirements are requirements that are related to specific technologies. They include semantic data enrichment, data integration and sharing, data privacy and security, as well as data quality. A major prerequisite for big data applications and analytics is the availability of data in an appropriate digital form. Many appropriate technologies are available to fulfil and support this requirement (e.g. speech recognition). Therefore no emphasis is put on data digitalization. The lack of appropriate digital data in healthcare is mostly caused by the limited adoption of data digitalization approaches in the everyday routine and familiar workflows of clinicians.

Semantic Data Enrichment As the IDC market research institute estimates, approximately 90 % of health data will be available in an unstructured manner in the upcoming years (Lünendonk GmbH 2013). To facilitate and guarantee seamless processing of such data, semantic data enrichment is needed. This means that health data, such as medical reports, images, videos, or communications, need to be enriched by so-called semantic labels. The major challenge with semantic data enrichment is that technological progress needs to be achieved with the analysis of several different types of data.

Data Integration and Sharing In order to avoid data silos or data cemeteries, big data has to be efficiently integrated from various different data sources and shared seamlessly. Currently, the adoption of technology to exchange data is lacking behind in Europe (Accenture 2012). In the United Kingdom less than 46 % of healthcare providers perform healthcare information exchanges, and in Germany and France this rate is even lower (approximately 25 %). This requirement goes hand in hand with the need for structured or semantically enriched data in order to make data easily accessible. A major prerequisite for medical research is the possibility to integrate data from various different sources to obtain a longitudinal view of the patients' history.

Data Security and Privacy   When talking about processing, integrating, or sharing medical data, a strong emphasis must be put on data security and privacy. Medical data is categorized as highly sensitive personal data and therefore protection from unauthorized access, manipulation, or damage has to be guaranteed. Hence the nature of big data might bypass established privacy protection approaches (e.g. when aggregating big data from different data sources). Big health data applications need to focus even more strongly on data privacy and security. For instance, anonymization is known to be a popular approach to de-identify health-related personal data. By aggregating big data from various different data sources, anonymized data could be unintentionally re-identified. Therefore, existing privacy enhancing methods need to be evaluated to find out whether they can meet all privacy requirements even when dealing with big data. If data privacy cannot be guaranteed by a specific method, this method needs to be adapted in order to satisfy the need for privacy or new methods and approaches need to be developed. Apart from the technical challenges, a common international legal framework together with guidelines needs to be established in order to provide a common basis for international exchange and integration of health-related big data.

Data Quality   High quality of available datasets is a major prerequisite for big data applications in the healthcare domain. The benefit of an application is strongly correlated with the quality of the data. In the healthcare domain, the quality of the available data is often unclear. The frequency of missing or incorrect values is an indicator of data quality. Usually the quality of data improves when data is captured and processed using high-quality information technology (IT) tools. Such tools can be integrated into everyday work routines and perform certain data quality checks (e.g. plausibility checks) during the data capturing or entering process. In order to generate valuable results or decision support when analysing health data, big data applications need to fulfil high quality standards.

10.7   Technology Roadmap for Big Data in the Health Sector

The following roadmap outlines and describes technologies and the underlying research questions, which meet the requirements defined in the previous section. Figure 10.1 visualizes and aligns them with the specific technical requirements.

10.7.1   Semantic Data Enrichment

In order to semantically enrich medical data a framework needs to be provided. Therefore, semantic enrichment techniques are needed that go beyond the mere extraction of relevant information from unstructured text or medical images. Semantic labels, which express and define the meaning of information, render the original content semantically accessible as well as automatically processable and machine-readable. For instance, medical procedure and diagnosis entities in unstructured text such as medical reports are recognized and the describing passages are linked. Therefore sophisticated text analysis techniques are needed (Bretschneider et al. 2013). Furthermore, a standardized enrichment framework, which is supporting the technical integration, is needed. To facilitate and improve

Technical Requirement	Technology	Research Question
Semantic Data Enrichment	Medical IE Algorithm	Identification of Relevant Information Entities
	Medical Image Understanding	Automated detection of abnormal structures
	Medical Annotation Framework	Standards fostering IE algorithm integration
Data Sharing and Integration	Semantic Data Representation	Creation of mature data models
	Semantic Knowledge Models	Improvement of existing biomedical ontologies
	Context Representation	Provenance, data usage, licence
Data Privacy and Security	Hash algorithms	Hash algorithms
	Secure Data Exchange	IHE profiles
	De-identification Algorithms	Anonymization, Pseudonymization, k-Anonymity
Data Quality	Provenance Management	Trust & permission management mechanism
	Human-Data Interaction	Natural language UI & schema agnostic queries
	Unstructured Data Integration	Unstructured Data Integration

Fig. 10.1 Mapping requirements to research questions in the healthcare sector

semantic enrichment of medical data, advances are needed for the following technologies:

- **Information extraction from medical texts** brings up new challenges to classical information extraction techniques, as negation, temporality, and further contextual features need to be taken into account. Several studies (Fan and Friedman 2011; Savova et al. 2010) show advances towards the specials needs of parsing medical text. As the ongoing research mainly focuses on clinical text in the English language, adaptations to other European languages are needed.
- **Image understanding algorithms** to formally capture automatically detected image information, such as anatomical structures, abnormal structures, and semantic image annotations, are desired. Therefore, additional research targeting and considering the complexity of the human body as well as the different medical imaging technologies is needed.
- **Standardized medical annotation frameworks** that include standardized medical text processing and support the technical integration of annotation technologies. Even though there are some frameworks available (e.g. UIMA[3]), adaptations are needed in order to meet the specific challenges and requirements of the healthcare domain.

10.7.2 Data Sharing and Integration

Efficient data integration and seamless sharing relies on standardized coding schemes and terminologies as well as data models. Currently standardized coding systems are either used for high-level information coding (e.g. diseases, laboratory values, medications) or not internationally used. A lot of information is not available in coded format at all. For the usage of standardized data models, the HL7 Reference Information Model[4] (RIM) is considered to become the standard data model for EHR implementations. Nevertheless a high percentage of technology providers still rely on their own data models when it comes to data integration. In order to advance data integration and sharing, coding schemes as well as data models need to be improved and standardized.

- **Semantic data models** enable the unambiguous representation of data. Existing models (e.g. HL7 RIM) have several issues that make it difficult to implement. Further research activities, such as the Model for Clinical Information (MCI) (Oberkampf et al. 2013) that integrate patient models on the basis of ontologies, are ongoing.
- **Semantic knowledge models** such as biomedical domain ontologies and terminologies are used in combination with semantic data models and help to

---

[3] http://uima.apache.org/

[4] http://www.hl7.org/implement/standards/rim.cfm

facilitate semantic interoperability. There are several different models (e.g. SNOMED CT[5]) available, but further research in order to improve these standards, as well as to develop new standards, is needed.

- **Context information** is needed in order to provide information about data provenance, usage, or ownership. Therefore standards for describing context information are needed.

10.7.3 Data Privacy and Security

In order to fulfil the high demand for big health data privacy and security, different aspects need to be taken into account. Besides the national data protection laws, a common legal framework for the European Union is needed in order to facilitate international approaches or cooperation. When talking about big health data privacy and security, it is often necessary to re-identify patients (e.g. for longitudinally assessing the patient's health status). The aggregation of data from various different data sources brings up two major challenges for big data privacy and security. First, the aggregation of data from heterogeneous data sources is difficult and data for patient has to be aligned properly. Also the nature of big data may bypass certain privacy enhancing methods when aggregating data from various different data sources. Therefore advances are needed for the following technologies:

- **Hash algorithms** are often used as an encryption method. Its one-way function can also be used to generate pseudo-identifiers and therefore facilitate secure pseudonymization. However it is crucial that hash algorithms are robust and collision resistant.
- **Secure data exchange** across institutional and country boundaries is essential for several interesting visions for the healthcare domain (e.g. international EHR). Therefore, Integrating the Healthcare Enterprise (IHE)[6] profiles are widely used (e.g. IHE cross-enterprise document sharing) although they are still the focus of research activities.
- **De-identification algorithms**, such as anonymization or pseudonymization, need to be improved in order to guarantee data privacy even when aggregating big data from different data sources. K-anonymity (El Emam and Dankar 2008) is a promising approach that envisions ensuring anonymity even in the big data context.

---

[5] http://ihtsdo.org/snomed-ct/
[6] http://www.ihe.net/

10.7.4   Data Quality

Good data quality is a key-enabler for big health data applications. It depends on four different aspects: (1) the data quality of the original data sources, (2) the coverage and level of detail of the collected data, (3) common semantics as described before, and (4) the handling of media-disruptions. In order to improve the data quality of these four aspects, advances for the following technologies are needed:

- An improvement of **provenance management** is needed in order to allow reliable curation of health data. Therefore data-level trust and permission management mechanisms need to be implemented.
- **Human-data interaction technologies** [e.g. natural language interfaces, schema–agnostic query formulation (Freitas and Curry 2014)] improve data quality as they facilitate ease-of-use interaction that is perfectly integrated in particular workflows.
- Reliable **information extraction approaches** are needed in order to facilitate the processing of unstructured medical data (e.g. medical reports, medical images). Therefore existing approaches (e.g. natural language processing) have to be improved for the purpose of addressing the specific characteristics of health information and data.

Roadmap developments are usually accomplished for a single company. There is a need to develop a roadmap for the European market that depends on (a) the degree to which the non-technical requirements will be addressed and (b) the extent to which European organizations are willing to invest in big data developments and use case implementations. As such it was not possible to come up with an exact timeline of technology milestones, but with an estimated timeline depicted in Table 10.1.

10.8   Conclusion and Recommendations for Health Sector

Big data technologies and health data analytics provide the means to address the efficiency and quality challenges in the health domain. For instance, by aggregating and analysing health data from disparate sources, such as clinical, financial, and administrative data, the outcome of treatments in relation to the resource utilization can be monitored. This analysis in turn helps to improve the efficiency of care. Moreover, the identification of high-risk patients with predictive models leads towards proactive patient care allowing for the delivery of high quality care.

A comprehensive analysis of domain needs and requirements indicated that the highest impact of big data applications in the healthcare domain is achievable when it becomes possible to not only acquire data from one single source, but various data sources such that different aspects can be combined to gain new insights. Therefore, the availability and integration of all related health data sources, such as clinical

Table 10.1 Timeframe of the major expected outcomes for the health sector

Technical requirement	Year 1	Year 2	Year 3	Year 4	Year 5
Data enrichment		Standardized formats and interfaces for annotation modules	Knowledge-based information extraction algorithm	Algorithm for anomaly detection in images Data enrichment technologies available for a large number of different text types and multiple languages	Definition and implementation of medical annotation framework
Data integration	Context representation for data repositories	Aligned semantic knowledge models and terminologies	Common semantic data model for structured patient data	Common semantic data model for unstructured patient data	Context representation for all patient data
Data security and privacy		IHE profiles for secure data exchange		Privacy enhancing through hash algorithms	Anonymization, pseudonymization and k-anonymity approaches for big data
Data quality	Methods for trust and permission management		Natural language UI and schema agnostic queries	Integrated workflows for trust and permission management	Context-aware integration of unstructured data

data, claims, cost, and administrative data, pharmaceutical and R&D data, patient behaviour, and sentiment data as well as the health data on the web, is of high relevance.

However, access to health data is currently only possible in a very constrained manner. In order to enable seamless access to healthcare data, several technical requirements need to be addressed, including (1) the content of unstructured health data (such as images or reports) is enhanced by semantic annotation; (2) data silos are conquered by means of efficient technologies for semantic data sharing and exchange; (3) technical means backed by legal frameworks ensure the regulated sharing and exchange of health data; and (4) techniques for assessing and improving data quality are available.

The availability of the technologies will not be sufficient for fostering widespread adoption of big data in the healthcare domain. The critical stumbling block is the lack of business cases and business models. As big data fosters a new dimension of value proposition in healthcare delivery, with insights on the effectiveness of treatments to significantly improve the quality of care, new reimbursement models that reward quality instead of quantity of treatments are needed.

References

Accenture. (2012). *Connected health: The drive to integrated healthcare delivery*. Online: www. acccenture.com/connectedhealthstudy

Bretschneider, C., Zillner, S., & Hammon, M. (2013). Grammar-based lexicon enhancement for aligning German radiology text and images. In *Proceedings of the Recent Advances in Natural Language Processing (RANLP 2013)*, Hissar, Bulgaria.

Centers for Medicare and Medicaid Services. (2010). *Medicare accountable care organizations – Shared savings program – New Section 1899 of Title XVIII, Preliminary questions and answers*. Online retrieved January 10, 2010.

El Emam, K., & Dankar, F. K. (2008). Protecting privacy using k-anonymity. *Journal of the American Medical Information Association, 15*(5), 627–37.

Fan, J. W., & Friedman, C. (2011). Deriving a probabilistic syntacto-semantic grammar for biomedicine based on domain-specific terminologies. *Journal of Biomedical Informatics, 44*(5), 805–14.

Freitas, A., & Curry, E. (2014). Natural language queries over heterogeneous linked data graphs: A distributional-compositional semantics approach. *18th International Conference on Intelligent User Interfaces* (pp. 279–288). Haifa, Israel: ACM.

Korster, P., & Seider, C. (2010). The world's 4 trillion dollar challenge. *Executive Report of IBM Global Business Services*, online.

Lünendonk GmbH. (2013). Trendpapier 2013: Big Data bei Krankenversicherungen. Bewältigung der Datenmengen in einem veränderten Gesundheitswesen. Online.

Ma Ching-To Albert (1994). Health care payment systems: Cost and quality incentives. *Journal of Economics and Management Strategy, 3*(1), Spring

McKinsey Company. (2011). *Big data: The next frontier for innovation, competition, and productivity*, online.

Oberkampf, H., Zillner, S., Bauer, B., & Hammon, M. (2013). An OGMS-based Model for Clinical Information (MCI). In *Proceedings of International Conference on Biomedical Ontology, Montreal*, Canada.

PricewaterhouseCoopers. (2009). *Transforming healthcare through secondary use of health data*.

Savova, G. K., Masanz, J. J., Ogren, P. V., Zheng, J., Sohn, S., Kipper-Schuler, K. C., & Chute, C. G. (2010). Mayo clinical Text Analysis and Knowledge Extraction System (cTAKES): Architecture, component evaluation and applications. *Journal of American Medical Informatics Association, 17*(5), 507–513.

Soderland, N., Kent, J., Lawyer, P., & Larsson, S. (2012). Progress towards value-based health care. Lessons from 12 countries. The Boston Consulting Group, online.

Zillner, S., Lasierra, N., Faix, W., & Neururer, S. (2014a). User needs and requirements analysis for big data healthcare applications. In *Proceeding of the 25th European medical informatics conference (MIE 2014)*, Istanbul, Turkey, September 2014.

Zillner, S., Rusitschka, S., Munne, R., Lippell, H., Vilela, F. L., & Hussain, K., et al. (2014b). *D2.3.2. Final version of the sectorial requisites*. Public Deliverable of the EU-Project BIG (318062; ICT-2011.4.4).

Chapter 11
Big Data in the Public Sector

Ricard Munné

11.1 Introduction

The public sector is becoming increasingly aware of the potential value to be gained from big data. Governments generate and collect vast quantities of data through their everyday activities, such as managing pensions and allowance payments, tax collection, national health systems, recording traffic data, and issuing official documents. This chapter takes into account current socio-economic and techno-logical trends, including boosting productivity in an environment with significant budgetary constraints, the increasing demand for medical and social services, and standardization and interoperability as important requirements for public sector technologies and applications. Some examples of potential benefits are as follows:

- **Open government and data sharing:** The free flow of information from organizations to citizens promotes greater trust and transparency between citizens and government, in line with open data initiatives.
- **Citizen sentiment analysis:** Information from both traditional and new social media (websites, blogs, twitter feeds, etc.) can help policy makers to prioritize services and be aware of citizens' interests and opinions.
- **Citizen segmentation and personalization while preserving privacy:** Tailoring government services to individuals can increase effectiveness, efficiency, and citizen satisfaction.
- **Economic analysis:** Correlation of multiple sources of data will help government economists with more accurate financial forecasts.
- **Tax agencies:** Automated algorithms to analyse large datasets and integration of structured and unstructured data from social media and other sources will help them validate information or flag potential frauds.

R. Munné (✉)
Atos Spain, S.A., Av. Diagonal, 200, 08018 Barcelona, Spain
e-mail: ricard.munne@atos.net

- **Smart city and Internet of things (IoT) applications:** The public sector is increasingly characterized by applications that rely on sensor measurements of physical phenomena such as traffic volumes, environmental pollution, usage levels of waste containers, location of municipal vehicles, or detection of abnormal behaviour. The integrated analysis of these high volume and high velocity IoT data sources has the potential to significantly improve urban management and positively impact the safety and quality of life of its citizens.
- **Cyber security:** Collect, organize, and analyse vast amounts of data from government computer networks with sensitive data or critical services, to give cyber defenders greater ability to detect and counter malicious attacks.

11.1.1 Big Data for the Public Sector

As of today, there are no broad implementations of big data in the public sector. Compared to other sectors, the public sector has not been traditionally using data mining technologies intensively. However, there is a growing interest in the public sector on the potentials of big data for improvement in the current financial environment.

Some examples of the global growing awareness are the Joint Industry/Government Task Force to drive development of big data in Ireland, announced by the Irish Minister for Jobs, Enterprise and Innovation in June 2013 (Government of Ireland 2013), or the announcement made by the Obama administration (The White House 2012), on the "Big Data Research and Development Initiative" where six Federal departments and agencies announce more than $200 million in new commitments to greatly improve the tools and techniques needed to access, organize, and glean discoveries from huge volumes of digital data.

11.1.2 Market Impact of Big Data

There is no direct market impact nor competition, as the public sector is not a productive sector, although its expenditure represented 49.3 % of GDP in 2012 of the EU28. The major part of the sector's income is collected through taxes and social contributions. Hence, the impact of big data technologies is in terms of efficiency: the more efficient the public sector is, the better off are citizens, as less resources (taxes) are needed to provide the same level of service. Therefore, the more effective the public sector is, the more positive the impact on the economy, by transition for the rest of productive sectors, and more positive impact on society. Additionally, the quality of services provided, for example, education, health, social services, active policies, and security, can also be improved by making use of big data technologies.

11.2   Analysis of Industrial Needs in the Public Sector

The benefits of big data in the public sector can be grouped into three major areas, based on a classification of the types of benefits:

Big Data Analytics This area covers applications that can only be performed through automated algorithms for advanced analytics to analyse large datasets for problem solving that can reveal data-driven insights. Such abilities can be used to detect and recognize patterns or to produce forecasts.

Applications in this area include fraud detection (McKinsey Global Institute 2011); supervision of private sector regulated activities; sentiment analysis of Internet content for the prioritization of public services (Oracle 2012); threat detection from external and internal data sources for the prevention of crime, intelligence, and security (Oracle 2012); and prediction for planning purposes of public services (Yiu 2012).

Improvements in Effectiveness Covers the application of big data to provide greater internal transparency. Citizens and businesses can take better decisions and be more effective, and even create new products and services thanks to the information provided. Some examples of applications in this area include data availability across organizational silos (McKinsey Global Institute 2011); sharing information through public sector organizations [e.g. avoiding problems from the lack of a single identity database (e.g. in the UK) (Yiu 2012)]; open government and open data facilitating the free flow of information from public organizations to citizens and businesses, reusing data to provide new and innovative services to citizens (McKinsey Global Institute 2011; Ojo et al. 2015).

Improvements in Efficiency This area covers the applications that provide better services and continuous improvement based on the personalization of services and learnings from the performance of such services. Some examples of applications in this area are personalization of public services to adapt to citizen needs and improving public services through internal analytics based on the analysis of performance indicators.

11.3   Potential Big Data Applications for the Public Sector

Four potential applications for the public sector were described and developed in Zillner et al. (2013, 2014) for demonstrating the use of big data technologies in the public sector (Table 11.1).

Table 11.1 Summary of application scenarios for the public sector

Name	Monitoring and supervision of regulated activities for online gambling operators
Summary	Large volumes of data available make it difficult to effectively regulate and supervise activities
Synopsis	To monitor the online gambling operators for the control of regulated activities and detection of fraud. The user of this application is the public body in charge of the supervisory activity. This procedure is a regulatory obligation from the public administration; the online gambling operators must provide the information to the regulatory public through a specific communication channel. Real-time data is received from gambling operators every 5 min.
Business objectives	Ensure compliance with regulations, fraud prevention and detection, and criminal investigation.
Name	Operative efficiency in labour agency
Summary	Extract value from available large volumes of unused data
Synopsis	Enable a new range of personalized services, improve customer services and cut operation costs in German Federal Labour agency. All unemployed workers were receiving the same standard services despite having different profiles. Historical data on their customers was analysed, including profiles, interventions, and the time it took to find a job. Based on this analysis, customer segmentation was developed.
Business objectives	Reduce the cost and improve the quality of the service: now they are able to find a new job in a shorter period of time.
Name	Public Safety in Smart Cities
Summary	Large volumes of data available from sensors, social media, and emergency calls can be combined to provide effective public safety.
Synopsis	Smart cities equipped with sensors and communication infrastructures help the public sector keep cities and their citizens safe. Having accurate and up-to-date information allows better and faster responses during emergencies and results in less damage and casualties. Typical sources for obtaining such information can come from emergency response calls, surveillance cameras, and mobile forces (such as a police patrol car) that arrived at a site. In recent years social media have shown interesting potential for gathering information that aids in obtaining an accurate situational awareness picture (van Kasteren et al. 2014). All gathered information is collected in a command and control centre where an operator can decide how to steer available mobile forces.
Business objectives	Quick response to emergencies, prevention of damages, and less casualties.
Name	Predictive policing using open data
Summary	Reuse of public open data to provide predictive policing
Synopsis	Governments around the world have started open data initiatives to make public sector data available to the public for the sake of transparency and to allow third parties to offer services based on the data. One such service can be described as predictive policing where historical crime data is used to automatically discover trends and patterns. The identified patterns help in gaining insights into crime-related problems a city is facing and allow a more effective and efficient deployment of police forces (Wang et al. 2013; PredPol 2013).
Business objectives	Significant decrease in crime, efficient use of mobile forces.

11.4   Drivers and Constraints for Big Data in the Public Sector

The key drivers and constraints of big data technologies in the public sector are:

11.4.1   Drivers

The following **drivers** were identified for big data in the public sector:

- **Governments can act as catalysts** in the development of a data ecosystem through the opening of their own datasets, and actively managing their dissemination and use (World Economic Forum 2012).
- **Open data initiatives** are a starting point for boosting a data market that can take advantage from open information (content) and the big data technologies. Therefore active policies in the area of open data can benefit the private sector, and in return facilitate the growth of this industry in Europe. In the end this will benefit public budgets with an increase of tax incomes from a growing European data industry.

11.4.2   Constraints

The **constraints** for big data in the public sector can be summarized as follows:

- **Lack of political willingness** to make the public sector take advantage of these technologies. It will require a change in mind-set of senior officials in the public sector.
- **Lack of skilled business-oriented people** aware of where and how big data can help to solve public sector challenges, and who may help to prepare the regulatory framework for the successful development of big data solutions.
- **New General Data Protection Regulation and the PSI directives display some uncertainties** about the impact on the implementation of big data and open data initiatives in the public sector. Specifically, open data is set to be a catalyst from the public sector to the private sector to establish a powerful data industry.
- **Gaining adoption momentum.** Today, there is more marketing around big data in the public sector than real experiences from which to learn which applications are more profitable, and how it should be deployed. This requires the development of a standard set of big data solutions for the sector.
- **Numerous bodies in public administration** (especially in those which are widely decentralized), so much energy is lost and will remain so until a common strategy is realized for the reuse of cross technology platforms.

11.5   Available Public Sector Data Resources

In Directive 2003/98/EC (The European Parliament and the Council of The
European Union 2003), on the re-use of public sector information, public sector
information (PSI) is defined as follows: "It covers any representation of acts, facts
or information – and any compilation of such acts, facts or information – whatever
its medium (written on paper, or stored in electronic form or as a sound, visual or
audio-visual recording), held by public bodies. A document held by a public sector
body is a document where the public sector body has the right to authorise re-use."

According to Correia (2004), concerning the availability of the information
produced by those public bodies, and in the absence of specific guidelines, the
producing body is free to decide how to make it available: directly to the end users,
establishing a public/private partnership, or outsourcing the commercial exploitation of that information to private operators. The Directive 2003/98/EC clarifies
that activities falling outside the public task: "will typically include supply of
documents that are produced and charged for exclusively on a commercial basis
and in competition with others in the market".

On the nature of the PSI available, there are several approaches. The Green paper
on PSI (European Commission 1998) proposes some classifications such as:

- PSI distinction between administrative and non-administrative
- PSI distinction regarding its relevance for the public

Additionally it can be distinguished according to its potential market value, and
in some cases according to the content of personal data:

- PSI distinction according to its anonymity

The most important amount of data produced by public sector is textual or
numerical, versus other sectors like healthcare that produces a large amount of
electronic images. As a result of e-government initiatives of the past 15 years, a
great part of this data is created in digital form, 90 % according to McKinsey
(McKinsey Global Institute 2011).

According to the survey performed for the formulation of the European Big Data
Value Partnership to public sector representatives (Zillner et al. 2014), the key data
asset is the whole system of public sector, registries, databases, and information
systems, of which the most significant are:

- Citizens, business, and properties (e.g. base registries, transactions)
- Fiscal data
- Security data
- Document management especially as the electronic transactions are growing
- Public procurement and expenses
- Public bodies and employees
- Geographical data mainly related to cadastral
- Content related to culture, education, and tourism
- Legislative documents

- Statistical data (socio-economic data that could be used by private sector)
- Geospatial data

11.6   Public Sector Requirements

The requirements of the public sector were broken down into non-technical and technical requirements.

11.6.1   Non-technical Requirements

Privacy and Security Issues The aggregation of data across administrative boundaries on a non-request-based manner is a real challenge, since this inform-ation may reveal highly sensitive personal and security information when combined with various other data sources, not only compromising individual privacy but also civil security. Access rights to the required datasets for an operation must be justified and obtained. When a new operation is performed over existing data, a notification or a license must be obtained from the Data Privacy Agency. Anonym-ity must be preserved in these cases, so data dissociation is required. Individual privacy and public security concerns must be addressed before governments can be convinced to share data more openly, not only publicly but sharing in a restricted manner with other governments or international entities. Another dimension is the regulation for the use of cloud computing in a way that public sector can trust cloud providers. Furthermore, the lack of European big data cloud computing providers within the European market is also a barrier for adoption.

Big Data Skills There's a lack of skilled data scientists and technologists who can capture and process these new data sources. When big data technologies become increasingly adopted in business, skilled big data professionals will become harder to find. Public body agencies could go a fair distance with the skills they already have, but then they will need to make sure those skills advance (1105 Government Information Group n.d.). Besides the technical oriented people, there is a lack of knowledge in business-oriented people who are aware of what big data can do to help them solve public sector challenges.

Other Requirements Other non-technical requirements include:

- Willingness to supply and to adopt big data technologies, and also to know how to use it.
- Need for common national or European approaches (policies)—like the European policies for interoperability and open data. Lack of leadership in this field.

- A general mismatch between business intelligence in general and big data in particular in the public sector.

11.6.2 Technical Requirements

Below is a detailed description of each of the eight technical requirements that were distilled from the four big data applications selected for the Public Sector Forum.

Pattern Discovery Identifying patterns and similarities to detect specific criminal or illegal behaviours in the application scenario of monitoring and supervision of online gambling operators (and also for similar monitoring scenarios within the public sector). This requirement is also applicable in the scenario to improve operative efficiency in the labour agency, and in the predictive policing scenario.

Data Sharing/Data Integration Required to overcome lack of standardization of data schemas and fragmentation of data ownership. Integration of multiple and diverse data sources into a big data platform.

Real-Time Insights Enable analysis of fresh/real-time data for instant decision-making, for obtaining real-time insights from the data.

Data Security and Privacy Legal procedures and technical means that allow the secure and privacy preserving sharing of data. The solutions to this requirement may unlock the widespread use of big data in public sector. Advances in the protection and privacy of data are key for the public sector, as it may allow the analysis of huge amounts of data owned by the public sector without disclosing sensitive information. These privacy and security issues are preventing the use of cloud infrastructures (processing, storage) by many public agencies that deal with sensitive data.

Real-Time Data Transmission Because the capability of placing sensors is increasing in smart city application scenarios, there is a high demand for real-time data transmission. It will be required to provide distributed processing and cleaning capabilities for image sensors so as not to collapse the communication channels and provide just the required information to the real-time analysis, which will be feeding situational awareness systems for decision-makers.

Natural Language Analytics Extract information from unstructured online sources (e.g. social media) to enable sentiment mining. Recognition of data from natural language inputs like text, audio, and video.

Predictive Analytics As described in the application scenario for predictive policing, where the goal is to distribute security forces and resources according to the prediction of incidents, provide predictions based on the learning from previous situations to forecast optimal resource allocation for public services.

Modelling and Simulation Domain-specific tools for modelling and simulation of events according to data from past events to anticipate the results from decisions taken to influence the current conditions in real-time, for example, in scenarios of public safety.

11.7 Technology Roadmap for Big Data in the Public Sector

For each requirement in the sector, this section presents applicable technologies and the research questions to be developed (Fig. 11.1). All references presented here are from Curry et al. (2014).

11.7.1 Pattern Discovery

- Data Analysis Technology: Semantic pattern technologies including stream pattern matching.
  - Research Question: Scalable complex pattern matching. Reaching trillions over datasets will take 5 years.
- Data Curation Technology: Validation of pattern analytics outputs with humans via curation.
  - Research Question: Curation at scale depends on the interplay between automated curation platforms and collaborative approaches leveraging large pools of data curators. Commercial application results could be reached in 6–10 years.
- Data Storage Technology: Analytical Databases, Hadoop, Spark, Mahout.
  - Research Question: Standard Array Query Language. Currently there is a lack of standardized query languages but efforts such as ArrayQL are on their way. Currently there is no widespread adoption and existing DBs (SciDB, Rasdaman) are used in the scientific community. This may change in 3–5 years from now.

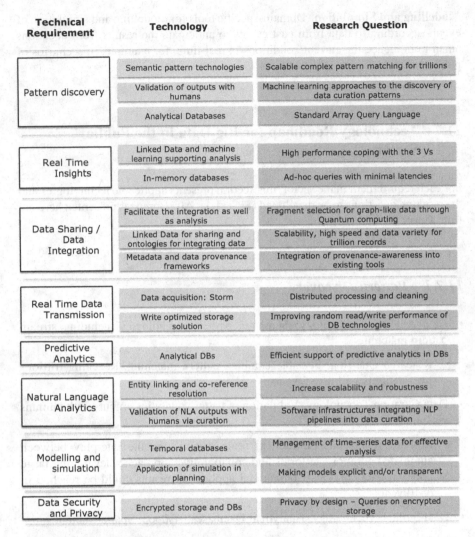

Technical Requirement	Technology	Research Question
Pattern discovery	Semantic pattern technologies	Scalable complex pattern matching for trillions
	Validation of outputs with humans	Machine learning approaches to the discovery of data curation patterns
	Analytical Databases	Standard Array Query Language
Real Time Insights	Linked Data and machine learning supporting analysis	High performance coping with the 3 Vs
	In-memory databases	Ad-hoc queries with minimal latencies
Data Sharing / Data Integration	Facilitate the integration as well as analysis	Fragment selection for graph-like data through Quantum computing
	Linked Data for sharing and ontologies for integrating data	Scalability, high speed and data variety for trillion records
	Metadata and data provenance frameworks	Integration of provenance-awareness into existing tools
Real Time Data Transmission	Data acquisition: Storm	Distributed processing and cleaning
	Write optimized storage solution	Improving random read/write performance of DB technologies
Predictive Analytics	Analytical DBs	Efficient support of predictive analytics in DBs
Natural Language Analytics	Entity linking and co-reference resolution	Increase scalability and robustness
	Validation of NLA outputs with humans via curation	Software infrastructures integrating NLP pipelines into data curation
Modelling and simulation	Temporal databases	Management of time-series data for effective analysis
	Application of simulation in planning	Making models explicit and/or transparent
Data Security and Privacy	Encrypted storage and DBs	Privacy by design – Queries on encrypted storage

Fig. 11.1 Mapping requirements to research questions in the public sector

11.7.2 Data Sharing/Data Integration

- Data Acquisition Technology: To facilitate the integration as well as analysis.

  - Research Question: Data fragment selection, sampling and scalability. Solutions will be brought about by quantum computers (predicted to be available in 5–10 years, but 15–20 years seems more realistic.)

- Data Analysis Technology: Linked data provides the best technology set for sharing data on the Web. Linked data and ontologies provide mechanisms for integrating data (map to same ontology; map between ontologies/schemas/instances).

  - Research Question: Scalability, dealing with high speed of data and high variety. Dealing with trillions of nodes will take 3–5 years.
  - Research Question: Making semantic systems easy to use by non-semantic (logic) experts. It will take 5 years at least to have a comprehensive tooling support.

- Data Curation/Storage Technology: Metadata and data provenance frameworks.

  - Research Question: What are standards for common data tracing formats? Provenance on certain storage types, e.g. graph databases, is still computationally expensive. The integration of provenance-awareness into existing tools can be achieved in the short term (2–3 years) once this reaches a critical market demand.

11.7.3 Real-Time Insights

- Data Analysis Technology: Linked data and machine learning technologies can support automated analysis, which is required for gaining real-time insights.

  - Research Question: High performance while coping with the 3 Vs (volume, variety and velocity). Real-time deep analytics is more than 5 years away.

- Data Storage Technology: Google Data Flow, Amazon Kinesis, Spark, Drill, Impala, in-memory databases.

  - Research Question: How can ad hoc and streaming queries on large datasets be executed with minimal latencies? This is an active research field and may reach further maturity in a few years' time.

11.7.4 Data Security and Privacy

- Data Storage Technology: Encrypted storage and DBs; proxy re-encryption between domains; automatic privacy protection (e.g. differential privacy).

  - Research Question: Advances in "privacy by design" to link analytics needs with protective controls in processing and storage. A legal framework, e.g., the General Data Protection Regulation (GDPR), has to be harmonized among EU member states. Beyond legislation, data and social commons are required (Curry et al. 2014). This will require at least a further 3 years of research.

11.7.5   Real-Time Data Transmission

- Data Acquisition Technology: Kafka, Flume, Storm, etc., Curry et al. (2014).

  - Research Question: Distributed processing and cleaning. Current approaches should be able to let the user know the type of resources that they require to perform tasks specified by the user (e.g. process 10 GB/s). First approaches towards these ends are emerging and they should be available on the market within the next 5 years.

- Data Storage Technology: Current best practice: write optimized storage solution (e.g. HDFS), columnar stores.

  - Research Question: How to improve random read/write performance of database technologies. The Lambda Architecture described by Marz and Warren reflects the current best practice standard for persisting high velocity data. Effectively it addresses the shortcoming of insufficient random/read write performances of existing DB technologies. Performance increases will be continuous and incremental and simplify overall development of big data technology stacks. Technologies could reach a level of maturity that leads to simplified architectural blueprints in 3–4 years.

11.7.6   Natural Language Analytics

- Data Analysis Technology: Information extraction, named entity recognition, machine learning, linked data. Entity linking and co-reference resolution.

  - Research Question: Increasing scalability and robustness. Robust scalable solutions are at least 3–5 years away.

- Data Curation Technology: Validation of Natural Language Analytics (NLA) outputs with humans via curation.

  - Research Question: Curation at scale depends on the interplay between automated curation platforms and collaborative approaches leveraging large pools of data curators. Technically, this integration can be achieved in the short term (2–3 years).

11.7.7   Predictive Analytics

- Data Storage Technology: Analytical databases.

  - Research Question: How can databases efficiently support predictive analytics? From a storage point of view, analytical databases address the problem of better performance as the DB itself is able to execute analytical code.

Currently there is a lack of standardized query languages but efforts such as ArrayQL are on their way. This may change in 3–5 years from now.

11.7.8 Modelling and Simulation

- Data Storage Technology: Best practices; batch and in-stream processing (Lambda architecture), temporal databases.

  - Research Question: How can time-series data be managed in a general way for effective analysis? Spatiotemporal databases are an active research field and results may be beyond a 5-year time scale.

- Data Usage Technology: Standards in (semantic) modelling; application of simulation in planning (e.g. plant planning).

  - Research Question: Making models explicit and/or transparent. This is a research question with a long timeline (beyond 2020).

11.8 Conclusion and Recommendations for the Public Sector

The findings after analysing the requirements and the technologies currently available show that there are a number of open research questions to be addressed in order to develop the technologies such that competitive and effective solutions can be built. The main developments are required in the fields of scalability of data analysis, pattern discovery, and real-time applications. Also required are improvements in provenance for the sharing and integration of data from the public sector.

It is also extremely important to provide integrated security and privacy mechanisms in big data applications, as the public sector collects vast amounts of sensitive data. In many countries legislation limits the use of the data only for purposes for which it was originally obtained. In any case, respecting the privacy of citizens is a mandatory obligation in the European Union.

Other areas, especially interesting for the safety applications in public sector, are the analysis of natural language, which can be useful as a method to gather unstructured feedback from citizens, e.g. from social media and networks. The development of effective predictive analytics, as well as modelling and simulation tools for the analysis of historical data, are key challenges to be addressed by future research.

References

1105 Government Information Group. (n.d.). *The chase for Big Data skills*. Retrieved March 26, 2013, from GCN.com: http://gcn.com/microsites/2012/snapshot-managing-big-data/04--chasing-big-data-skill-sets.aspx

Correia, Z. P. (2004). Toward a stakeholder model for the co-production of the public-sector information system. *Information Research*, 10(3), paper 228. Retrieved February 27, 2013, from InformationR.net: http://InformationR.net/ir/10-3/paper228.html

Curry, E., Ngonga, A., Domingue, J., Freitas, A., Strohbach, M., Becker, T. et al. (2014). D2.2.2. Final version of the technical white paper. Public deliverable of the EU-Project BIG (318062; ICT-2011.4.4).

European Commission. (1998). COM(1998)585. *Public sector information: A key resource for Europe. Green paper on public sector information in the information society*. European Commission.

Government of Ireland. Department of Jobs, Enterprise and Innovation. (2013, June 24). *Joint Industry/Government Task Force to drive development of Big Data in Ireland – Minister Bruton*. Retrieved February 17, 2013, from Working for Jobs, Enterprise and Innovation: http://www.djei.ie/press/2013/20130624.htm

McKinsey Global Institute. (2011, June). *Big Data: The next frontier for innovation, competition, and productivity*. McKinsey & Company.

Ojo, A., Curry, E., & Sanaz-Ahmadi, F. (2015). A tale of open data innovations in five smart cities. 48th Annual Hawaii International Conference on System Sciences, IEEE (pp. 2326–2335)

Oracle. (2012). *Big Data: A big deal for public sector organizations*. Oracle.

PredPol. (n.d.). Retrieved September 08, 2013, from PredPol Web site: http://www.predpol.com/

The European Parliament and the Council of The European Union. (2003, November 17). Directive 2003/98/EC of the European Parliament and of the Council of 17 November 2003 on the re-use of public sector information. Official Journal L 345, 31/12/2003 P. 0090 - 0096. Brussels: The European Parliament and the Council of the European Union.

The White House. (2012, March 29). *Big Data is a Big Deal*. Retrieved January 18, 2013, from The White House: http://www.whitehouse.gov/blog/2012/03/29/big-data-big-deal

van Kasteren, T., Ulrich, B., Srinivasan, V., & Niessen, M. (2014). Analyzing tweets to aid situational awareness. *36th European Conference on Information Retrieval*.

Wang, T., Rudin, C., Wagner, D., & Sevieri, R. (2013). Detecting patterns of crime with series finder. *Proceedings of the European Conference on Machine Learning and Principles and Practice of Knowledge Discovery in Databases*.

World Economic Forum. (2012). *Big Data, Big Impact: New possibilities for international development*. Geneva: The World Economic Forum.

Yiu, C. (2012). *The Big Data Opportunity. Making government faster, smarter and more personal*. London: Policy Exchange.

Zillner, S., Rusitschka, S., Munné, R., Lippell, H., Lobillo, F., Hussain, K. et al. (2013): *D2.3.1. First draft of the sectorial requisites*. Public Deliverable of the EU-Project BIG (318062; ICT-2011.4.4).

Zillner, S., Neururer, S., Munné, R., Prieto, E., Strohbach, M., van Kasteren, T. et al. (2014). *D2.3.2. Final version of the sectorial requisites*. Public Deliverable of the EU-Project BIG (318062; ICT-2011.4.4).

Chapter 12
Big Data in the Finance and Insurance Sectors

Kazim Hussain and Elsa Prieto

12.1 Introduction

The finance and insurance sector by nature has been an intensively data-driven industry for many years, with financial institutes having managed large quantities of customer data and using data analytics in areas such as capital market trading. The business of insurance is based on the analysis of data to understand and effectively evaluate risk. Actuaries and underwriting professionals depend upon the analysis of data to be able to perform their core roles; thus it is safe to state that this data is a dominant force in the sector.

There is however an increase in prevalence of data which falls into the domain of big data, i.e. high volume, high velocity, and high variety of information assets born out of the advent of new customer, market, and regulatory data surging from multiple sources. To add to the complexity is the co-existence of structured and un-structured data. Unstructured data in the financial services and insurance industry can be identified as an area where there is a vast amount of un-exploited business value. For example, there is much commercial value to be derived from the large volumes of insurance claim documentation which would predominately be in text form and contains descriptions entered by call centre operators, notes associated with individual claims and cases. With the help of big data technologies not only can value be more efficiently extracted from such a data source, but the analysis of this form of unstructured data in conjunction with a wide variety of datasets to extract faster, targeted commercial value. An important characteristic of big data in this industry is value—how can a business not only collect and manage big data, but how can the data which holds value be identified and how can organizations forward-engineer (as opposed to retrospectively evaluate) commercial value from the data.

K. Hussain • E. Prieto (✉)
Atos Spain, S.A., Albarracín, 25 28037 Madrid, Spain
e-mail: kazim.hussain@atos.net; elsa.prieto@atos.net

© The Author(s) 2016
J.M. Cavanillas et al. (eds.), *New Horizons for a Data-Driven Economy*,
DOI 10.1007/978-3-319-21569-3_12

12.1.1   Market Impact of Big Data

The market for big data technology in the financial and insurance domains is one of the most promising. According to TechNavio's forecast (Technavio 2013), the global big data market in the financial services sector will grow at a CAGR of 56.7 % over the period 2012–2016. One of the key factors contributing to this market growth is the need to meet financial regulations, but the lack of skilled resources to manage big data could pose a challenge.

The key vendors dominating this space include Hewlett-Packard, IBM, Microsoft, and Oracle that are global well-established players with a generalist profile. However, the appeal of the market will be a pull factor on new entrants in the coming years.

With data being the most important asset, this technology is especially favourable and differentiating for financial services organizations, as said by the IBM Institute for Business Value's report "Analytics: The real-world use of big data in financial services" (IBM 2013). By leveraging this asset, banks and financial markets firms can gain a comprehensive understanding of markets, customers, channels, products, regulations, competitors, suppliers, and employees that will let them better compete. Therefore, this is a positive trend in the market and is expected to drive the growth of the global big data market in the financial services sector.

In terms of data strategy, financial services organizations are taking a business-driven approach to big data: business requirements are identified in the first place and then existing internal resources and capacities are aligned to support the business opportunity, before investing in the sources of data and infrastructures. However, not all financial organizations are keeping the same pace. According to the IBM report, while 26 % are focused on understanding the principal notions (compared with 24 % of global organizations), the majority are either defining a roadmap related to big data (47 %) or already conducting big data pilots and implementations (27 %).

Where they lag behind their cross-industry peers is in using more varied data types within their big data implementations. Slightly more than 21 % of these firms are analysing audio data (often produced in abundance in retail banks' call centres), while slightly more than 27 % report analysing social data (compared to 38 % and 43 %, respectively, of their cross-industry peers). This lack of focus on unstructured data is attributed to the on-going struggle to integrate the organizations' massive structured data.

12.2 Analysis of Industrial Needs in the Finance and Insurance Sectors

The advent of big data in financial services can bring numerous advantages to financial institutions. Benefits that come with the greatest commercial impact are highlighted as follows:

Enhanced Levels of Customer Insight, Engagement, and Experience With the digitization of financial products and services and the increasing trend of customers interacting with brands or organizations in the digital space, there is an opportunity for financial services organizations to enhance their level of customer engagement and proactively improve the customer experience. Many argue that this is the most crucial area for financial institutes to start leveraging big data technology to stay ahead, or even just keep up with competition. To help achieve this, big data technologies and analytical techniques can help derive insight from newer unstructured sources such as social media.

Enhanced Fraud Detection and Prevention Capabilities Financial services institutions have always been vulnerable to fraud. There are individuals and criminal organizations working to defraud financial institutions and the sophistication and complexity of these schemes is evolving with time. In the past, banks analysed just a small sample of transactions in an attempt to detect fraud. This could lead to some fraudulent activities slipping through the net and other "false positives" being highlighted. Utilization of big data has meant these organizations are now able to use larger datasets to identify trends that indicate fraud to help minimize exposure to such a risk.

Enhanced Market Trading Analysis Trading the financial markets started becoming a digitized space many years ago, driven by the growing demand for the faster execution of trades. Trading strategies that make use of sophisticated algorithms to rapidly trade financial markets are a major benefactor of big data.

Market data can be considered itself, as big data. It is high in volume, it is generated from a variety of sources, and it is generated at a phenomenal velocity. However, this big data does not necessarily translate into actionable information. The real benefit from big data lies in effectively extracting actionable information and integrating this information with other sources. Market data from multiple markets and geographies as well as a variety of asset classes can be integrated with other structured and unstructured sources to create enriched, hybrid datasets (a combination of structured and unstructured data). This provides a comprehensive and integrated view of the market state and can be used for a variety of activities such as signal generation, trade execution, profit and loss (P&L) reporting, and risk measurement, all in real-time hence enabling more effective trading.

12.3   Potential Big Data Applications in Finance and Insurance

Three potential applications for the finance and insurance sector were described and developed in Zillner et al. (2013, 2014) as representatives of the application of big data technologies in the sector (Table 12.1).

Table 12.1 Summary of big data application scenarios for the finance and insurance sector

Name	Market manipulation detection.
Summary	Detection of false rumours that try to manipulate the market.
Synopsis	Financial markets are often influenced by rumours. Sometimes false rumours are intentionally placed in order to distract and mislead other market participants. These behaviours differ based on the intended outcome of the manipulation. Examples of market abuse are market sounding (the illegal dissemination of untrue information about a company whose stock is traded on exchanges) and pump and dump (false positive reports are published about a company whose shares are tradable with the goal of encouraging other market participants to buy stock in the corresponding company; an increase in demand would cause the price of the stock to rise to an artificial level).
Business objectives	Identifying hoaxes and assessing the consistency of new information with other reliable sources.
Name	Reputational risk management.
Summary	Assessment of exposure to reputational risk connected to consulting services offered by banks to their customers.
Synopsis	A negative perception can adversely affect a bank's ability to maintain existing, establish new business relationships, or continued access to sources of funding. The increase in the probability of default (issuer credit risk), the price volatility, and the difficulties to exchange specific financial products on restricted markets have all contributed to the increase of the reputational and operational risk associated with brokerage and advisory services. Banks and financial institutions usually offer third party financial products. This implies that a lack of performance of a third party product could have real impacts on the relationship between the bank and its customers.
Business objectives	To monitor third parties' reputation and the effects of reputation disruption on the direct relationship between banks and customers.
Name	Retail brokerage.
Summary	Discover topic trends, detect events, or support the portfolio optimization/asset allocation.
Synopsis	A general trend in the whole industry of retail brokerage and market data is to come up with functionalities that offer actionable information. The focus is no longer on figures based on quantitative historical data, e.g. key figures or performance data. Instead, investors look for signals that have some kind of predictive element yet are easy to understand. In that sense, the extraction of sentiments and topics from textual sources is a perfect add-on for the conventional data and functionalities that are already offered by retail brokerage companies.
Business objectives	Collecting and reviewing various sources of financial information (on markets, companies, or financial institutions) repeatedly by automation of this task.

12.4 Drivers and Constraints for Big Data in the Finance and Insurance Sectors

The successful realization of big data in finance and insurance has several drivers and constraints.

12.4.1 Drivers

The following **drivers** were identified for big data in the finance and insurance sector:

- **Data Growth:** Financial transaction volumes are increasing, leading to data growth in financial services firms. In capital markets, the presence of electronic trading has led to an increase in the number of trades. Data growth is not limited to capital markets businesses. The Capgemini/RBS Global Payments study for 2012 (Capgemini 2012) estimates that the global number of electronic payment transactions is about 260 billion and growing between 15 and 22 % for developing countries.
- **Increasing scrutiny from regulators:** Regulators of the industry now require a more transparent and accurate view of financial and insurance businesses, this means that they no longer want reports; they need raw data. Therefore financial institutions need to ensure that they are able to analyse their raw data at the same level of granularity as the regulators.
- **Advancements in technology mean increased activity:** Thanks largely to the digitization of financial products and services, the ease and affordability of executing financial transactions online has led to ever-increasing activity and expansion into new markets. Individuals can make more trades, more often, across more types of accounts, because they can do so with the click of a button in the comfort of their own homes.
- **Changing business models:** Driven by the aforementioned factors, financial institutions find themselves in a market that is fundamentally different from the market of even a few years ago. Adoption of big data analytics is necessary to help build business models for financial institutions geared towards retention of market share from the increasing competition coming from other sectors.
- **Customer insight:** Today the relationship between banks and consumers has been reversed: consumers now have transient relationships with multiple banks. Banks no longer have a complete view of their customer's preferences, buying patterns, and behaviours. Big data technologies therefore play a focal role in enabling customer centricity in this new paradigm.

12.4.2 Constraints

The **constraints** for big data in the finance and insurance sector can be summarized as follows:

- **Old culture and infrastructures:** Many banks still depend on old rigid IT infrastructure, with data siloes and a great many legacy systems. Big data, therefore, is an add-on, rather than a completely new standalone initiative. The culture is an even bigger barrier to big data deployment. Many financial organizations fail to implement big data programs because they are unable to appreciate how data analytics can improve their core business.
- **A lack of skills:** Some organizations have recognized the data and the opportunities the data presents; however they lack human capital with the right level of skills to be able to bridge the gap between data and potential opportunity. The skills that are "missing" are those of a data scientist.
- **Data "Actionability":** The next main challenge can be seen in making big data actionable. Big data technology and analytical techniques enable financial services institutions to get deep insight into customer behaviour and patterns, but the challenge still lies in organizations being able to take specific action based on this data.
- **Data privacy and security:** Customer data is a continuing cause for concern. Regulation remains a big unknown: what is and is not legally permissible in the ownership and use of customer data remains ill-defined, and that is an inhibiting factor to rapid and large-scale adoption.

12.5 Available Finance and Insurance Data Resources

The financial service system has several major pools of data that are held by different stakeholders/parties. Data are classified into three major categories:

Structured Data This refers to information with a high degree of organization, such that inclusion in a relational database is seamless and readily searchable by simple, straightforward search engine algorithms, or other search operations. Examples of financial structured data sources are:

- Trading systems (transaction data)
- Account systems (data on account holdings and movements)
- Market data from external providers
- Securities reference data
- Price information
- Technical indicators

Unstructured Data Although the financial industry has previously focused on high velocity market data, it is now moving towards unstructured data to changing trading dynamics. Examples of financial unstructured data are:

- Daily stock feeds
- Company announcements (ad-hoc news)
- Online news media
- Articles/blogs
- Customers' feedback/experiences

Semi-structured Data A form of structured data that does not conform to the formal structure of data models associated with relational databases or other forms of data tables, but even so contains tags or markers to separate semantic elements and enforce hierarchies of records and fields within the data. Examples of semi-structured data are expressed in meta-languages (mostly XML-based) such as:

- Financial products Markup Language (FpML)
- Financial Information eXchange (FIX)
- Interactive Financial eXchange (IFX)
- Market Data Definition Language (MDDL)
- Financial Electronic Data Interchange (FEDI)
- Open Financial eXchange (OFX)
- eXtensible Business Reporting Language (XBRL)
- SWIFTStandards

Nowadays the amount of unstructured information in enterprises is around 80–85 %. The financial and insurance industry has vast repositories of structured data in comparison to other industries, with a large amount of this information having its origin inside the organization.

12.6   Finance and Insurance Sector Requirements

12.6.1   Non-technical Requirements

Data Protection and Privacy Particularly in the EU, there are numerous data protection and privacy issues to consider when undertaking big data analytics. Regulatory requirements dictate that personal data must be processed for specified and lawful purposes and that the processing must be adequate, relevant, and not excessive. The impact of these principles for financial services organizations is significant, with individuals being able to ask financial services organizations to remove or refrain from processing their personal data in certain circumstances.

This requirement could lead to increased costs for financial services organizations, as they deal with individuals' requests. This removal of data may also lead to the dataset being skewed, as certain groups of people will be more active and aware of their rights than others.

Confidentiality and Regulatory Requirements Any information related by a third party that is subject to big data analytics is likely to be confidential information. Therefore, financial services organizations will need to ensure that they comply with their obligations and that any use of such data does not give rise to a breach of their confidentiality or regulatory obligations.

Liability Issues Just because big data contains an enormous amount of information, it does not mean that it reflects a representative sample of the population. Therefore there is a risk of misinterpreting the information produced and liability may arise where reliance is placed on that information. This is a factor that financial services organizations have to take into account when looking at using big data in analytical models and ensuring that any reliance placed upon the output comes with relevant disclaimers attached.

12.6.2 Technical Requirements

Data Extraction and Sentiment Classification Though the definition of sentiment is vague, in general, a sentiment on an object is a positive or negative view, attitude, emotion, or appraisal on or from a document author or actor.

Sentiment is often expressed in a domain-specific way, and using non-domain-specific vocabulary may lead to misclassifications. The goal is to extract facts and sentiments concerning the financial use cases: financial instruments, situations, conditions, indicators, and experts' assessments regarding these instruments, as well as investors' sentiment, etc. The classification of sentiment can be done at several levels: words, phrases, sentences, paragraphs, documents, and even multiple documents, and then aggregate.

Data extraction needs to cope with noise, misinformation, irony, bias, or uncertainty. In addition, with sentiment it is important not only to determine the sentiment of a piece of information, but how words affect the semantic orientation and how sentiment changes.

Data Quality The more timely, accurate, and relevant the data (along with good analytics), the better the assessment of the current financial state is. This requires better processes of identifying and maintaining the data sources of interest, verifying, cleaning, transforming, integrating, and deduplicating data. Due to the large amount of available data, there is a need for automation and scalability processes. Language detection methods also need to be refined to improve precision and reliability.

Data Acquisition For banks and financial services providers, the volume of data they generate, consume, store, and access will increase exponentially year over year. The applications depend on acquiring and accessing massive amounts of

historical heterogeneous information and live feeds of unstructured, semi structured, and structured information. A significant amount of data comes from internal
structured data, though there is a growing trend towards external unstructured data
(from news, blogs, articles, social networks, and websites). Even when there can be
a wide variety of data sources to access, the actual ones that are required depend on
the design for a specific application.

Data Integration/Sharing This describes the task to overcome the heterogeneity
of disparate data sources in terms of hardware, software, syntax, and/or semantics
by providing access tools that enable interoperability.

The data is usually scattered among different heterogeneous sources with differing conceptual representations (different structures and data semantics) but it is
encapsulated into a single, homogeneous data source to the end user.

The motivation for integration may be based on strategic or operational considerations. Regarding strategic considerations and analysis, it may not be required to
constantly integrate the data but to integrate data snapshots at a certain point in
time. For operational analysis a real-time integration of the most up-to-date information may be required.

Typically data integration is not a once-off conversion but an on-going task,
therefore poses the additional constraint that the chosen solution needs to be robust
in terms of adaptability, extensibility, and scalability. Approaches leveraging
standards such as eXtensible Business Reporting Language (XBRL) and Linked
Data show promise (O'Riáin et al. 2012).

This rapid generation of continuous streams of information has challenged the
storage, computation, and communication capabilities in computing systems, as
they impose high resource requirements on data stream processing systems.

Decision Support Systems (DSS) Model-driven DSS emphasises access to and
manipulation of statistical, financial, optimization, and/or simulation models.
Models use data and parameters to aid decision-makers in analysing a situation,
for instance, assessing and evaluating decision alternatives and examining the
effect of changes. This requires integrating information from the knowledge base
into financial event detection models, visualization models, decision-models, and
for scalable execution of these models.

For some application scenarios, the response of the system should support real-
time or near-real-time insights. The velocity of the response is subject to the end
user requirements.

In DSS, visualization is an extremely useful tool for providing overviews and
insights into overwhelming amounts of data to support the decision-making
process.

Data Privacy and Security Top priorities for the financial sector today include
on-going regulatory compliance [e.g. Sarbanes-Oxley (SOX) Act, U.S. Government
(2002); EU data protection directive, Parliament (1995); cyber security directive,
Parliament (2013)] and risk mitigation, continued adaptation to the expectations of

consumers for anywhere/anytime service, reducing operational costs, and increasing efficiencies through use of cloud-based services.

Banking and financial institutions need to secure the storage, transit, and use of corporate and personal data across business applications, including online banking and electronic communications of sensitive information and documents.

The increasingly global nature and high-interconnectivity of the industry makes it necessary to comprehensively address international data security and privacy regulations, from the front to the back-end, and along the full supply chain, including third parties. Data is not always stored in-house but with third parties. Using commercial "cloud" services as data storage locations poses potential privacy and security problems since the terms of service for these products are often poorly understood.

12.7 Technology Roadmap for Big Data in the Finance and Insurance Sectors

For each requirement in the sector, this section presents applicable technologies and the research questions to be developed (Fig. 12.1; Table 12.2). All references presented here are from Curry et al. (2014).

12.7.1 Data Acquisition

- Acquisition pipeline technology.

  - Research Question: Data stream management. Current data analysis in the stored-data domain shall need to move to management of data in the data stream itself.

- Proprietary APIs technology.

  - Research Question: Privacy and anonymization at collection time. The data collection process shall require intrinsic data anonymization and/or decoupling of personal data from data emanating from business processes or otherwise.
  - Research Question: Social APIs. Moving ahead of existing proprietary (or even open) APIs, social APIs into financial services datasets need to be investigated.

Technical Requirement	Technology	Research Question
Data Acquisition	Acquisition pipeline	Data stream management
	APIs technology	Privacy and anonymization at collection time
		Social APIs
Data quality	Manual processing and validation	Scalable data curation and validation
		New methods to improve precision and reliability
Data extraction	Language modelling	Statistical language models
	Machine Learning	Required inference functionality
	Scalability in real-time	Processing of large datasets
Data integration / sharing	Wrappers/mediators to encapsulate distributed & automatic data and schema mapping	User-specific integration
		Data variety: sentiments, quantitative information
		Scaling methods for large data volumes and near-real time processing.
Decision support	Multi-attribute decision models	Stream-based data mining
		Machine learning adaptation to evolving content
	Resource allocation in mining data streams	Improved storage, computation and communication capabilities
Data privacy & security	Roles-based IdM and access control	Privacy by design | Security by design
		Data Security for public-private hybrid environments
		Enhanced Compliance management
	Database encryption NoSQL	Apply external encryption and authentication controls

Fig. 12.1 Mapping requirements to research questions in the finance and insurance sectors

12.7.2 Data Quality

- Manual processing and validation technology.

  - Research Question: Scalable data curation and validation.
  - Research Question: New methods to improve precision and reliability.

12.7.3 Data Extraction

- Language modelling technology.

  - Research Question: Obtaining keywords and key-phrases by using statistical language models.

220

K. Hussain and E. Prieto

Table 12.2 Timeframe of the major expected outcomes of the big data roadmap for the finance and insurance sector

Technical requirement	Year 1	Year 2	Year 3	Year 4	Year 5
Data acquisition			Social APIs		Data stream management. Privacy and anonymization at collection time
Data quality			Scalable data curation and validation		New methods to improve precision and reliability
Data extraction		Statistical language models	New machine learning techniques to satisfy the newly required inference functionality		Processing of large datasets
Data integration/ sharing					User-specific integration Data variety: sentiments, quantitative information Scaling methods for large data volumes and near-real-time processing
Decision support		Stream-based data mining			Machine learning adaptation to evolving content Improved storage, computation, and communication capabilities
Data privacy and security		Apply external encryption and authentication controls	Privacy by design	Security by design		Data security for public-private hybrid environments Enhanced compliance management

- Machine Learning technology.

  – Research Question: The size of datasets in financial services makes it necessary for new machine learning techniques to satisfy the newly required inference functionality.

- Scalability in real-time technology: Real-time information is of interest in some application scenarios of financial services.

- Research Question: The challenge of processing large datasets represents a requirement for research in the scalability of data processing in real-time as datasets grow in size and number.

12.7.4 Data Integration/Sharing

- Wrappers/mediators to encapsulate distributed data and automatic data and schema mapping technology: Sources of data in the financial services industry can be distributed across organizations, or across time and space.

  - Research Question: User-specific integration. Integration of data for the benefit of specific users (namely, business processes, or target end user organizations).
  - Research Question: Data variety: sentiments, quantitative information.
  - Research Question: Scaling methods for large data volumes and near-real-time processing. This research challenge is in relation to the "scalability in real time" described earlier, under "data extraction".

12.7.5 Decision Support

- Multi-attribute decision-models technology: The availability of information from multiple sources will provide multiple attribute types that become available to include in decision-models.

  - Research Question: Stream-based data mining.
  - Research Question: Machine learning adaptation to evolving content.

- Resource allocation in mining data streams technology: Elastic computing today allows for dynamic resource allocation as required. Improvements may be required in resource allocation for near real-time support to decision-making.

  - Research Question: Improved storage, computation, and communication capabilities.

12.7.6 Data Privacy and Security

- Roles-based identity management and access control technology: access control in the context of large datasets will pose a problem when sensitive data (business process related) begins to be exploited in large datasets and integrated with other data, and accessed by third parties.

- Research Question: Privacy by design | Security by design.
- Advances in "privacy by design" to link analytics needs with protective controls in processing and storage.
- Research Question: Data Security for public-private hybrid environments.
- The advent of cloud storage and computation services, however, comes at the expense of data security and user privacy.
- Research Question: Enhanced Compliance management (data protection, others). Research has already been initiated, but needs to continue in providing methodologies and infrastructures that facilitate the monitoring, enforcement, and audit of quantifiable indicators on the security of a business process.
- Database encryption technology: The security concept of NoSQL databases generally relies on external enforcing mechanisms.
- Research Question: Review the security architecture and policies of the overall system and apply external encryption and authentication controls to safeguard NoSQL databases. Data security for public-private hybrid environments.

12.8 Conclusion and Recommendations for the Finance and Insurance Sectors

The Finance and insurance sector analysis for the roadmap is based on four major application scenarios based on exploiting banks and insurance companies' own data to create new business value. The findings of this analysis show that there are still research challenges to develop the technologies to their full potential in order to provide competitive and effective solutions. These challenges appear at all levels of the big data value chain and involve a wide set of different technologies, which would make necessary a prioritization of the investments in R&D. In broad terms there seems to be a general agreement on real-time aspects, better data quality techniques, scalability of data management and processing, better sentiment classification methods, and compliance with security requirements along the supply chain. However, it is worth mentioning the importance of the application scenario and the real needs of the end user in order to determine these priorities. At the same time, apart from the technological aspects, there are organizational, cultural, and legal factors that will play a key role in how the financial services market takes on big data for its operations and business development.

References

Capgemini. (2012). *World payments report 2012*. Available at http://www.capgemini.com/resource-file-access/resource/pdf/The_8th_Annual_World_Payments_Report_2012.pdf. Accessed 2014.

Curry, E., Ngonga, A., Domingue, J., Freitas, A., Strohbach, M., Becker, T. et al. (2014). D2.2.2. Final version of the technical white paper. Public deliverable of the EU-Project BIG (318062; ICT-2011.4.4).

IBM. (2013). *Analytics: The real-world use of big data in financial services*. IBM Institute for Business Value. Available at http://www-935.ibm.com/services/multimedia/Analytics_The_real_world_use_of_big_data_in_Financial_services_Mai_2013.pdf. Accessed 2014.

O'Riáin, S., Curry, E., & Harth, A. (2012). XBRL and open data for global financial ecosystems: A linked data approach. *International Journal of Accounting Information Systems, 13*, 141–162. doi:10.1016/j.accinf.2012.02.002.

Parliament, E. (1995). *Directive 95/46/EC of the European Parliament and of the Council of 24 October 1995 on the protection of individuals with regard to the processing of personal data and on the free movement of such data*. Available at http://eur-lex.europa.eu/legal-content/en/ALL/?uri=CELEX:31995L0046. Accessed 2014.

Parliament, E. (2013). *Proposal for a Directive of the European Parliament and of the Council concerning measures to ensure a high common level of network and information security across the Union, from European Commission*. Available at http://ec.europa.eu/information_society/newsroom/cf/dae/document.cfm?doc_id=1666. Accessed 2014.

Technavio. (2013). *Global big data market in the financial services sector 2012-2016*. Retrieved from http://www.technavio.com. Accessed 2014.

U.S. Government. (2002). *Sarbanes-Oxley Act of 2002*. Available at 107th Congress Public Law 204. http://www.gpo.gov/fdsys/pkg/PLAW-107publ204/html/PLAW-107publ204.htm

Zillner, S., Rusitschka, S., Munné, R., Lippell, H., Lobillo, F., Hussain, K. et al. (2013). *D2.3.1. First draft of sector's roadmap*. Public Deliverable of the EU-Project BIG (318062; ICT-2011.4.4).

Zillner, S., Neururer, S., Munné, R., Prieto, E., Strohbach, M., van Kasteren, T. et al. (2014). *D2.3.2. Final version of the sectorial requisites*. Public Deliverable of the EU-Project BIG (318062; ICT-2011.4.4).

Chapter 13
Big Data in the Energy and Transport Sectors

Sebnem Rusitschka and Edward Curry

13.1 Introduction

The energy and transport sectors are currently undergoing two main transformations: digitization and liberalization. Both transformations bring to the fore typical characteristics of big data scenarios: sensors, communication, computation, and control capabilities through increased digitization and automation of the infrastructure for operational efficiency leading to high-volume, high-velocity data. In liberalized markets, big data potential is realizable within consumerization scenarios and when the variety of data across organizational boundaries is utilized.

In both sectors, there is a connotation that the term "big data" is not sufficient: the increasing computational resources embedded in the infrastructures can also be utilized to analyse data to deliver "smart data". The stakes are high, since the multimodal optimization opportunities are within critical infrastructures such as power systems and air travel, where human lives could be endangered, not just revenue streams.

In order to identify the industrial needs and requirements for big data technologies, an analysis was performed of the available data sources in energy and transport as well as their use cases in the different categories for big data value: operational efficiency, customer experience, and new business models. The energy and transport sectors are quite similar when it comes to the prime characteristics regarding big data needs and requirements as well as future trends. A special area is

S. Rusitschka (✉)
Corporate Technology, Siemens AG, Munich, Germany
e-mail: sebnem.rusitschka@siemens.com

E. Curry
Insight Centre for Data Analytics, National University of Ireland Galway, Lower Dangan, Galway, Ireland
e-mail: edward.curry@insight-centre.org

the urban setting where all the complexity and optimization potentials of the energy and transport sectors are focused within a concentrated regional area.

The main need of the sectors is a virtual representation of the underlying physical system by means of sensors, smart devices, or so-called intelligent electronic devices as well as the processing and analytics of the data from these devices. A mere deployment of existing big data technologies as used by the big data natives will not be sufficient. Domain-specific big data technologies are necessary in the cyber-physical systems for energy and transport. Privacy and confidentiality preserving data management and analysis is a primary concern of all energy and transport stakeholders that are dealing with customer data. Without satisfying the need for privacy and confidentiality, there will always be regulatory uncertainty and barriers to customer acceptance of new data-driven offerings.

13.2   Big Data in the Energy and Transport Sectors

The following section examines the dimensions of big data in energy and transport to identify the needs of business and end users with respect to big data technologies and their usage.

Electricity Industry   Data is coming from digitalized generator substations, transformer substations, and local distribution substations in an electric grid infrastructure of which the ownership has been unbundled. Information can come in the form of service and maintenance reports from field crews about regular and unexpected repairs, health sensor data from self-monitoring assets, data on end usage and power feed-in from smart meters, and high-resolution real-time data from GPS-synchronized phasor measurement units or intelligent protection and relay devices. An example use case comes from Électricité de France (EDF) (Picard 2013), where they currently "do a standard meter read once a month. With smart meters, utilities have to process data at 15-min intervals. This is about a 3000-fold increase in daily data processing for a utility, and it's just the first wave of the data deluge. Data comes from individual load curves, weather data, contractual information; network data 1 measure every 10 min for a target of 35 million customers. The estimated annual data volume would be 1800 billion records or 120 TB of raw data. The second wave will include granular data from smart appliances, electric vehicles, and other metering points throughout the grid. That will exponentially increase the amount of data being generated."

Oil and Gas Industry   Data comes from digitalized storage and distribution stations, but wells, refineries, and filling stations are also becoming data sources in the intelligent infrastructure of an integrated oil and gas company. Down hole sensors from production sites deliver data on a real-time basis including pressure, temperature, and vibration gauges, flow meters, acoustic and electromagnetic, circulation solids. Other data comes from sources such as vendors, tracking service crews, measurements of truck traffic, equipment and hydraulic fracturing, water usage; Supervisory Control and Data Acquisition (SCADA) data from valve and pump events, asset operating parameters, out of condition alarms; unstructured reserves data, geospatial data, safety incident notes, and surveillance video streams. An example use case comes from Shell (Mearian 2012) where "optical fiber attached to down hole sensors generate massive amounts of data that is stored at a private isolated section of the Amazon Web Services. They have collected 46 petabytes of data and the first test they did in one oil well resulted in 1 petabyte of information. Knowing that they want to deploy those sensors to approximately 10,000 oil wells, we are talking about 10 Exabytes of data, or 10 days of all data being created on the Internet. Because of these huge datasets, Shell started piloting with Hadoop in the Amazon Virtual Private Cloud". Others examples in the industry include (Nicholson 2012): "Chevron proof-of-concept using Hadoop for seismic data processing; Cloudera Seismic Hadoop project combining Seismic Unix with Apache Hadoop; PointCross Seismic Data Server and Drilling Data Server using Hadoop and NoSQL".

Transportation In transportation the number of data sources is increasing rapidly. Air and seaports, train and bus stations, logistics hubs, and warehouses are increasingly employing sensors: Electronic on board recorders (EOBRs) in trucks delivering data on load/unload times, travel times, driver hours, truck driver logs, pallet or trailer tags delivering data on transit and dwell times, information on port strikes, public transport timetables, fare systems and smart cards, rider surveys, GPS updates from vehicle fleet, higher volumes of more traditional data from established sources such as frequent flyer programs, etc. An example use case comes from the City of Dublin (Tabbitt 2014) where the "road and traffic department is now able to combine big data streaming from an array of sources—bus timetables, inductive-loop traffic detectors, closed-circuit television cameras, and GPS updates that each of the city's 1000 buses transmits every 20 s—to build a digital map of the city overlaid with the real-time positions of Dublin's buses using stream computing and geospatial data. Some interventions have led to a 10–15 % reduction in journey times".

13.3 Analysis of Industrial Needs in the Energy and Transport Sectors

Business needs can be derived from the previous dimensioning of big data and examples from within the energy and transport sectors:

Ease of use regarding the typical big data technologies will ultimately ensure wide-scale adoption. Big data technologies employ new paradigms and mostly offer programmatic access. Users require software development skills and a deep understanding of the distributed computing paradigm as well as knowledge of the application of data analytics algorithms within such distributed environments. This is beyond the skillset of most business users.

Semantics of correlations and anomalies that can be discovered and visualized via big data analytics need to be made accessible. Currently only domain and data experts together can interpret the data outliers; business users are often left with guesswork when looking at the results of data analytics.

Veracity of data needs to be guaranteed before it is used in energy and transport applications. Because the increase in data that will be used for these applications will be magnitudes bigger, simple rules or manual plausibility checks are no longer applicable.

Smart data is often used by industrial stakeholders to emphasize that an industrial business user needs refined data—not necessarily all raw data (big data)—but without losing information by concentrating only on small data that is of relevance today. In cyber-physical systems as opposed to online businesses, there is information and communication technology (ICT) embedded in the entire system instead of only in the enterprise IT backend. Infrastructure operators have the opportunity to pre-process data in the field, aggregate data, and distribute the intelligence for data analytics along the entire ICT infrastructure to make the best use of computing and communication resources to deal with volume and velocity of mass sensor data.

Decision support and automation becomes a core need as the pace and structure of business changes. European grid operators today need to intervene almost daily to prevent potentially large-scale blackouts, e.g. due to integration of renewables or liberalized markets. Traffic management systems become more and more elaborate as the amount of digitized and controllable elements increase. Business users need more information than "something is wrong". Visualizations can be extremely useful, but the question of what needs to be done remains to be answered either in real-time or in advance of an event, i.e. in a predictive manner.

Scalable advanced analytics will push the envelope on the state of the art. For example, smart metering data analytics (Picard 2013) include segmentation based on load curves, forecasting on local areas, scoring for non-technical losses, pattern recognition within load curves, predictive modelling, and real-time analytics in a fast and reliable manner in order to control delicate and complex systems such as the electricity grid (Heyde et al. 2010). In the US transportation sector, the business value of scalable real-time analytics is already being reaped by using big data systems for full-scale automation applications, e.g. automated rescheduling that helps trains to dynamically adapt to events and be on time across a wide area.[1]

Big data analytics offer many improvements for the end users. Operational efficiency ultimately means energy and resource efficiency and timeliness, which will improve quality of life—especially in urban mobility settings.

Customer experience and new business models related to big data scenarios are entirely based on better serving the end user of energy and mobility. However, both

---

[1] https://www.mapr.com/blog/why-transportation-industry-getting-board-big-data-hadoop

scenarios need personalized data in higher resolution. There is significant value in cross-combining a variety of data, which on the downside can make pseudonymization or even anonymization ineffective in protecting the identity and behavioural patterns of individuals, or the business patterns and the strategies of companies. New business models based on monetizing the collected data, with currently unclear regulations, leave end users entirely uninformed, and unprotected against secondary use of their data for purposes they might not agree with, e.g. insurance classification, credit rating, etc.

Reverse transparency is at the top of the wish list of data-literate end users. Data analytics need to empower end users to grasp the usage of their data trails. The access and usage of an end users' data should become efficiently and dynamically configurable by the end users. End users need *practical access to information on what data is used by whom, and for what purpose* in an easy-to-use, manageable way. *Rules and regulations* are needed for granting such transparency for end users.

Data access, exchange, and sharing for both business and end users. In today's complex electricity or intermodal mobility markets, there is almost no scenario where all the required data for answering a business, or engineering, question comes from one department's databases. Nonetheless, most of the currently installed advanced metering infrastructures have a lock-in of the acquired energy usage data to the utilities' billing systems. The lock-in makes it cumbersome to use the energy data for other valuable analytics. These data silos have traditional roots from when most European infrastructure businesses were vertically integrated companies. Also, the amount of data to be exchanged was much less, such that interfaces, protocols, and processes for data exchange were rather rudimentary.

13.4   Potential Big Data Applications for the Energy and Transport Sectors

In the pursuit of collecting the many sectorial requirements towards a European big data economy and its technology roadmap, big data applications in energy and transport have been analysed. A finding that is congruent with Gartner's study on the advancement of analytics (Kart 2013) is that big data applications can be categorized as "operational efficiency", "customer experience", and "new business models".

Operational efficiency is the main driver (Kart 2013) behind the investments for digitization and automation. The need for operational efficiency is manifold, such as increasing revenue margins, regulatory obligations, or coping with the loss of retiring skilled workers. Once pilots of big data technologies are set up to analyse the masses of data for operational efficiency purposes, the businesses realize that they are building a digital map of their businesses, products, and infrastructures—and that these maps combined with a variety of data sources can also deliver additional insight in other areas of the business such as asset conditions, end usage patterns, etc.

The remainder of this section details big data scenarios and the key challenge that prevents these scenarios from uptake in Europe.

13.4.1 Operational Efficiency

Operational efficiency subsumes all use cases that involve improvements in maintenance and operations in real time, or in a predictive manner, based on the data which comes from infrastructure, stations, assets, and consumers. Technology vendors who developed the sensorization of the infrastructure are the main enablers. The market demand for enhanced technologies is increasing, because it helps the businesses in the energy sector to better manage risk. The complexity of the pan-European interconnected electricity markets, with the integration of renewables and liberalization of electricity trading, requires more visibility of the underlying system and of the energy flows in real time. As a rule of thumb, anything with the adjective "smart" falls into this category: smart grid, smart metering, smart cities, and smart (oil, gas) fields. Some examples of big data use cases in operational efficiency are as follows:

- Predictive and real-time analysis of disturbances in power systems and cost-effective countermeasures.
- Operational capacity planning, monitoring, and control systems for energy supply and networks, dynamic pricing.
- Optimizing multimodal networks in energy as well as transportation especially in urban settings, such as city logistics or eCar-sharing for which the energy consumption and feed-in to the transportation hubs could be cross-optimized with logistics.

All of the scenarios in this category have the *main big challenge of the connecting of data silos*: be it across departments within vertically integrated companies, or across organizations along the electricity value chain. The big data use cases in the operational efficiency scenario require seamless integration of data, communication, and analytics across a variety of data sources, which are owned by different stakeholders.

13.4.2 Customer Experience

Understanding big data opportunities regarding customer needs and wants is especially interesting for companies in liberalized consumerized markets such as electricity, where entry barriers for new players as well as the margins are decreasing. Customer loyalty and continuous service improvement is what enables energy players to grow in these markets.

Some examples of using big data to improve customer experience are as follows:

- Continuous service improvement and product innovation, e.g. individualized tariff offerings based on detailed customer segmentation using smart meter or device-level consumption data.
- Predictive lifecycle management of assets, i.e. data from machines and devices combined with enterprise resource planning and engineering data to offer services such as intelligent on-demand spare-parts logistics.
- Industrial demand-side management, which allows for energy efficient production and increases competitiveness of manufacturing businesses.

The core challenge is handling confidentiality and privacy of domestic and business customers while getting to know and anticipate their needs. The data originator, data owner, and data user are different stakeholders that need to collaborate and share data to realize these big data application scenarios.

13.4.3 New Business Models

New business models revolve around monetizing the available data sources and existing data services in new ways. There are quite a few cases in which data sources or analysis from one sector represents insights for stakeholders within another sector. An analysis of energy and mobility data start-ups shows that there is a whole new way of generating business value if the end user owns the resources. Then the business is entirely customer- and service-oriented; whereas the infrastructures of energy and transport with their existing stakeholders are utilized as part of the service. These are called intermediary business models.

Energy consumer segment profiles, such as prosumer profiles for power feed-in from photovoltaic, or combined heat and power units; or actively managed demand-side profile, etc., from metering service providers could also be offered for smaller energy retailers, network operators, or utilities who can benefit from improvements on the standard profiles of energy usage but do not yet have access to high resolution energy data of their own customers.

The core challenge is to provide clear regulation around the secondary use of energy and mobility data. The connected end user is the minimal prerequisite for these consumer-focused new business models. The new market segments are diversified through big data energy start-ups like Next: Kraftwerke, who "merge data from various sources such as operational data from our virtual power plant, current weather and grid data as well as live market data. This gives Next Kraftwerke an edge over conventional power traders" (Kraftwerke 2014).

In transportation, cars are parked 95 % of the time (Barter, 2013) and according to a recent study, one car-sharing vehicle displaces 32 new vehicle purchases (AlixPartners 2014). Businesses that previously revolved around the product now become all about data-driven services. On the contrary to the energy sector, this bold move shows the readiness of the transportation incumbents to seize the big data value potential of a data-driven business.

13.5 Drivers and Constraints for Big Data in Energy and Transport

13.5.1 Drivers

The key drivers in the energy and transport sectors are as follows:

- **Efficiency increase** of the energy and transportation infrastructure and associated operations.
- **Renewable energy sources** have transformed whole national energy policies, e.g. the German *"Energiewende"*. Renewable energy integration requires optimization on multiple fronts (e.g., grid, market, and end usage or storage) and increases the dependability of electrification on weather and weather forecasts.
- **Digitization and automation** can substantially increase efficiency in the operation of flow networks such as in electricity, gas, water, or transport networks. These infrastructure networks will become increasingly sensorized, which adds considerably to the volume, velocity, and variety of industrial data.
- **Communication and connectivity** is needed to collect data for optimization and control automation. There needs to be bidirectional and multidirectional connectivity between field devices, e.g. intelligent electronic devices in an electricity grid substation or traffic lights.
- **Open data:** Publication of operational data on transparency platforms[2] by grid network operators, by the energy exchange market, and by the gas transmission system operators is a *regulatory obligation* that fosters grass-roots projects. Open Weather Map[3] and Open Street Map[4] are examples of user-generated free of charge data provisioning which are very important for both sectors.
- **The "skills shift":** As a result of retiring of skilled workers, such as truck drivers or electricity grid operators, a know-how shortage is being created that needs to be filled fast. This directly translates to increasing prices for the customers, because higher salaries need to be paid to attract the few remaining skilled workers in the market.[5] In the mid to long term, efficiency increases and more

---

[2] www.entsoe.net, www.transparency.eex.com, http://www.gas-roads.eu/

[3] http://openweathermap.org/

[4] http://www.openstreetmap.org/

[5] http://www.businessweek.com/articles/2013-08-29/germany-wants-more-truck-drivers

automation will be the prevailing trends: such as driverless trucks[6] in transportation or wide area monitoring protection and control systems in energy.

13.5.2 Constraints

Constraints in the energy and transport sectors are as follows:

- **Skills:** There are comparatively few people who can apply big data management and analytics knowledge together with domain know-how within the sectors.
- **Interpretation:** Implicit or tacit models are in the heads of the (retiring) skilled workers. Scalable domain model extraction becomes key, e.g. in traffic management systems rule bases grow over years to unmanageable complexities.
- **Digitization has not yet reached the tipping point:** Digitization and automation of infrastructure requires upfront investments, which are not well considered, if at all, by the incentive regulation by which infrastructure operators are bound. Real-time higher-resolution data is still not widely available.
- **Uncertainty regarding digital rights and data protection laws:** Unclear views on data ownership hold back big data in the end user facing segments of the energy and transport sectors (e.g. smart metering infrastructure).
- **"Digitally divided" European union:** Europe has fragmented jurisdiction when it comes to digital rights.
- **"Business-as-usual" trumps "data-driven business":** In established businesses it is very hard to change running business value chains. Incumbents will need to deal with a lot of changes: change in the existing long innovation cycles, change to walled garden views of closed systems and silos, and a change in the mind-set so that ICT becomes an enabler if not a core competency in their companies.
- **Missing end user acceptance:** In the energy sector it is often argued that people are not interested in energy usage data. However, when missing end user acceptance of a technology is argued, it is more a statement that a useful service using this technology is not yet deployed.
- **Missing trust:** Trust is an issue that could and should be remedied with technology data protection and with regulatory framework (i.e., appropriate privacy protection laws).

---

[6] http://www.techhive.com/article/2046262/the-first-driverless-cars-will-actually-be-a-bunch-of-trucks.html

13.6 Available Energy and Transport Data Resources

As the potential for big data was explored within the two sectors, the clearer it became that the list of available data sources will grow and still not be exhaustive. A key observation is that the variety of data sources utilized to find an answer to a business or engineering question is the differentiator from business-as-usual.

- **Infrastructure data** includes power transmission and distribution lines, and pipelines for oil, gas, or water. In transportation, infrastructure consists of motorways, railways, air and seaways. The driving question is *capacity*. Is a road congested? Is a power line overloaded?
- **Stations** are considered part of the infrastructure. In business and engineering questions they play a special role as they include the main assets of an infra- structure in a condensed area, and are of high economic value. The main driving question is current *status* and utilization levels, i.e. the effective capacity of the infrastructure. Is a transmission line open or closed? Is it closed due to a fault on the line? Is a subway delayed? Is it due to a technical difficulty?
- **Time-stamped and geo-tagged data** are required and increasingly available, especially GPS-synchronized data in both sectors, but also GSM data for tracing mobility and extracting mobility patterns.
- **Weather data**, besides **geo-location data**, is the most used data source in both sectors. Most energy consumption is caused by heating and cooling, which are highly weather-dependent consumption patterns. With renewable energy resources power feed-in into the electrical grid becomes weather dependent.
- **Usage data and patterns**, indicators, and derived values of *end usage of the respective resource and infrastructure*, in both energy or transport, can be harvested by many means, e.g. within the smart infrastructure, via metering at stations at the edges of the network, or smart devices.
- **Behavioural patterns** both .affect energy usage and mobility patterns and can be predicted. Ethical and social aspects become a major concern and stumbling block. The positive effects such as better consumer experience, energy effi- ciency, more transparency, and fair pricing must be weighed against the negative side effects.
- Data sources in the **horizontal IT landscape**, including data coming from sources such as CRM tools, accounting software, and historical data coming from ordinary business systems. The value potential from cross-combining historical data with new sources of data which come from the increased digiti- zation and automation in energy and transportation systems is high.
- Finally a myriad of **external third-party data or open data sources** are important for big data scenarios in energy and transport sectors, including macro-economic data, environmental data (meteorological services, global weather models/simulation), market data (trading info, spot and forward, busi- ness news), human activity (web, phone, etc.), energy storage information,

geographic data, predictions based on Facebook and Twitter, and information communities such as Open Energy Information.[7]

13.7 Energy and Transport Sector Requirements

The analysed business user and end user needs, as well as the different types of data sharing needs directly translate into technical and non-technical requirements.

13.7.1 Non-technical Requirements

Several non-technical requirements in the sectors were identified:

- **Investment in communication and connectedness:** Broadband communication, or ICT in general, needs to be widely available across all of Europe and alongside energy and transportation infrastructure for real-time data access. Connectedness needs to extend to end users to allow them to be continuously connected.
- **A digitally united European union:** Roaming costs have been preventing European end users using data-intensive apps across national borders. European data-driven service providers—especially start-ups looking for scalability of their business models—have mainly focused on the US market, and not the 27 other EU member states due to different data-related regulations. European stakeholders require reliable minimally consistent rules and regulations regarding digital rights and regulations. A digital bill of rights[8] as called for by the inventor of the Web, Tim Berners-Lee, is globally the right move and should be supported by Europe.
- **A better breeding ground for start-ups and start-up culture** is required, especially for techno-economic paradigm shifts like big data and the spreading digitization, where new business widely deviates from business-as-usual. Energy and mobility start-ups require more than just financial investments but also freedom for exploration and experimentation with data. Without this freedom innovation has little chance, unless of course the aforementioned techniques for privacy preserving analytics are not feasible.
- **Open data** in this regard is a great opportunity; however, *standardization* is required. Practical migration paths are required to simplify the adoption of state-of-the-art standards. Data model and representation standards will enable the

---

[7] http://en.openei.org
[8] http://www.wired.com/2014/03/web25

growth of a *data ecosystem* with collaborative data mining, shareable granularity of data, and accompanying techniques that prevent de-anonymization.

- **Data skilled people:** Programming, statistics, and associated tools need to be a part of engineering education. Traditional data analysts need to grasp the distributed computing paradigm, e.g. how to design algorithms that run on massively parallel systems, how to move algorithms to data, or how to engineer entirely new breeds of algorithms.

13.7.2 Technical Requirements

Several technical requirements were identified in the sectors:

- **Abstraction:** from the actual big data infrastructure is required to enable (a) ease of use, and (b) extensibility and flexibility. The analysed use cases have such diverse requirements that there is no single big data platform or solution that will empower the future utility businesses.
- **Adaptive data and system models** are needed so that new knowledge extracted from domain and system analytics can be redeployed into the data analytics framework without disrupting daily business. The abstraction layer should accommodate plug-in adaptive models.
- **Data interpretability** must be assured without the constant involvement of domain experts. The results must be traceable and explainable. Expert and domain know-how must be blended into data management and analytics.
- **Data analytics** is required as part of every step from data acquisition to data usage. In data acquisition embedded in-field analytics can enhance the veracity of data and can support different privacy and confidentiality settings on the same data source for different data users, e.g. service providers.
- **Real-time analytics** is required to support decisions, which need to be made in ever-shorter time spans. In smart grid settings, near real-time dynamic control requires insights at the source of the data.
- **Data lake** is required in terms of low-cost off-the-shelf storage technology combined with the ability to efficiently deploy data models on demand ("schema-on-read"), instead of the typical data warehouse solution of extract-transform-load (ETL).
- **Data marketplaces, open data, data logistics**, standard protocols capable of handling the variety, volume, and velocity of data, as well as data platforms are required for data sharing and data exchange across organizational boundaries.

13.8   Technology Roadmap for the Energy and Transport Sectors

The big data value chain for infrastructure- and resource-centric systems of energy and transport businesses consists of three main phases: data acquisition, data management, and data usage. *Data analytics, as indicated by business user needs, is implicitly required within all steps and is not a separate phase.*

The technology roadmap for fulfilling the key requirements along the data value chain for the energy and transport sectors focuses on technology that is not readily available and needs further research and development in order to fulfil the more strict requirements of energy and transport applications (Fig. 13.1).

13.8.1   Data Access and Sharing

Energy and transport are resource-centric infrastructure businesses. Access to usage data creates the opportunity to analyse the usage of a product or service to improve it, or gain efficiency in sales and operations. Usage data needs to be combined with other available data to deliver reliable predictive models. Currently there is a trade-off between enhancing interpretability of data and preserving privacy and confidentiality. The following example of mobility usage data combined with a variety

Technical Requirement	Technology	Research Question
Data Access & Sharing ▪ Interpretability of data & scalability of access ▪ Privacy & Confidentiality	Linked Data	Automating data linkage, Scalability
	Encrypted Storage	Analytics on encrypted data
	Data Provenance, Differential Privacy	Efficient computing, Scalability
Real-Time Analytics ▪ spatio-temporal, high-dimensional, high-speed	Machine Learning (ML)	Deep learning, such as Convolutional neural networks, Tensor modeling
	Distributed stream computing	Infrastructure awareness, Advanced elasticity, Federation
Prescriptive Analytics ▪ In support of usage for automation and control	Prediction & Optimization	Efficient computing, Scalability
	Embedded analytics	Distributed Data Analytics
	Linked Data & ML	Large-scale reasoning & ML in real-time
Abstraction ▪ Ease-of-use ▪ Flexibility & extensibility	Linked Data	Scalable knowledge modeling and retrieval
	Data abstraction layers	Data type agnostic architectures

Fig. 13.1 Mapping requirements to research questions in the energy and transport sectors

of other data demonstrates the privacy challenge. de Montjoye et al. (2013) show that "4 spatio-temporal points (approximate places and times) are enough to uniquely identify 95 % of 1.5 M people in a mobility database. The study further states that these constraints hold even when the resolution of the dataset is low". The work shows that mobility datasets combined with metadata can circumvent anonymity.

At the same time, insufficient privacy protection options can hinder the sourcing of big data in the first place, as experiences from smart metering rollouts in the energy businesses show. In the EU only 10 % of homes have smart meters (Nunez 2012). Although there is a mandate that the technology reaches 80 % of homes by 2020, European rollouts are stagnant. A survey from 2012 (Department of Energy and Climate Change 2012) finds that "with increasing reading frequency, i.e. from monthly to daily, to half hourly, etc., energy consumption data did start to feel more sensitive as the level of detail started to seem intrusive... Equally, it was not clear to some [participants] why anyone would want the higher level of detail, leaving a gap to be filled by speculation which resulted in some [participants] becoming more uneasy".

Advances are needed for the following technologies for data access and sharing:

- **Linked data** is a lightweight practice for exposing and connecting pieces of data, information, or knowledge using basic web standards. It promises to open up siloed data ownership and is already an enabler of open data and data sharing. However, with the increasing number of data sources already linked, the various types of new data that will come from intelligent infrastructures, and always connected end users in energy and mobility, scalability and cost-efficacy becomes an issue. One of the open research questions is how to (semi-) automatically extract data linkage to increase current scalability.
- **Encrypted data storage** can enable integrated, data-level security. As cloud storage becomes commonplace for domestic and commercial end users, better and more user-friendly data protection becomes a differentiation factor (Tanner 2014). In order to preserve privacy and confidentiality the use of encrypted data storage will be a basic enabler of data sharing and shared analytics. However, analytics on encrypted data is still an ongoing research question. The most widely pursued research is called fully homomorphic encryption. Homomorphic encryption theoretically allows operations to be carried out on the cipher text. The result is a cipher text that when decrypted matches the result of operation on plaintext. Currently only basic operations are feasible.
- **Data provenance** is the art of tracking data through all transformations, analyses, and interpretations. Provenance assures that data that is used to create actionable insights are reliable. The metadata that is generated to realize provenance across the big variety of datasets from differing sources also increases interpretability of data, which in turn could improve automated information extraction. However, scaling data provenance across the dimensions of big data is an open research question.

- **Differential privacy** (Dwork and Roth 2014) is the mathematically rigorous definition of privacy (and its loss) with the accompanying algorithms. The fundamental law of information recovery (Dwork and Roth 2014) states that too many queries with too few errors will expose the real information. The purpose of developing better algorithms is to push this event as far away as possible. This notion is very similar to the now mainstream realization that there is no unbreakable security, but that barriers if broken need to be fixed and improved. The cutting-edge research on differential privacy considers distributed databases and computations on data streams, enabling linear scalability and real-time processing for privacy preserving analytics. Hence, this technique could be an enabler of privacy preserving analytics on big data, allowing big data to gain user acceptance in mobility and energy.

13.8.2   Real-Time and Multi-dimensional Analytics

Real-time and multi-dimensional analytics enable real-time, multi-way analysis of streaming, spatiotemporal energy, and transport data. Examples from dynamic complex cyber-physical systems such as power networks show that there is a clear business mandate. Global spending on power utility data analytics is forecast to top $20 billion over the next 9 years, with an annual spend of $3.8 billion globally by 2020 (GTM Research 2012). However cost-efficacy of the required technologies needs to be proven. Real-time monitoring does not justify the cost if actions cannot be undertaken in real time. Phasor measurement technology, enabling high-resolution views of the current status of power networks in real time, is a technology that was invented 30 years ago. Possible applications have been researched for more than a decade. Initially there was no business need for it, because the power systems of the day were well engineered and well structured, hierarchical, static, and predictable. With increased dynamics through market liberalization and the integration of power generation technology from intermittent renewable sources like wind and solar, real-time views of power networks becomes indispensable.

Advances are needed for the following technologies:

- **Distributed stream computing** is currently gaining traction. There are two different strains of research and development of stream computing: (1) stream computing as in complex event processing (CEP), which has had its main focus on analysing data of high-variety and high-velocity, and (2) distributed stream computing, focusing on high-volume and high-velocity data processing. Complementing the missing third dimension, volume and variety, respectively, in both strains is the current research direction. It is argued that distributed stream computing, which already has linear scalability and real-time processing capabilities, will tackle high-variety data challenges with semantic techniques (Hasan and Curry 2014) and *Linked data*. A further open question is how to ease development and deployment for the algorithms that make use of distributed stream computing as well as other computing and storage solutions, such as plain old data warehouses and RDBMS. Since cost-effectiveness is the main enabler for big data value, advanced elasticity with computing and storage on demand as the algorithm requires must also be tackled.

• **Machine learning** is a fundamental capability needed when dealing with big data and dynamic systems, where a human could not possibly review all data, or where humans just lack the experience or ability to be able to define patterns. Systems are becoming increasingly more dynamic with complex network effects. In these systems humans are not capable of extracting reliable cues in real time—but only in hindsight during post-mortem data analysis (which can take significant time when performed by human data scientists). Deep learning, a research field that is gaining momentum, concentrates on more complex non-linear data models and multiple transformations of data. Some representations of data are better for answering a specific question than others, meaning multiple representations of the same data in different dimensions may be necessary to satisfy an entire application. The open questions are: how to represent specific energy and mobility data, possibly in multiple dimensions— and how to design algorithms that learn the answers to specific questions of the energy and mobility domains better than human operators can—and do so in a verifiable manner. The main questions for machine learning are cost-effective storage and computing for massive amounts of high-sampled data, the design of new efficient data structures, and algorithms such as tensor modelling and convolutional neural networks.

13.8.3 *Prescriptive Analytics*

Prescriptive analytics enable real-time decision automation in energy and mobility systems. The more complex and dynamic the systems are becoming, the faster insights from data will need to be delivered to enhance decision-making. With increasing ICT installed into the intelligent infrastructures of energy and transport, decision automation becomes feasible. However, with the increasing digitization, the normal operating state, when all digitized field devices deliver actionable information on how to operate more efficiently, will overwhelm human operators. The only logical conclusion is to either have dependable automated decision algorithms, or ignore the insights per second that a human operator cannot reasonably handle at the cost of reduced operational efficiency.

Advances are needed for the following technologies:

• **Prescriptive analytics:** Technologies enabling real-time analytics are the basis for prescriptive analytics in cyber-physical systems with resource-centric infrastructures such as energy and transport. With prescriptive analytics the simple predictive model is enhanced with possible actions and their outcomes, as well as an evaluation of these outcomes. In this manner, prescriptive analytics not only explains what might happen, but also suggests an optimal set of actions. Simulation and optimization are analytical tools that support prescriptive analytics.

- **Machine readable engineering and system models:** Currently many system models are not machine-readable. Engineering models on the other hand are semi-structured because digital tools are increasingly used to engineer a system. Research and innovation in this area of work will assure that machine learning algorithms can leverage system know-how that today is mainly limited to humans. Linked data will facilitate the semantic coupling of know-how at design and implementation time, with discovered knowledge from data at operation time, resulting in self-improving data models and algorithms for machine learning (Curry et al. 2013).

- **Edge computing:** Intelligent infrastructures in the energy and mobility sectors have ICT capability built-in, meaning there is storage and computing power along the entire cyber-physical infrastructure of electricity and transportation systems, not only in the control rooms and data centres at enterprise-level. Embedded analytics, and distributed data analytics, facilitating the in-network and in-field analytics (sometimes referred to as edge-computing) in conjunction with analytics carried out at enterprise-level, will be the innovation trigger in energy and transport.

13.8.4 Abstraction

Abstraction from the underlying big data technologies is needed to enable ease of use for data scientists, and for business users. Many of the techniques required for real-time, prescriptive analytics, such as predictive modelling, optimization, and simulation, are data and compute intensive. Combined with big data these require distributed storage and parallel, or distributed computing. At the same time many of the machine learning and data mining algorithms are not straightforward to parallelize. A recent survey (Paradigm 4 2014) found that "although 49 % of the respondent data scientists could not fit their data into relational databases anymore, only 48 % have used Hadoop or Spark—and of those 76 % said they could not work effectively due to platform issues".

This is an indicator that big data computing is too complex to use without sophisticated computer science know-how. One direction of advancement is for abstractions and high-level procedures to be developed that hide the complexities of distributed computing and machine learning from data scientists. The other direction of course will be more skilled data scientists, who are literate in distributed computing, or distributed computing experts becoming more literate in data science and statistics. Advances are needed for the following technologies:

- **Abstraction** is a common tool in computer science. Each technology at first is cumbersome. Abstraction manages complexity so that the user (e.g., programmer, data scientist, or business user) can work closer to the level of human problem solving, leaving out the practical details of realization. In the evolution of big data technologies several abstractions have already simplified the use of distributed file systems by extracting SQL-like querying languages to make them similar to database, or by adapting the style of processing to that of familiar online analytical processing frameworks.

- **Linked data** is one state-of-the-art enabler for realizing an abstraction level over large-scale data sources. The semantic linkage of data without prior knowledge and continuously linking with discovered knowledge is what will allow scalable knowledge modelling and retrieval in a big data setting. A further open question is how to manage a variety of data sources in a scalable way. Future research should establish a thorough understanding of data type agnostic architectures.

13.9 Conclusion and Recommendations for the Energy and Transport Sectors

The energy and transport sectors, from an infrastructure perspective as well as from resource efficiency, global competitiveness, and quality of life perspectives, are very important for Europe.

The analysis of the available data sources in energy as well as their use cases in the different categories of big data value, operational efficiency, customer experience, and new business models helped in identifying the industrial needs and requirements for big data technologies. In the investigation of these requirements, it becomes clear that a mere utilization of existing big data technologies as employed by online data businesses will not be sufficient. Domain- and device-specific adaptations for use in cyber-physical energy and transport systems are necessary. Innovation regarding privacy and confidentiality preserving data management and analysis is a primary concern of the energy and transport sector stakeholders. Without satisfying the need for privacy and confidentiality there will always be regulatory uncertainty, and uncertainty regarding user acceptance of a new data-driven offering.

Among the energy and transport sector stakeholders, there is a sense that "big data" will not be enough. The increasing intelligence embedded in infrastructures will be able to analyse data to deliver "smart data". This seems to be necessary, since the analytics involved will require much more elaborate algorithms than for other sectors. In addition, the stakes in energy and transport big data scenarios are very high, since the optimization opportunities will affect critical infrastructures.

There are a few examples in the energy and transport sectors, where a technology for data acquisition, i.e. a smart device, has been around for many years, or that the stakeholders have already been measuring and capturing a substantial amount of data. However the business need was unclear, making it difficult to justify investment. With recent advances it is now possible for the data to be communicated, stored, and processed cost-effectively. Hence, some stakeholders run the danger of not acknowledging the technology push. On the other hand, unclear regulation on what usage is allowed with the data keeps them from experimenting.

Many of the state-of-the-art big data technologies just await adaptation and usage in these traditional sectors. The technology roadmap identifies and elaborates the high-priority requirements and technologies that will take the energy and transport sectors beyond state of the art, such that they can concentrate on generating value by adapting and applying those technologies within their specific application domains and value-adding use cases.

References

AlixPartners. (2014). AlixPartners car sharing outlook study. Retrieved from: http://www.alixpartners.com/en/MediaCenter/PressReleases/tabid/821/articleType/ArticleView/articleId/950/AlixPartners-Study-Indicates-Greater-Negative-Effect-of-Car-Sharing-on-Vehicle-Purchases.aspx

Barter, P. (2013, February 22). 'Cars are parked 95% of the time'. Let's check! [Online article]. Available: http://www.reinventingparking.org/2013/02/cars-are-parked-95-of-time-lets-check.html

Curry, E., O'Donnell, J., Corry, E., et al. (2013). Linking building data in the cloud: Integrating cross-domain building data using linked data. *Advanced Engineering Informatics, 27,* 206–219.

de Montjoye, Y.-A., Hidalgo, C. A., Verleysen, M., & Blondel, V. D. (2013). Unique in the crowd: The privacy bounds of human mobility. *Sci Rep, 3,* 1376. doi:10.1038/srep01376.

Department of Energy and Climate Change. (2012, December). Smart metering data access and privacy – Public attitudes research. [Whitepaper]. Available: https://www.gov.uk/government/uploads/system/uploads/attachment_data/file/43045/7227-sm-data-access-privacy-public-att.pdf

Dwork, C., & Roth, A. (2014). The algorithmic foundations of differential privacy. *Foundations and Trends in Theoretical Computer Science, 9*(3–4), 211–407. doi:10.1561/0400000042.

GTM Research. (December 2012). The soft grid 2013-2020: Big data and utility analytics for smart grid. [Online]. Available: www.sas.com/news/analysts/Soft_Grid_2013_2020_Big_Data_Utility_Analytics_Smart_Grid.pdf

Hasan, S., & Curry, E. (2014b). Thematic event processing. In *Proceedings of the 15th international middleware conference on - middleware'14*, ACM Press, New York, NY, pp 109–120. doi:10.1145/2663165.2663335.

Heyde, C. O., Krebs, R., Ruhle, O., & Styczynski, Z. A. (2010). Dynamic voltage stability assessment using parallel computing. In *Proceeding of: Power and energy society general meeting, 2010 IEEE.*

Kart, L. (April 2013). Advancing analytics. Online Presentation, p. 6. Available: http://meetings2. informs.org/analytics2013/Advancing%20Analytics_LKart_INFORMS%20Exec%20Forum_ April%202013_final.pdf

Kraftwerke. (2014). http://www.next-kraftwerke.com/

Mearian, L. (2012, April 4). Shell oil targets hybrid cloud as fix for energy-saving, agile IT [Online article]. Available: http://www.computerworld.com/article/2502623/cloud-computing/shell-oil-targets-hybrid-cloud-as-fix-for-energy-saving--agile-it.html

Nicholson, R.(2012). Big data in the oil and gas industry. IDC energy insights. Presentation. Retrieved from https://www-950.ibm.com/events/wwe/grp/grp037.nsf/vLookupPDFs/RICK%20-%20IDC_ Calgary_Big_Data_Oil_and-Gas/$file/RICK%20-%20IDC_Calgary_ Big_Data_Oil_and-Gas.pdf

Nunez, C. (2012, December 12). Who's watching? Privacy concerns persist as smart meters roll out [Online article]. Available: http://news.nationalgeographic.com/news/energy/2012/12/ 121212-smart-meter-privacy/

Paradigm 4. (2014, July 1). Leaving data on the table: New survey shows variety, not volume, is the bigger challenge of analyzing big data. Survey. Available: http://www.paradigm4.com/wp-content/uploads/2014/06/P4PR07012014.pdf

Picard, M.-L. (2013, June 26). A smart elephant for a smart-grid: (Electrical) Time-series storage and analytics within hadoop [Online]. Available: http://www.teratec.eu/library/pdf/forum/ 2013/Pr%C3%A9sentations/A3_03_Marie_Luce_Picard_EDF_FT2013.pdf

Tabbitt, S. (2014, 17 February). Big data analytics keeps Dublin moving [Online article]. Available: http://www.telegraph.co.uk/sponsored/sport/rugby-trytracker/10630406/ibm-big-data-analytics-dublin.html

Tanner, A. (2014, July 11). The wonder (and woes) of encrypted cloud storage [Online article]. Available: http://www.forbes.com/sites/adamtanner/2014/07/11/the-wonder-and-woes-of-encrypted-cloud-storage/

Chapter 14
Big Data in the Media and Entertainment Sectors

Helen Lippell

14.1 Introduction

The media and entertainment industries have frequently been at the forefront of adopting new technologies. The key business problems that are driving media companies to look at big data capabilities are the need to reduce the costs of operating in an increasingly competitive landscape and, at the same time, the need to generate revenue from delivering content and data through diverse platforms and products.

It is no longer sufficient merely to publish a daily newspaper or broadcast a television programme. Contemporary operators must drive value from their assets at every stage of the data lifecycle. The most nimble media operators nowadays may not even create original content themselves. Two of the biggest international video streaming services, Netflix and Amazon, are largely aggregators of others' content, though also offering originally commissioned content to entice new and existing subscribers.

Media industry players are more connected with their customers and competitors than ever before. Thanks to the impact of disintermediation, content can be generated, shared, curated, and republished by literally anyone with an Internet-enabled device. Global revenues from such devices, including smartphones, tablets, desktop PCs, TVs, games consoles, e-readers, wearable gadgets, and even drones were expected to be around \$750 billion in 2014 (Deloitte 2014). This means that the ability of big data technology to ingest, store, and process many different data sources, and in real-time, is a valuable asset to the companies who are prepared to invest in it.

The Media Sector is in many respects an early adopter of big data technologies, but much more evolution has to happen for the full potential to be realized. Better integration between solutions along the data value chain will be essential in order to convince decision-makers to invest in innovation, especially in times of economic

H. Lippell (✉)
Press Association, London, UK
e-mail: helenlippell@gmail.com

© The Author(s) 2016
J.M. Cavanillas et al. (eds.), *New Horizons for a Data-Driven Economy*,
DOI 10.1007/978-3-319-21569-3_14

uncertainty. Also, the solutions market is dominated by US, and, increasingly, Asian firms. Therefore, there is an economic imperative for Europe to both develop and use big data technologies more extensively. Media and entertainment content and platforms have a global reach that many companies in other sectors, even retail and manufacturing, would be envious of.

Case studies of successful big data projects in media have tended to come from the left-hand end of the data value chain (i.e. data acquisition and analysis). However, there is a need to identify both exemplars and gaps in the curation and usage of big data, as these are significant areas of competitive advantage for media organizations. Big data contributes to the bottom line by enabling organizations to pursue digital transformation. According to PWC (2014), this forges the trust of consumers, creates the confidence to innovate with speed and agility, and empowers innovation.

Unlike some other sectors, the vast majority of actionable data in the media sector is already in digital form (and analogue products such as newspapers have been created through digital technologies for some years now). However, this does not mean that organizations are deriving the fullest possible financial benefit or cost efficiencies from both their existing data and new sources of data. There is a growing body of evidence that there is much work to do at research and policy levels to support the burgeoning ecosystem of diverse businesses engaged in analysing, enhancing, and delivering content and data.

14.2 Analysis of Industrial Needs in the Media and Entertainment Sectors

The media sector has always generated data, whether from research, sales, customer databases, log files, and so on. Equally, the vast majority of publishers and broadcasters have always faced the need to compete right from the earliest days of newspapers in the eighteenth century. Even government or publicly funded media bodies have to continually prove their relevance to their audiences, in order to stay relevant in a world of extensive choice and to secure future funding. But the big data mind-set, technical solutions, and strategies offer the ability to manage and disseminate data at speeds and scales that have never been seen before.

There are three main areas where big data has the potential to disrupt the status quo and stimulate economic growth within the media and entertainment sectors:

1. **Products and Services:** Big data-driven media businesses have the ability to *publish* content in more sophisticated ways. Human expertise in, e.g., curation, editorial nous, and psychology can be complemented with quantitative insights derived from analysing large and heterogeneous datasets. But this is predicated on big data analysis tools being easy to use for data scientists and business users alike.
2. **Customers and Suppliers:** Ambitious media companies will use big data to find out more about their customers—their preferences, profile, attitudes—and they

will use that information to build more engaged relationships. With the tools of social media and data capture now widely available to more or less anyone, individuals are also suppliers of content back to media companies. Many organizations now back social media analysis into to their orthodox journalism processes, so that consumers have a richer, more interactive relationship with news stories. Without big data applications, there will be a wasteful and random approach to finding the most interesting content.

3. **Infrastructure and Process:** While start-ups and SMEs can operate efficiently with open source and cloud infrastructure, for larger, older players, updating legacy IT infrastructure is a challenge. Legacy products and standards still need to be supported in the transition to big data ways of thinking and working. Process and organizational culture may also need to keep pace with the expectations of what big data offers. Failure to transform the culture and skillset of staff could impact companies who are profitable today but cannot adapt to data-driven business models.

14.3   Potential Big Data Applications for the Media and Entertainment Sectors

Six application scenarios for the media sector were described and further developed in Zillner et al. (2013, 2014a). All of these scenarios represent tangible business models for organizations; however, without support from big data technologies, companies will not be able to mature their existing pilots or small-scale projects into future revenue opportunities (Table 14.1).

14.4   Drivers and Constraints for Big Data in Media and Entertainment Sectors

Like all businesses, media companies aim to maximize revenue, minimize costs, and improve decision-making and business processes.

14.4.1   Drivers

Specific to the media and entertainment sectors though are the following drivers:

- Aim to **understand customers** on a very detailed level, often by analysing many different types of interaction (e.g. product usage, customer service interactions, social media, etc.).

Table 14.1 Summary of six application big data scenarios for the media sector

Name	Data journalism
Summary	Large volumes of data become available to a media organization.
Synopsis	Single or multiple datasets require analysis to derive insight, find interesting stories, and generate material. This can then be enhanced and ultimately monetized by selling to customers.
Business objectives	– Improve quality of journalism and therefore enhance the brand – Analyse data more thoroughly for less cost – Enable data analysis to be performed by a wider range of users
Name	Dynamic semantic publishing
Summary	Scalable processing of content for efficient targeting
Synopsis	Using semantic technologies to both produce and target content more efficiently
Business objectives	– Manage content and scarce staff resources more efficiently – Add value to data to differentiate services from competitors
Name	Social media analysis
Summary	Processing of large user-generated content datasets.
Synopsis	Batch and real-time analysis of millions of tweets, images, status updates to identify trends and content that can be packaged in value-added services.
Business objectives	– Create value-added services for clients – Perform large-scale data processing in a cost-effective manner
Name	Cross-sell of related products
Summary	Developing recommendation engines using multiple data sources.
Synopsis	Applications that exploit collaborative filtering, content-based filtering, and hybrids of both approaches.
Business objectives	– Generate more revenue from customers
Name	Product development
Summary	Using predictive analytics to commission new services
Synopsis	Data mining to support development of new and enhanced products for the marketplace
Business objectives	– Offer innovative new products and services – Enable development in a more quantitative way than is currently possible
Name	Audience insight
Summary	Using data from multiple sources to build up a comprehensive 360° view of a customer
Synopsis	Extension of scenario "Product Development"—mining of data external to the organization for information about customer habits and preferences
Business objectives	– Reduce costs of customer retention and acquisition – Use insights to aid commissioning of new products and services – Maximize revenue from customers

- **Operate in crowded sub-sectors** such as digital marketing or book publishing, where very few players have dominance, and consumer preferences and fashions can change very rapidly.

- **Diversify service offerings** wherever possible. Most significant European media companies operate in many areas, for example, newspaper publishers, websites, and commercial apps; or broadcasters may also sell broadband access.
- **Communicate to build influence within society**, e.g. politically. This is less tangible than just selling products but seen as equally important by media owners or governments.

14.4.2 Constraints

The **constraints** for big data in the media and entertainment sectors can be summarized as follows:

- **Increased consumer awareness** and concern about how personal data is being used. There is regulatory uncertainty for European businesses that handle personal data, which potentially puts them at a disadvantage compared to, say, US companies who operate within a much more relaxed legal landscape.
- **Insufficient access to finance** for media start-ups and SMEs. While it is relatively easy to start a new company producing apps, games, or social networks, it is much harder to scale up without committed investors.
- The **labour market** across Europe is not providing enough data professionals able to manipulate big data applications, e.g. for data journalism and product management.
- Fear of **piracy and consumer disregard for copyright** may disincentive creative people and companies from taking risks to launch new media and cultural products and services.
- **Large US players** dominate the content and data industry. Companies such as Apple, Amazon, and Google between them have huge dominance in many sub-sectors including music, advertising, publishing, and consumer media electronics.
- Differences in **penetration of high-speed broadband** provision across member countries, in cities, and in rural areas. This is a disincentive for companies looking to deliver content that requires high bandwidth, e.g. streaming movies, as it reduces the potential customer base.

14.5 Available Media and Entertainment Data Resources

Table 14.2 is intended to give a flavour of the data sources that most media companies routinely handle. One table lists some categories of data that are generated by the companies themselves, while the second shows third-party sources that are or can be processed by those in the media sector, depending on their particular line of business.

Each type of data source is matched to a key characteristic of big data. Customarily, the technology industry has talked of "the three Vs of big data", that is, volume, variety, and velocity. Kobielus (2013) also discusses a fourth characteristic—veracity. This is important for the media sector because consumer products and services can quickly fail if the content lacks authoritativeness, or it is of poor quality, or it has uncertain provenance. According to IBM (2014), 27 % of respondents to a US survey were unsure even *how much* of their data was inaccurate—suggesting the scale of the problem is underestimated.

Table 14.2 Media data resources mapped to "V" characteristics of big data

Internally generated data	*Key "V" characteristic*
Consumer profile details including customer service interactions.	Volume—Large amounts of data to be stored and potentially mined. Variety applies when considering the different ways customers may interact with a media service provider—and hence the opportunity for the business to "join up the dots" and better understand them.
Network logging (e.g. for web or entertainment companies operating their own networks).	Velocity—Network issues must be identified in real-time in order to resolve problems and retain consumer trust.
Organizations own data services to end users.	Characteristic(s) will depend on business objective of the data, e.g., a news agency will prioritize speed of delivery to customers, a broadcaster will be focused on streaming content in multiple formats to multiple types of device.
Consumer preferences inferred from sources including click stream data, product usage behaviour, purchase history, etc.	Volume—Large amounts of data can be gathered. Velocity will become pertinent where the service needs to be responsive to user action, e.g., online gaming networks which upsell extra features to players.
Third-party data	*Key "V" characteristic*
Commercial data feeds, e.g., sports data, press agency newswires.	Velocity—Being first to use data such as sports or news events builds competitive advantage.
Network information (where external networks are being used, e.g., messaging apps that piggyback on mobile networks).	Velocity—Network issues must be identified in real-time in order to ensure continuity of service.
Public sector open datasets.	Veracity—Open data may have quality, provenance, and completeness issues.
Free structured and/or linked data, e.g., Wikidata/DBpedia	Veracity—crowdsourced data may have quality, provenance, and completeness issues.
Social media data, e.g., updates, videos, images, links, and signals such as "likes".	Volume, variety, velocity, and veracity—Media companies must prioritize processing based on expected use cases. As one example, data journalism requires a large volume of data to be prepared for analysis and interpretation. On the other hand, a media marketing business might be more concerned with the variety of social data across many channels.

14.6   Media and Entertainment Sector Requirements

The Media and Entertainment Sectorial Forum were able to identify and name several requirements, which need to be addressed by big data application in the domain. The requirements are distinguish between non-technical and technical requirements.

14.6.1   Non-technical Requirements

It is important to note that the widespread uptake of big data within the media industry is not solely dependent on successful implementation of specific technologies and solutions. In Zillner et al. (2014b), a survey was undertaken among European middle and senior managers from the media sector (and also the telecoms sector, where large players are increasingly moving into areas that were once considered purely the realm of broadcasters, publishers, etc.). Respondents were asked to rank several big data priorities based on how important they would be to their own organizations.

It is striking that all survey participants identified the need for a European framework for shared standards, a clear regulatory landscape, and a collaborative ecosystem—implying that businesses are suffering from a lack of confidence in their ability to see through the hype and really get to grips with big data in their enterprises. Another area ranked as very important by a notable proportion of respondents was making solutions usable and attractive for business users (i.e. not just data scientists).

14.6.2   Technical Requirements

Table 14.3 lists 37 requirements that were distilled from the work of the Media Sector Forum. Each requirement is matched to a business objective (although of course in practice some requirements could meet more than one objective). The five columns at the right-hand side of the table place each requirement in its appropriate place(s) along the big data value chain. Media, as a mostly customer-facing, revenue-generating economic sector, has many critical needs in data curation and usage.

Table 14.3 Big data technical requirements of the media sector

Big data requirement	Business objective	Acquisition	Analysis	Curation	Storage	Usage
Curate heterogeneous data sources in a content and origin agnostic manner	Improve business processes	X		X		
Programmatically interrogate data for trends	Improve business processes		X			
Quickly start processing new data types as they become needed	Improve business processes	X	X	X	X	
Analyse unstructured data with regard to sentiment, topic, and other intangible aspects of text	Improve business processes		X	X		
Transform and augment open data from the public sector with regard to format, semantics, and quality	Improve business processes	X	X	X	X	
Scalable tools for search and discovery applications	Improve business processes				X	X
Visualize data for analytics and metrics (especially for business-technical users)	Improve business processes		X			X
Automatically create and apply metadata to datasets	Improve business processes	X	X	X		
Quickly and accurately process data in near real-time	Improve decision-making	X	X		X	
Apply models and ontologies to data to extract relationships	Improve decision-making	X	X		X	
Transform streams from sensors into actionable views	Improve decision-making	X			X	
Analytics tools which enable powerful querying and manipulation by non-programmers or statisticians	Improve decision-making		X		X	
Inference engines to analyse semantic graph data	Improve decision-making		X	X		

(continued)

Table 14.3 (continued)

Big data requirement	Business objective	Acquisition	Analysis	Curation	Storage	Usage
Derive value from proprietary datasets	Increase revenue	X	X	X	X	X
Derive value from public open datasets	Increase revenue		X	X		X
Deliver tailored data and content to customers	Increase revenue			X		X
Human-centred editorializing of curated data streams	Increase revenue		X	X		X
Algorithms to crunch data to produce more interesting recommendations than "more of the same"	Increase revenue					X
Algorithm management tools for non-technical users	Increase revenue			X		X
Enrich multimedia content such as images and videos with semantic metadata	Increase revenue		X	X		X
Blend user-generated content with commercially produced media to create new digital products	Increase revenue	X		X		X
Generate insights from data to enable new business models (e.g. cross-selling based on viewing habits)	Increase revenue		X			X
Increase conversions from offline marketing activities (e.g. direct mail) by analysing online data	Increase revenue		X			X
Predictive analytics solutions that can identify trends, segments, and patterns without these explicitly being modelled	Increase revenue		X			
Return more relevant search results in consumer-facing	Increase revenue					X

(continued)

Table 14.3 (continued)

Big data requirement	Business objective	Acquisition	Analysis	Curation	Storage	Usage
applications using semantic analysis						
Database solutions that can be set-up more quickly than with traditional applications	Reduce costs				X	
Capability to use crowdsourced data curation to complement internal subject matter expertise	Reduce costs			X		
Manage large-scale data in graph databases	Reduce costs				X	
Translate unstructured data (e.g. text or voice) to one or many languages	Reduce costs	X	X		X	
High-volume data scraping and crawling tools	Reduce costs	X			X	
Identify patterns in data to drive insights about consumer behaviour	Understand customers		X			
Take account of many factors (e.g. location, device, user profile, usage context) to better target content delivery	Understand customers	X				
Connect data from all customer interactions to form a 360° view	Understand customers	X	X		X	
Ingest data from new classes of device (e.g. wearables)	Understand customers	X				
Drill down into consumer behaviour in more granular detail	Understand customers		X			X
Foster a more engaged relationship with audiences and customers through unstructured social data analysis	Understand customers					X
Clear policy direction on use of personal data within the EU	Understand customers				X	X

14.7   Technology Roadmap for Big Data in the Media and Entertainment Sectors

Of all the sectors discussed in this book, media is arguably the one that changes most suddenly and most often. New paradigms can emerge extremely quickly and become commercially vital in a short space of time (e.g. Twitter was founded only in 2006 and now has a market capitalization of many billions of dollars). The year 2015 onwards will see many media players and consumers alike experimenting with drones (more strictly, "unmanned aerial vehicles", or UAVs) to see if captured footage can be monetized either directly as content or indirectly to attract advertising.

Figure 14.2 and Table 14.4 consolidate the outcomes of the research completed in Zillner et al. (2013, 2014a), along with additional background research. Figure 14.1 maps out the methodology used to derive the sector roadmap, showing how iterative engagement with industry supported at every stage the definition of the needs and technologies around big data for the media sector.

Any roadmap must be cognisant of the risk that it will be out of date before it is even published. Nevertheless, the key headings shown in the figures in this section are strongly predicted to remain highly relevant to the sector for the following reasons.

14.7.1   Semantic Data Enrichment

Semantics is a long-established and now fast-developing field that is finally fulfilling its academic promise. Major media applications such as "intelligent personal assistants", e.g. Siri and Cortana, are underpinned by "artificial intelligence" and semantic analysis technology. More development is needed to help commercial organizations in Europe exploit the potential of ontologies, graph databases, and curation platforms.

14.7.2   Data Quality

The key technological developments in this area include open data and data standards generally to aid interoperability. Also key are capabilities for processing unstructured (especially natural language) data streams. Finally, there is a need for back-end systems that can absorb different types of data with as little friction as possible, by minimizing the need to define data schemas upfront.

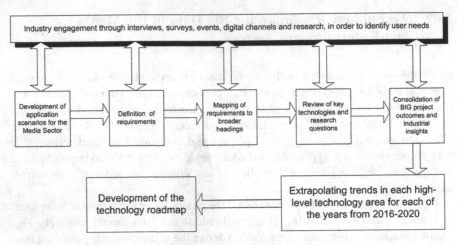

Fig. 14.1 Methodology for deriving the media sector roadmap

Technical Requirement	Technology	Research Question
Semantic Data Enrichment	Common and open ontologies	Relation extraction
	Graph databases	Scalability of non-relational databases
	Crowdsourced curation platform	Blended algorithmic & manual curation at scale
Data Quality	Open data platforms	Data standardisation & interoperability
	Unstructured data processing	Natural language processing at scale
	Heterogeneous data storage	Data-agnostic storage architectures
Data-driven Innovation	Machine learning (ML)	Integrating ML approaches into databases
	Networks, sensors, wearable tech	Commercialisation of auto-generated data
	Customer recommendation tools	Improving algorithmic recommendations
Data Analysis	Descriptive analytics	Data mining for subjective factors e.g. sentiment
	Data visualisation solutions	Business-user friendly applications
	Customer relationship platforms	Understand contexts to enhance data delivery

Fig. 14.2 Mapping requirements to research questions in the media sector

14.7.3 *Data-Driven Innovation*

Three key technologies underpinning the drive for high-quality innovation are machine learning at enterprise scale; the Internet of Things (IoT), which will exponentially increase the volume and diversity of data streams available to anyone

Table 14.4 Big data technology roadmap for the media sector

Technical requirement	Year 1	Year 2	Year 3	Year 4	Year 5
Semantic data enrichment	Large media firms with resources create and publish open ontologies	Common ontologies for specific use cases in media and entertainment industries	Ontology management and manipulation tools available for a wide range of commercial uses	Relation extraction technology available at scale and affordability	Semantic inference to support predictive analysis of data, e.g., user behaviour, tracking news stories
Data quality	Limited open data available to companies looking to generate new business models	Open data published in machine-readable formats by more public and private sector bodies	Natural language processing tools scalable to large volumes of data (including speech)	Standardization of data acquisition protocols	Data-agnostic architectures enable diverse data streams to be analysed simultaneously and in real-time
Data-driven innovation	Curation platforms to enhance value-add of data products	Scalable recommendation tools for non-technical users	Machine learning frameworks embedded into decision-making tools	Real-time aggregation of streams generated by networks, sensors, body-worn devices	Product development platforms for rapid iteration of data-driven services
Data analysis	More detailed segmentation of customers based on subjective factors	Intuitive data visualization tools for interactive applications	Convergence of business intelligence and product analytics applications	Actionable predictive analytics of events or trends across large, dispersed data streams	Combinable analytics approaches enable deep insights into patterns based on context

involved in media or data-driven storytelling; and finally, tools to better interpret customer interactions with products and services.

14.7.4 Data Analysis

Media and entertainment companies need to analyse data not only at the customer and product levels, but also at network and infrastructure levels (e.g. streaming video suppliers, Internet businesses, television broadcasters, and so on). Key technologies in the coming years will be descriptive analytics, more sophisticated customer relationship management solutions, and lastly data visualization solutions that are accessible to a wide range of users in the enterprise. It is only by "humanizing" these tools that big data will be able to deliver the benefits that data-driven businesses increasingly demand (Table 14.4).

14.8 Conclusion and Recommendations for the Media and Entertainment Sectors

Europe has much to offer in culture and content to the global market. European publishers and TV companies are globally renowned, but no EU-based competitor has emerged to the multinational giants of Google, Amazon, Apple, or Facebook. Differences between the European and US economies, such as ease of access to venture capital, would seem to preclude this happening. Therefore, the best way forward for Europe is to build on its strengths of creativity and free movement of people and services, in order to bring together communities of industrial players, researchers, and government to tackle the following priorities:

- Making sense of data streams, whether text, image, video, sensors, and so on. Sophisticated products and services can be developed by extracting value from heterogeneous sources.
- Exploiting big data step changes in the ability to ingest and process raw data, so as to minimize risks in bringing new data-driven offerings to market.
- Curating quality information out of vast data streams, using algorithmic scalable approaches and blending them with human knowledge through curation platforms.
- Accelerating business adoption of big data. Consumer awareness is growing and technical improvements continue to reduce the cost of storage and analytics tools among other things. Therefore, it is more important than ever that businesses have confidence that they understand what they want from big data and that the non-technical aspects such as human resources and regulation are in place.

References

Deloitte. (2014). *Technology, media and telecommunications predictions 2014*. Retrieved from http://www.deloitte.co.uk/tmtpredictions/assets/downloads/Deloitte-TMT-Predictions-2014.pdf

IBM. (2014). *Infographic – The four V's of big data*. Retrieved from http://www.ibmbigdatahub.com/enlarge-infographic/1642

Kobielus, J. (2013). *Measuring the business value of big data*. Retrieved from http://www.ibmbigdatahub.com/blog/measuring-business-value-big-data

PWC. (2014). *Global entertainment and media outlook 2014-2018 – key industry themes*. Retrieved from http://www.pwc.com/gx/en/global-entertainment-media-outlook/insights-and-analysis.jhtml

Zillner, S., Neurerer, S., Munné, R., Lippell, H., Vilela, L., Prieto, E. et al. (2013). *D2.4.1 first draft of sectors roadmap*. Public deliverable of the EU-Project BIG (318062; ICT-2011.4.4).

Zillner, S., Neurerer, S., Munné, R., Lippell, H., Vilela, L., Prieto, E. et al. (2014a). *D2.3.2. Final version of the sectorial requisites*. Public deliverable of the EU-Project BIG (318062; ICT-2011.4.4).

Zillner, S., Neurerer, S., Munné, R., Lippell, H., Vilela, L., Prieto, E. et al. (2014b). *D2.4.2 Final version of sectors roadmap*. Public deliverable of the EU-Project BIG (318062; ICT-2011.4.4).

Part IV
A Roadmap for Big Data Research

Chapter 15
Cross-sectorial Requirements Analysis for Big Data Research

Tilman Becker, Edward Curry, Anja Jentzsch, and Walter Palmetshofer

15.1 Introduction

This chapter identifies the cross-sectorial requirements for big data research necessary to define a prioritized research roadmap based on expected impact. The aim of the roadmaps is to maximize and sustain the impact of big data technologies and applications in different industrial sectors by identifying and driving opportunities in Europe. The target audiences for the roadmaps are the different stakeholders involved in the big data ecosystem including industrial users of big data applications, technical providers of big data solutions, regulators, policy makers, researchers, and end users.

The first step toward the roadmap was to establish a list of cross-sectorial business requirements and goals from each of the industrial sectors covered in part of this book and in Zillner et al. (2014). The consolidated results comprise a prioritized set of cross-sector requirements that were used to define the technology, business, policy, and society roadmaps with action recommendations. This chapter presents a condensed version of the cross-sectorial consolidated requirements. It discusses each of the high-level and sub-level requirements together with the associated challenges that need to be tackled. Finally the chapter concludes with

T. Becker (✉)
German Research Centre for Artificial Intelligence (DFKI), Stuhlsatzenhausweg 3, 66123
Saarbrücken, Germany
e-mail: tilman.becker@dfki.de

E. Curry
Insight Centre for Data Analytics, National University of Ireland Galway, Lower Dangan,
Galway, Ireland
e-mail: edward.curry@insight-centre.org

A. Jentzsch • W. Palmetshofer
Open Knowledge Foundation (OKF), Singerstr. 109, 10179 Berlin, Germany
e-mail: anja.jentzsch@okfn.org; walter.palmetshofer@okfn.org

© The Author(s) 2016
J.M. Cavanillas et al. (eds.), *New Horizons for a Data-Driven Economy*,
DOI 10.1007/978-3-319-21569-3_15

a prioritization of the cross-sectorial requirements. As far as possible, the roadmaps have been quantified to allow for a well-founded prioritization and action plans (e.g. policies).

15.2   Cross-sectorial Consolidated Requirements

In order to establish a common understanding of requirements as well as technology descriptions across domains, the sector-specific requirement labels were aligned. Each sector provided their requirements with the associated user needs, and similar and related requirements were merged, aligned, or restructured to create a homogenous set.

While most of the requirements exist within each of the sectors, the level of importance for the requirement in each sector varies. For the cross-sector analysis, any requirements that were identified by at least two sectors as being a significant requirement for that sector were included into the cross-sector roadmap definition. Thus, the initial list of 13 high-level requirements and 28 sub-level requirements was reduced to 5 high-level requirements and 12 sub-level requirements (see Table 15.1). Within this chapter, the discussion on each cross-sectorial requirement has been condensed and minor updates applied. Full details are available in Becker et al. (2014).

15.2.1   Data Management Engineering

The high-level requirement *data management engineering* aims at efficient strategies to manage heterogeneous data sources and technologies. Data management engineering has four sub-requirements:

- *Data enrichment*
- *Data integration*
- *Data sharing*
- *Real-time data transmission*

15.2.1.1   Data Enrichment

The sub-requirement *data enrichment* aims to make unstructured data understandable across domains, application, and value chains.

In the *health sector*, data enrichment is of high relevance, since 90 % of health data is only available in unstructured formats without semantic labels informing applications on the content of the data. In particular, approaches for the semantic annotation of medical images and medical text are needed.

Table 15.1 Consolidated cross-sectorial requirements (and demanding sectors)

Technological Requirement	Number of Demanding Sectors	Health	Public	Finance & Insurance	Energy & Transport	Telecom & Media	Retail	Manufacturing
Data Management Engineering	3		X			X	X	
Data Enrichment	2	X				X		
Data Integration	5	X	X	X		X	X	
Data Sharing	4	X	X	X	X			
Real-Time Data Transmission	3		X				X	X
Data Quality	3	X		X			X	
Data Improvement	2						X	X
Data Security and Privacy	7	X	X	X	X	X	X	X
Data Visualization and User Experience	2						X	X
Deep Data Analytics	3		X	X			X	
Modelling Simulation	3		X				X	X
Natural Language Analytics	3		X				X	X
Pattern Discovery	3		X	X		X		
Predictive Analytics	2		X			X		
Prescriptive Analytics	3				X	X	X	
Real-Time Insights	5		X		X	X	X	X
Usage Analytics	2			X		X		

In the *telecom and media sector*, data enrichment includes ontologies (e.g. eTOM SID), data transformation, addition of metadata, formats, etc., taking into account that the data sources are heterogeneous (including social media information, audio, customer data, and traffic data, for example). Data coming from different sources and in different formats, produced by heterogeneous systems, have to be processed together. In order to address these requirements, the following challenges need to be tackled:

- Information extraction from text
- Image understanding algorithms
- Standardized annotation framework

15.2.1.2 Data Sharing and Integration

The sub-requirement *data sharing and integration* aims to establish a basis for the seamless integration of multiple and diverse data sources into a big data platform. The lack of standardized data schemas, semantic data models, as well as the fragmentation of data ownership are important aspects that need to be tackled.

As of today, less than 30 % of *health data* is shared between healthcare providers (Accenture 2012). In order to enable seamless data sharing in the health and other domains, a standardized coding system and terminologies as well as data models are needed.

In the *telecom* sector, data has been collected for years and classified according to business standards based on eTOM (2014), but the data reference model does not yet contemplate the inclusion of social media data. A unified information system is required that includes data from both the telecom operator and the customer. Once this information model is available, it should be incorporated in the eTOM SID reference model and taken into account in big data telecom-specific solutions for all data (social and non-social) to be integrated.

In the *retail sector*, standardized product ontologies are needed to enable sharing of data between product manufacturers and retailers. Services to optimize operational decisions in retail are only possible with semantically annotated product data.

In the *public sector*, data sharing and integration are important to overcome the lack of standardization of data schemas and fragmentation of data ownership, to achieve the integration of multiple and diverse data sources into a big data platform. This is required in cases where data analysis has to be performed from data belonging to different domains and owners (e.g. different agencies in the public sector) or integrating heterogeneous external data (from open data, social networks, sensors, etc.).

In the *financial sector*, several factors have put organizations in a situation where a large number of different datasets lack interconnection and integration. Financial organizations recognize the potential value of interlinking such datasets to extract information that would be of value either to optimize operations, improve services to customers, or even create new business models. Existing technology can cover most of the requirements of the financial services industry, but the technology is still not widely implemented.

In order to address these requirements, the following challenges need to be tackled:

- Semantic data and knowledge models
- Context information
- Entity matching
- Scalable triple stores, key/value stores
- Facilitate core integration at data acquisition
- Best practice for sharing high-velocity and high-variety data
- Usability of semantic systems
- Metadata and data provenance frameworks

- Scalable automatic data/schema mapping mechanisms

15.2.1.3   Real-Time Data Transmission

The sub-requirement *real-time data transmission* aims at acquiring (sensor and event) information in real time.

In the *public sector*, this is closely related with the increasing capability of deploying sensors and Internet of Things scenarios, like in public safety and smart cities. Image sensors have followed Moore's Law, doubling megapixel density per dollar every 2 years (PWC 2014). Distributed processing and cleaning capabilities are required for image sensors in order to avoid overloading the transmission channels (Jobling 2013) and provide the required real-time analysis to feed situational awareness systems for decision-makers.

In the *manufacturing sector*, sensor data must be acquired at high sample rates and needs to be transmitted close to real time in order to be used effectively. Decisions can be made at central planning, command, and control points, or can be made at a local level in a distributed fashion. Data transmission must be sufficiently close to real time, greatly improving on the currently long intervals (hourly or greater) in which inventory data is sampled. The hostile working environment in manufacturing may hamper data transmission.

For the *retail sector*, it is important that the data from sensors inside the store are acquired in real time. This includes visual data from cameras and customer locations from positioning sensors.

In order to address these requirements, the following challenges need to be tackled:

- Distributed data processing and cleaning
- Read/write optimized storage solutions for high velocity data
- Near real-time processing of data streams

15.2.2   Data Quality

The high-level requirement, *data quality*, describes the need to capture and store high-quality data so that analytic applications can use the data as reliable input to produce valuable insights. Data quality has one sub-requirement:

- *Data improvement*

Big data applications in the *health sector* need to fulfil high data quality standards in order to derive reliable insights for health-related decisions. For instance, the features and parameter list used for describing patient health status needs to be standardized in order to enable the reliable comparison of patient (population) datasets.

In the *telecom and media sectors*, despite the fact that data has been collected already for years, there are still data quality issues that make the information un-exploitable without pre-processing.

In the *financial sector*, data quality is not a major issue in internally generated datasets, but information collected from external sources may not be fully reliable.

In order to address these requirements, the following challenges need to be tackled:

- Provenance management
- Human data interaction
- Unstructured data integration

15.2.2.1 Data Improvement

The sub-requirement *data improvement* aims at removing noise/redundant data, checking for trustworthiness, and adding missing data.

In the *telecom and media sectors*, this relates to the ability to improve the commercial offering of the service provider based on the available information in traditional systems, as well as advanced techniques such as predictive, speech, or prescriptive analytics.

In the *retail sector*, both sensor data and data extracted from web sources (i.e. product data and customer data) are error prone and need to be checked for trustworthiness. Therefore data improvement procedures are required that help to remove incorrect/redundant data and noise.

- Human validation via curation
- Automatic removal of large amounts of noise at scale
- Scalable semantic validation

15.2.3 Data Security and Privacy

The high-level requirement *data security and privacy* describes the need to protect highly sensitive business and personal data from unauthorized access. Thus, it addresses the availability of legal procedures and the technical means that allow the secure sharing of data.

In *healthcare applications*, a strong emphasis has to be put on data privacy and security since some of the usual privacy protection approaches could be bypassed by the nature of big data. For instance, in terms of health-related data, anonymization is a well-established approach to de-identify personal data. Nevertheless, the anonymized data could be re-identified (El Emam et al. 2014) when aggregating big data from different data sources.

Big data applications in *retail* require the storage of personal information of customers in order for the retailer to be able to provide tailored services. It is very important that this data is stored securely to ensure the protection of customer privacy.

In the *manufacturing sector*, there are conflicting interests in storing data on products for easy retrieval and protection of data from unauthorized retrieval. Data collected during production and use may well contain proprietary information concerning internal business processes. Intellectual property needs to be protected as far as it is encoded in product and production data. Regulations for data ownership need to be established, e.g., what access may the manufacturer of a production machine have to its usage data.

Privacy protection for workers interacting in an Industry 4.0 environment needs to be established. Data encryption and access control into object memories needs to be integrated. European and worldwide regulations need to be harmonized. There is a need for data privacy regulations and transparent privacy protection.

In the *telecom and media sector*, one of the main concerns is that big data policies apply to personal data, i.e., to data relating to an identified or identifiable person. However, it is not clear whether the core privacy principles of the regulation apply to newly discovered knowledge or information derived from personal data, especially when the data has been anonymized or generalized by being transformed into group profiles. Privacy is a major concern which can compromise the end users' trust, which is essential for big data to be exploited by service providers. An Ovum (2013) Consumer Insights Survey revealed that 68 % of Internet users across 11 countries around the world would select a "Do-Not-Track" feature if it was easily available. This clearly highlights some amount of end users' antipathy towards online tracking. Privacy and trust is an important barrier since data must be rich in order for businesses to use it.

Finding solutions to ensure data security and privacy may unlock the massive potential of big data in the *public sector*. Advances in the protection and privacy of data are key for the public sector, as it may allow the analysis of huge amounts of data owned by the public sector without disclosing sensitive information. In many cases, the public sector regulations restrict the use of data for different purposes for which it was collected. Privacy and security issues are also preventing the use of cloud infrastructures (e.g. processing, storage) by many public agencies that deal with sensitive data. A new approach to security in cloud infrastructure may eliminate this barrier.

Data security and privacy requirements appear in the *financial sector* in the context of building new business models based on data collected by financial services institutions from their customers (individuals). Innovative services could be created with technologies that reconcile the use of data and privacy requirements. In order to address these requirements, the following challenges need to be tackled:

- Hash algorithms
- Secure data exchange
- De-identification and anonymization algorithms
- Data storage technologies to encrypted storage and DBs; proxy re-encryption between domains; automatic privacy-protection

- Advances in "privacy by design" to link analytics needs with protective controls in processing and storage
- Data provenance to enable usage transparency and metadata for privacy information

15.2.4 Data Visualization and User Experience

The high-level requirement *data visualization and user experience* describes the need to adapt the visualization to the user. This is possible by reducing the complexity of data, data inter-relations, and the results of data analysis.

In *retail* it will be very important to adapt the information visualization to the specific customer. An example of this would be tailored advertisements, which fit the profile of the customer.

In *manufacturing* human decision-making and guidance need to be supported on all levels: from the production floor to high-level management. Appropriate data visualization tools must be available and integrated to support browsing, controlling, and decision-making in the planning and execution process. This applies primarily to general big data but extends to and includes special visualization of spatiotemporal aspects of the manufacturing process for spatial and temporal analytics.

In order to address these requirements, the following challenges need to be tackled:

- Apply user modelling techniques to visual analytics
- High performance visualizations
- Large-scale visualization based on adaptive semantic frameworks
- Multimodal interfaces in hostile working environments
- Natural language processing for highly variable contexts
- Interactive visualization and visual queries

15.2.5 Deep Data Analytics

The high-level requirement *deep data analytics* is the application of sophisticated data processing techniques to yield information from multiple, typically large datasets comprised of both unstructured and semi-structured data. Deep data analysis has seven sub-requirements:

- *Modelling and simulation* covers domain-specific tools for modelling and simulation of events according to changes from past events.
- *Natural language analytics* aims at extracting information from unstructured sources (e.g. social media) to enable further analysis (for instance sentiment mining).

- *Pattern discovery* aims at identifying patterns and similarities.
- *Real-time insights* enable the analysis of real-time data for instant decision-making.
- *Usage analytics* provide analysis of the usage of product, service, resources, process, etc.
- *Predictive analytics* utilize a variety of statistical, modelling, data mining, and machine learning techniques to study recent and historical data to make predictions about the future.
- *Prescriptive analytics* focus on finding the best course of action for a given situation.

Prescriptive analytics belongs to a portfolio of analytic capabilities that include descriptive and predictive analytics. While descriptive analytics aims to provide insight into what has happened, and predictive analytics helps model and forecast what might happen, prescriptive analytics seeks to determine the best solution or outcome among various choices, given the known parameters.

In the *public sector*, deep data analytics can help in several scenarios where information should be extracted from data. In the scenario of monitoring and supervision of online gambling operators, the challenge is to detect specific criminal or illegal behaviours using pattern discovery to deliver real-time insights. Similar insights are needed in the supervision of markets regulated by the public sector (energy, telecommunications, stock markets, etc.).

Other application scenarios also need deep data analytics, as in the case of public safety in smart cities, where real-time insights can enable the analysis of fresh/real-time data for instant decision-making. In these scenarios, situational awareness systems can be built using real-time data provided by networks of sensors and near real-time data captured from social networks through natural language analytics. Smart cities situation awareness can also apply modelling and simulation tools for managing events (e.g. managing large crowds of people in public events) to anticipate the results from decisions taken to influence the current conditions in real-time.

Other application scenarios like predictive policing may require the use of predictive analytics to provide insights based on the learning from previous situations. This would allow for optimal security resources allocation, according to the prediction of incidents, which may be based on temporal patterns or related to specific events of any kind (sport events, weather conditions, or any other variable).

For the *telecom and media sectors*, deep data analytics are required in order to improve customer experience, either by tailoring the offerings, by improving customer care, or by proactively adapting resources (e.g. network) to meet the customer expectations in terms of service delivery. This can be achieved by obtaining a 360° customer view, which allows a better understanding of the customer and predicts their needs or demands. Advanced and flexible customer segmentation, knowing customer likes and dislikes, deeply analysing user habits, customer interactions, etc., help communication and content service providers to find patterns and sentiment out of the data, allowing cross selling based on multiple factors. Since Quality of Experience (QoE) and customer satisfaction can differ very quickly (as mood does), analytics should ideally provide the means to calculate and automate the best next action in real time.

Historical and online analytical processing of big data will be adopted as the insights gained will make planning and operations more precise. Real-time analytics on the other hand still faces some technological challenges, which may well be the reason for the lack of adoption of real-time analytics in energy and transportation. Manual steps in typical data analytics processes, such as data wrangling, for example, do not scale for the speed and volume of data to be analysed in operational efficiency scenarios in energy and transportation optimization.

In the *retail sector*, operational decisions can be optimized by analysing unstructured data from the web. This can be information about upcoming regional events, weather data, or even potential natural disasters that can be extracted from social networks using natural language analytics. Data, like visual data from cameras, acquired from sensors inside the store needs to be analysed to extract specific patterns, such as patterns of customer movement. Customer segmentation is possible by analysing customer–product and customer–staff interactions. This information can also be used to run prescriptive analytics. These are required to allow intelligent inventory, intelligent staff scheduling, and floor plan/ product location optimization.

In order to address these requirements, the following challenges need to be tackled:

- Data integration, linking, and semantics
- Sentiment analysis
- Machine learning
- Integrating semantics into large-scale modelling and simulation environments
- Increasing scalability and robustness of information extraction, named entity recognition, machine learning, linked data, entity linking, and co-reference resolution
- Validation of pattern analytics outputs and natural language analytics outputs with humans via curation
- Integration of natural language analytics into data usage scenarios
- Semantic pattern technologies including stream pattern matching and scalable complex pattern matching
- Analytical databases to efficiently support predictive analytics
- Combining large-scale reasoning with statistical approaches
- Predictive maintenance: predict failures, determine maintenance intervals Support for failure analysis
- Extend predictive analytics to prescriptive analytics
- Complex event processing applies business rules (or other frameworks) continuously on defined (short) interval of real-time data stream with low latency

- In-memory technology, new visualization and interaction techniques, automatic system reactions to enable ad hoc queries on large datasets to be executed with minimal latencies
- Real-time and in-stream analytical processing

15.3 Prioritization of Cross-sectorial Requirements

An actionable roadmap should have clear selection criteria regarding the priority of all actions. In contrast to a technology roadmap for the context of a single company, a European technology roadmap needs to cover developments across different sectors. The process of defining the roadmap included an analysis of the big data market and feedback received from stakeholders. Through this analysis, a sense of what characteristics indicate higher or lower potential of big data technical requirements was reached.

As the basis for the ranking, a table-based approach was used that evaluated each candidate according to a number of applicable parameters. In each case, the parameters were collected with the goal of being sector independent. Quantitative parameters were used where possible and available.

In consultation with stakeholders, the following parameters were used to rank the various technical requirements. The ranking parameters included:

- Number of affected sectors
- Size of affected sector(s) in terms of % of GDP
- Estimated growth rate of the sector(s)
- Possible prognosticated estimated growth rate by the sector due to big data technologies
- Estimated export potential of the sector(s)
- Estimated cross-sectorial benefits
- Short-term low-hanging fruit

Using these insights, a prioritization composed of multiple parameters was created, which give a relative sense of which technological requirements might be poised for greater gains and which would face the lowest barriers. The ranking of cross-sectorial technical requirements is presented in Table 15.2 and is illustrated in Fig. 15.1, where colour indicates the level of estimated importance, and the size of the bubble the estimated affected sectors of the industries. It is important to note that these indices do not offer a full picture, but they do offer a reasonable sense of both potential availability and capture across sectors. There are certain limitations to this approach. Not all relevant numbers and inputs were available as the speed of technology development and adoption relies on several factors. The ranking relies on forecasts and estimates from third parties and the project team. As a consequence, it is not always possible to determine precise numbers for timelines and

Table 15.2 Prioritization of technical cross-sectorial requirements

Prioritization	Technological requirements	Score
Level 1: Urgent		
	Data security and privacy	78
	Data management engineering—data integration	69.25
	Deep data analytics—real-time insights	61.5
	Data management engineering—data sharing	48.5
Level 2: Very important		
	Data quality	40.5
	Data management engineering—real-time data transmission	37
	Deep data analytics—modelling simulation	37
	Deep data analytics—natural language analytics	37
	Deep data analytics—pattern discovery	34.25
	Deep data analytics	31.75
	Data management engineering	31.5
Level 3: Important		
	Data management engineering—data enrichment	29.5
	Data visualization and user experience	29.5
	Deep data analytics—prescriptive analytics	29.5
	Deep data analytics—usage analytics	26.75
	Data quality—data improvement	24
	Deep data analytics—predictive analytics	20.75

specific impacts. Further investigation into these questions would be desirable for future research. Full details of the ranking process are available in (Becker, T., Jentzsch, A., & Palmetshofer, W. 2014).

15.4   Summary

The aim of the cross-sectorial roadmap is to maximize and sustain the impact of big data technologies and applications in the different industrial sectors by identifying and driving opportunities in Europe. While most of the requirements identified exist in some form within each sector, the level of importance of the requirements between specific sectors varies. For the cross-sector requirements, any requirements that were identified by at least two sectors as being a significant requirement for the sector were included into the cross-sector roadmap definition. This led to the

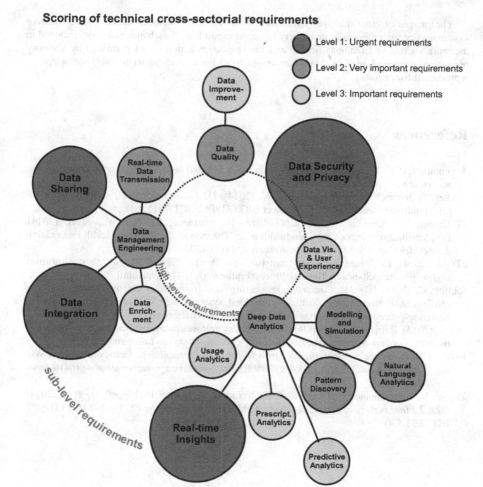

Scoring of technical cross-sectorial requirements

Level 1: Urgent requirements

Level 2: Very important requirements

Level 3: Important requirements

Fig. 15.1 Cross-sectorial requirements prioritized

identification of 5 high-level requirements and 12 sub-level requirements with associated challenges that need to be tackled.

Each cross-sectorial requirement was prioritized based on their expected impact. The consolidated results comprise a prioritized set of cross-sector requirements that were used to define the cross-sectorial roadmaps with associated action recommendations.

References

Accenture. (2012). *Connected health: The drive to integrated healthcare delivery*. Online: www.acccenture.com/connectedhealthstudy

Becker, T., Jentzsch, A., & Palmetshofer, W. (2014). *D2.5 Cross-sectorial roadmap consolidation*. Public deliverable of the EU-Project BIG (318062; ICT-2011.4.4).

El Emam, K., Arbuckle, L., Koru, G., Eze, B., Gaudette, L., Neri, E., et al. (2014). De-identification methods for open health data: The case of the Heritage Health Prize claims dataset. *Journal of Medical Internet Research, 14*(1), e33.

eTOM. (2014). *TM forum*. Retrieved from Business Process Framework: http://www.tmforum.org/BestPracticesStandards/BusinessProcessFramework/1647/Home.html

Jobling, C. (2013, July 31). *Capturing, processing, and transmitting video: Opportunities and challenges*. Retrieved from Military embedded systems: http://mil-embedded.com/articles/capturing-processing-transmitting-video-opportunities-challenges/

Ovum. (2013). Retrieved from http://ovum.com/press_releases/ovum-predicts-turbulence-for-the-internet-economy-as-more-than-two-thirds-of-consumers-say-no-to-internet-tracking/

PWC. (2014). *Image sensor: Steady growth for new capabilities*. Retrieved from PWC: http://www.pwc.com/gx/en/technology/mobile-innovation/image-sensor-steady-growth-new-capabilities.jhtml

Zillner, S., Bretschneider, C., Oberkampf, H., Neurerer, S., Munné, R., Lippell, H., et al. (2014). *D2.4.2 Final version of sectors roadmap*. Public deliverable of the EU-Project BIG (318062; ICT-2011.4.4).

Chapter 16
New Horizons for a Data-Driven Economy: Roadmaps and Action Plans for Technology, Businesses, Policy, and Society

Tilman Becker, Edward Curry, Anja Jentzsch, and Walter Palmetshofer

16.1 Introduction

A key objective of the BIG project was to define a big data roadmap that takes into consideration technical, business, policy, and society aspects. This chapter describes the integrated cross-sectorial roadmap and action plan.

The second objective of the BIG project was to set up an industrial-led initiative around intelligent information management and big data to contribute to EU competitiveness and position it in Horizon 2020. This objective was reached in collaboration with the NESSI European Technology Platform with the launch of the Big Data Value Association (BDVA).

Finally the implementation of the roadmaps required a mechanism to transform the roadmaps into real agendas supported by the necessary resources (economic investment of both public and private stakeholders). This was secured with the signature of the Big Data Value cPPP (BDVcPPP) between the BDVA and the European Commission. The cPPP was signed by Vice President Neelie Kroes, the then EU Commissioner for the Digital Agenda, and Jan Sundelin, the President of the Big Data Value Association (BDVA), on 13 October 2014 in Brussels. The BDV cPPP provides a framework that guarantees the industrial leadership,

T. Becker (✉)
German Research Centre for Artificial Intelligence (DFKI), Stuhlsatzenhausweg 3, 66123 Saarbrücken, Germany
e-mail: tilman.becker@dfki.de

E. Curry
Insight Centre for Data Analytics, National University of Ireland Galway, Lower Dangan, Galway, Ireland
e-mail: edward.curry@insight-centre.org

A. Jentzsch • W. Palmetshofer
Open Knowledge Foundation (OKF), Singerstr. 109, 10179 Berlin, Germany
e-mail: anja.jentzsch@okfn.org; walter.palmetshofer@okfn.org

J.M. Cavanillas et al. (eds.), *New Horizons for a Data-Driven Economy*,
DOI 10.1007/978-3-319-21569-3_16

investment, and commitment of both the private and public side to build a data-driven economy across Europe. The strategic objective of the BDVcPPP is to master the generation of value from big data and create a significant competitive advantage for European industry that will boost economic growth and jobs. The BDVA has produced a Strategic Research & Innovation Agenda (SRIA) on Big Data Value that was initially fed by the BIG technical papers and roadmaps and was extended with the inputs of a public consultation that included hundreds of additional stakeholders representing both the supply and the demand side.

This chapter describes the technology, business, policy, and society roadmaps defined by the BIG project. It then introduces the Big Data Value Association and the Big Data Value contractual Public Private Partnership and describes the role played by the BIG project in their establishment. The BDVA and the BDV cPPP will provide the necessary framework for industrial leadership, investment, and commitment of both the private and the public side to build a data-driven economy across Europe.

16.2 Enabling a Big Data Ecosystem

Big data is becoming a ubiquitous practice in both the public and private worlds. It is not a standalone solution and depends on many layers like infrastructure, Internet of Things, broadband, networks and open source, among many others. Furthermore, critical are the non-technical issues including policy, skills, regulation, and business models.

Big data has to be embedded in the European business agenda. Policymakers therefore need to act in a timely manner to promote an environment that is supportive to organizations seeking to benefit from this inevitable progression and the opportunities it presents. Failure to develop a comprehensive big data ecosystem in the next few years carries the risk of losing further competitive advantage in comparison to other global regions.

The roadmaps described in this chapter outline the most urgent and challenging issues for big data in Europe. They are based on over 2 years of research and input from a wide range of stakeholders with regard to policy, business, society, and technology. The roadmaps will foster the creation of a big data ecosystem. They will enable enterprises, business (both large and small), entrepreneurs, start-ups, and society to gain from the benefits of big data in Europe. This chapter presents a summary of the roadmaps; a full description is available in Becker et al. (2014).

16.3   Technology Roadmap for Big Data

In order to determine which technologies are needed at what point in time a systematic approach for predicting technology developments is needed. The sector-specific technology roadmaps developed establish such a framework by aligning user needs and associated requirements with technological advances and the related research questions. In contrast to a technology roadmap developed in the context of a single company, the approach taken here covers the development of a technology roadmap for the European market. As a consequence, it was not possible to come up with a precise timeline of technology milestones, as the speed of technology development and its adoption relies (a) on the degree to which the identified non-technical requirements will be addressed and (b) on the extent to which European organizations are willing to invest in and leverage big data.

Figure 16.1 depicts a consolidated technology roadmap for big data. For sector-specific technology roadmaps, refer to Part II of this book and Zillner et al. (2014). For a more detailed description of the consolidated technology roadmap, see Becker et al. (2014).

16.4   Business Roadmap for Big Data

The role of business is critical to the adoption of big data in Europe. Businesses need to understand the potential of big data technologies and have the capability to implement appropriate strategies and technologies for commercial benefit. The big data business roadmap is presented in Table 16.1.

Attitude of Change and Entrepreneurial Spirit The majority of European companies and their leaderships need to tackle the core issue of using data to drive their organization. This requires that data-driven innovation becomes a priority at the top level of the organization, not just in the IT department. An entrepreneurial spirit is needed in the leadership team to deal with fast changes and uncertainties in the big data business world. Change, even with the possible consequence of failure, should be embraced.

Business Models In the coming years, the business environment will undergo major changes due to transformation by big data. Existing business models may change and new models will emerge. Businesses are still unclear what data analyses are of relevance and value for their business, and the return on investment is often unclear. However, they recognize the need to analyse the data they amass for competitive advantage and to create new business opportunities. The adaption to these changes will be crucial to the success of many organizations.

Privacy by Design Privacy by design can gain more trust from customers and users. Europe needs to take a leading role in incorporating privacy by design with the business operations of all its sectors.

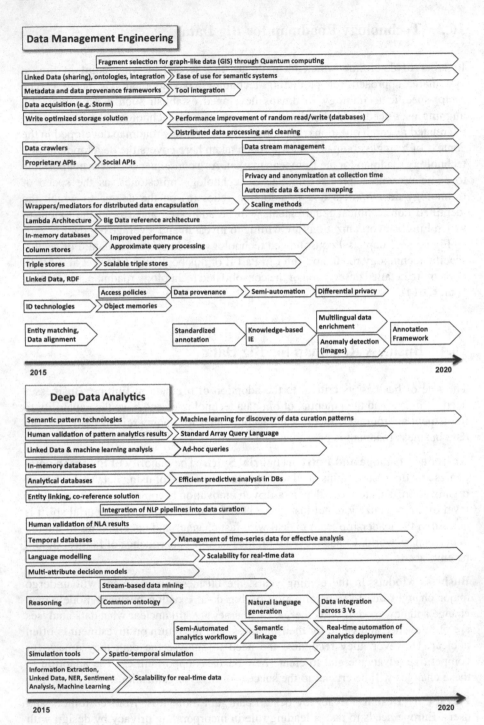

Fig. 16.1 (continued)

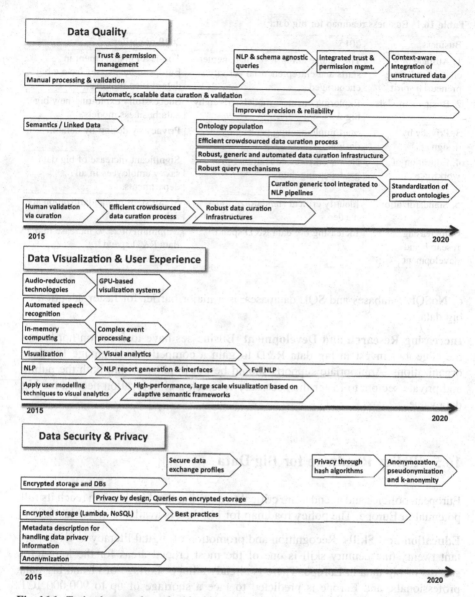

Fig. 16.1 Technology roadmap for big data

Education of Workforce There is a war for big data talent. Businesses should focus on training and educating all their staff, not just from the IT departments, with the necessary big data related skills.

Standardization Businesses need to work with other stakeholders and organizations to create the necessary technology and data standards to enable a big data ecosystem. The lack of standards, due to the non-interoperability, for example,

Table 16.1 Business roadmap for big data

Business	2015	2019 or earlier
1. Attitude of change and entre-preneurial spirit	The change at top-level management starts and entrepreneurial activity is encouraged.	Top-level management in European businesses have a big data-driven mind-set.
2. Business models	Exploring business models driven by big data.	Successfully exploiting new big data business models.
3. Privacy by design	Start implementing privacy by design.	Privacy by design by default.
4. Education of workforce	New workforce educational pro-grams on big data.	Significant increase of big data savvy employees in all departments.
5. Standardization	Identify critical standardization needed.	Major steps in standardization are achieved.
6. Increasing research and development	Increasing big data R&D spend.	Minimum of 25 % increase in big data R&D spend

of NoSQL databases and SQL databases, is a major barrier for faster adoption of big data.

Increasing Research and Development Businesses have to focus on not losing the edge and invest in big data R&D to gain a competitive advantage for their organizations. Appropriate supports should be put in place within both the public and private sectors to foster the necessary research and innovation needed for big data value.

16.5 Policy Roadmap for Big Data

European policies and agendas are critical to ensuring that big data can reach its full potential in Europe. The policy roadmap for big data is available in Table 16.2.

Education and Skills Recognition and promotion of digital literacy as an important twenty-first century skill is one of the most crucial areas for the long-term success of big data in Europe. There is already a huge shortage of IT and big data professionals, and Europe is predicted to face a shortage of up to 900,000 ICT professionals by 2020.[1] The skills shortage is risking the potential for growth and digital competitiveness. According to a number of studies, the demand for specific big data workers (e.g., data scientists, data engineers, architects, analysts) will further increase by up to 240 % in the next 5 years[2] which could result in an additional 100,000 data-related jobs by 2020. This problem affects not only the big

---

[1] http://europa.eu/rapid/press-release_IP-14-1129_en.htm

[2] http://ec.europa.eu/information_society/newsroom/cf/dae/document.cfm?doc_id=6243

Table 16.2 Policy roadmap for big data

Policies	2015	2019 or earlier
1. Education and skills	Big data education shortcomings are tackled.	Best continent for big data education.
2. Digital single market	Focus on creating a single European data market.	Single European data market for 500 million users established.
3. Funding for big data technology	Maintain current funding levels (850 Mio.).	Double the size of venture capital scene in Europe as of 2015.
4. Open data and data silos	Discussion on open government data by default.	Europe leading in open data. Minimized data silos.
5. Privacy and legal	Starting public debate, EU Data Protection signed.	Appropriate balance for people and businesses reached.
6. Foster technical infrastructure	Continue fostering the IT environment.	European infrastructure competitive with or surpasses US/Asia.

data domain, but also the whole digital landscape and has to be addressed in a general, broad, and urgent manner. Data and code-literacy should be integrated into standard curriculum from an early age. Specific big data skills like data engineering, data science, statistical techniques, and related disciplines should be taught in institutions of higher education. Easier access to work permits for non-Europeans should also be considered to help spur the European big data economy.

European Digital Single Market Despite the fact that the digital economy has existed for some time now, the EU's single market is still functioning best in more traditional areas like the trade of physical goods. It has so far failed to adapt to many of the challenges of the digital economy.

An established digital single market could lead the world in digital technology. Policymakers need to promote harmonization. This means combining 28 different regulatory systems, removing obstacles, tackling fragmentation, and improving technical standards and interoperability. Reaching this goal by 2019 is quite ambitious, but it is a necessary step towards a future European common data area.

Funding for Big Data Technology Create a friendlier start-up environment with increased access to funding. There is a lack of appropriate funding for research and innovation. Public supports and funding should increase. However, given the current budget constraints in Europe, alternative approaches also need to be considered (such as providing legal incentives for investment in big data, European Investment Bank, etc.).

Europe is also lacking an entrepreneurial atmosphere (i.e. venture capital spent per capita in comparison to USA or Israel). Fostering a better private financing environment for start-ups and SMEs is crucial.

Privacy and Legal Provide clear, understandable, reasonable rules regarding data privacy. When it comes to privacy rights and big data a double challenge is faced, lacking a European Digital Single Market, and the absence of unified user rights. This needs to be urgently addressed, since confidence and adoption of big data technology is dependent on the trust of the user. According to the latest indications EU Data Protection is expected to be signed in 2015, but a broader discussion will still be needed. Other areas that need to be considered are copyright and whether there is the right of data ownership.

No matter how quickly technology advances, it remains within the citizens' power to ensure that both innovation is encouraged and values are protected through law, policy, and the practices encouraged in the public and private sector. To that end, policymakers should set clear rules regarding data privacy so that organizations know what personal data they can store and for how long, and what data is explicitly protected by privacy regulations. Policy makers need to advance consumer and privacy laws to ensure consumers have clear, understandable, reasonable standards for how their personal information is used in the big data era.

Open Data and Data Silos Open data can create a cultural change within organizations towards data sharing and cooperation. From reducing the costs of data management to creating new business opportunities, many organizations are gaining benefits from opening up and sharing selected enterprise data. European governments need to start the discussion on *openness by default*. Harnessing data as a public resource to improve the delivery of public services. The sooner European governments open their data the higher the returns. *Big Open Data* should be the goal where possible.

Foster Technical Infrastructure Big data is not a standalone solution and depends on many layers like infrastructure, Internet of Things, broadband access for users, networks, open source, and many more. The cross-fertilization of these layers is vital to the success of big data. A technology push is needed to strengthen European technology providers to provide big data infrastructure that is competitive or leading when compared to other regions.

16.6 Society Roadmap for Big Data

In addition to the business and policy roadmaps presented, a roadmap for society in Europe has been defined. Without the support of the European citizen the up-take of big data technologies can be delayed and the opportunities available lost. A campaign to increase the awareness of the benefits of big data would be useful in order to motivate European citizens and society. This campaign could include the promotion of role models (especially females, and people with diverse backgrounds) and the positive long-term effects of the IT and innovation sectors. The society roadmap for big data is presented in Table 16.3.

Education and Skills Knowledge of mathematics and statistics, combined with coding and data skills is the basis for big data literacy. Improving big data literacy is important for the data-driven society. It is important that members of society develop fluency in understanding the ways in which data can be collected and

Table 16.3 Society roadmap for big data

Society	2015	2019 or earlier
1. Education and skills	Are you already coding?	Four times the coders and big data skilled people in Europe as in 2014.
2. Collaborative networks	Are you connected?	Leading continent with regard to a democratic big data community.
3. Open data	Are you already engaged in open data?	Europe is the leading open data society.
4. Entrepreneurship	Are you a data innovator?	Significant increase of big data entrepreneurship.
5. Civil engagement	Are you voting or staying in contact with your Member of the European Parliament (MEP)?	Europe is the most digital and political big data engaged society.
6. Privacy and trust	What's your stance on privacy? Do you trust big data?	Europe leading continent in privacy. Significant increase of trust in big data.

shared, how algorithms are employed, and for what purposes. It is important to ensure citizens of all ages have the ability and necessary tools to adequately protect themselves from data use and abuse. Initiatives such as "Code Week for Europe" are good exemplars for similar events in the big data domain.

Collaborative Networks All segments of society, from hacker spaces to start-ups, from SMEs to bigger businesses, from angle investors to politicians in Brussels, have to pull together to advance the big data agenda in Europe. Europe has the chance to become the continent to embrace big data through a bottom-up democratic process.

Open Data Open data is a good way to engage citizens and to illustrate the positive benefits of big data for organizational change, efficiency, and transparency (of course only with non-personal open government data). The goal should be big open data for Europe.

Entrepreneurship Current IT and big data developments impact the business world and society as a whole in a tremendous way. The opportunity to change things for the better for society needs to be taken. Affordable access to tools, data, technologies, and services are needed to foster an ecosystem of supports for both commercial and social entrepreneurs to exploit the potential of big data to create new products and services, establish start-ups, and drive new job creation.

Civil Engagement Every person in Europe can change the way Europe deals with the effects of big data by influencing the politics and policies in Brussels. Citizens need to understand that "Europe is you" and that their participation in the political life of the European community during this era of digital transition is needed. Civil society has to play a crucial role, which relies on every single citizen being an *engaged citizen*.

Privacy and Trust   An urgent point for the success of big data in Europe is the need for an open discussion on the pros and cons of big data and privacy to build the trust of citizens. The different points of view that exist in European member states and their citizens need to be addressed. Trust has to be established in a European digital single data market where both consumer and civil liberties are protected. Citizens have to raise their voice; otherwise their demands will not be heard in the on-going discussions on privacy.

16.7   European Big Data Roadmap

The final step was to create an integrated roadmap that takes into consideration technical, business, policy, and society aspects. The resulting European big data roadmap is a consensus reflecting roadmap with defined priorities and actions needed for big data in Europe. The roadmap (as illustrated Fig. 16.2) is the result of over 2 years of extensive analysis and engagement with stakeholders in the big data ecosystem. It is important to note that while actions are visualized sequentially, in reality many can and should be tackled at the same time in parallel, as detailed in specific roadmaps.

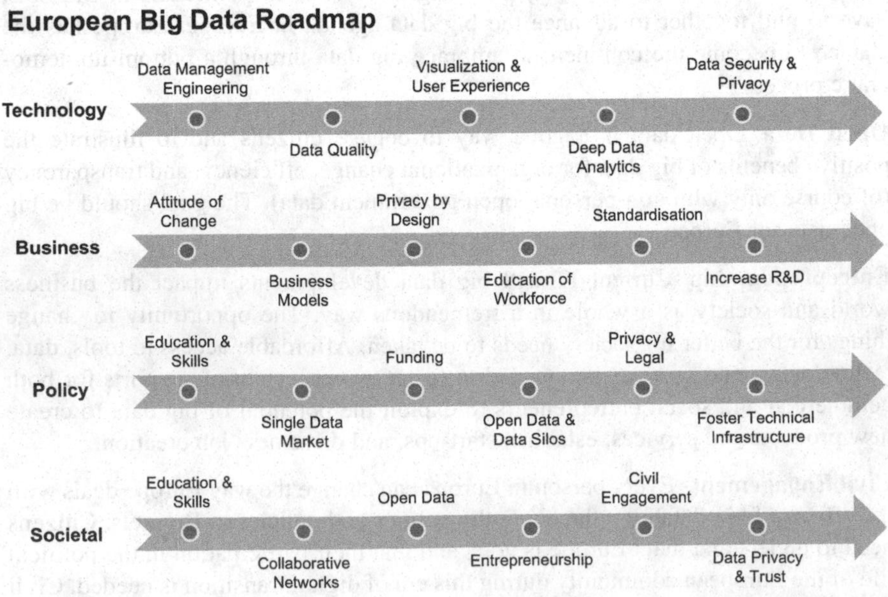

Fig. 16.2   European big data roadmap

16.8 Towards a Data-Driven Economy for Europe

In her many speeches as European Digital Commissioner, Neelie Krocs called for action from European stakeholders to mobilize across society, industry, academia, and research to enable a European big data economy. VP Kroes identified it was necessary to establish and support a framework to ensure there are enough high-skilled data workers (analysts, programmers, engineers, scientists, journalists, politicians, etc.) to be able to deliver the future technologies, products, and services needed for big data value chains and to ensure a sustainable stakeholder community in the future.

A key aim of the BIG project was to create new and enhance existing connections in the current European-wide big data ecosystem, by fostering the creation of new partnerships that cross sectors and domains. Europe needs to establish strong players in order to make the entire big data value ecosystem, and consequently Europe's economy, strong, vibrant, and valuable. BIG recognized the need to create venues that enable the interconnection and interplay of big data ideas and capabilities that would support the long-term sustainability, access, and development of a big data community platform. The linking of stakeholders would form the basis for a big data-driven ecosystem as a source for new business opportunities and innovation. The cross-fertilization of stakeholders is a key element for advancing the sustainable big data economy.

16.9 Big Data Value Association

The Big Data Public Private Forum, as it was initially called, was intended to create the path towards implementation of the roadmaps. The path required two major elements: (1) a mechanism to transform the roadmaps into real agendas supported by the necessary resources (economic investment of both public and private stakeholders) and (2) a community committed to making the investment and collaborating towards the implementation of the agendas.

The BIG consortium was convinced that achieving this outcome would require creating a broad awareness and commitment outside of the project. BIG took the necessary steps to contact major players and to liaise with the NESSI European Technology Platform to jointly work towards this endeavour. The collaboration was set up in the summer of 2013 and allowed the BIG partners to establish the necessary high-level connections at both industrial and political levels. The objective was reached in collaboration with NESSI with the launch of the Big Data Value Association (BDVA) and the Big Data Value contractual Public Private Partnership (BDV cPPP) within Horizon 2020.

The BDVA is a fully self-financed not-for-profit organization under Belgian law with 24 founding members from large and small industry and research, including many partners of the BIG project. The BDVA is an industrially led **representative**

community of stakeholders ready to commit to a big data value cPPP with a willingness to invest money and time.

The objective of the BDVA is to boost European big data value research, development, and innovation. It aims to:

- Strengthen competitiveness and ensure industrial leadership of providers and end users of big data value technology-based systems and services
- Promote the widest and most effective uptake of big data value technologies and services for professional and private use
- Establish scientific excellence as the base for the creation of value from big data

The BDVA will carry out a number of activities to achieve its objectives, these include:

- Developing strategic goals for European big data value research and innovation, and supporting their implementation
- Improving the industrial competitiveness of Europe through innovative big data value technologies, applications, services, and solutions
- Strengthening networking activities of the European big data value community
- Promoting European big data value offerings and organizations
- Reaching out to new and existing users
- Contributing to policy development, education, and the ramification of technology in ethical, legal, and societal areas

16.10   Big Data Value Public Private Partnership

The BDVA developed a **Strategic Research & Innovation Agenda (SRIA) on Big Data Value** (BDVA 2015) that was initially fed by the BIG technical papers and roadmaps and extended with the inputs of a public consultation that included hundreds of additional stakeholders representing both the supply and the demand side. The BDVA then developed a **cPPP (contractual PPP) proposal** as the formal step to set up a PPP on big data value. The cPPP proposal builds on the SRIA by adding additional content elements such as potential instruments that could be used for the implementation of the agenda.

A vital role in the European big data landscape will be fulfilled by the Big Data Value contractual Public Private Partnership (BDV cPPP). On 13 October 2014 the signature of BDV cPPP took place in Brussels, by the then European Commission Vice-President Neelie Kroes and the President of the BDVA Jan Sundelin, TIE Kinetix. The BDVA is the industry-led contractual counterpart to the European Commission for the implementation of the BDV cPPP. The main role of the BDVA will be to regularly update the Big Data Value SRIA, define and monitor the metrics of the BDV cPPP, and participate with the European Commission in the BDV cPPP partnership board.

The signature of the BDV cPPP is the first step towards building a thriving data community in the EU. The BDV cPPP is driven by the conviction that research and innovation focusing on a combination of business and usage needs is the best long-term strategy to deliver value from big data and create jobs and prosperity. The strategic objectives of the BDV cPPP as stated in the BDV SRIA (BDVA 2015) are:

- **Data:** To access, compose, and use data in a simple, clearly defined manner that allows the transformation of data into information.
- **Skills:** To contribute to the conditions for skills development in industry and academia.
- **Legal and Policy:** To contribute to policy processes for finding favourable European regulatory environments, and address the concerns of privacy and citizen inclusion.
- **Technology:** To foster European BDV technology leadership for job creation and prosperity by creating a European-wide technology and application base and building up competence. In addition, enable research and innovation, including the support of interoperability and standardization, for the future basis of BDV creation in Europe.
- **Application:** To reinforce the European industrial leadership and capability to successfully compete on a global-level in the data value solution market by advancing applications transformed into new opportunities for business.
- **Business:** To facilitate the acceleration of business ecosystems and appropriate business models with particular focus on SMEs, enforced by Europe wide benchmarking of usage, efficiency, and benefits.
- **Social:** To provide successful solutions for the major societal challenges that Europe is facing such as health, energy, transport, and the environment. And to increase awareness about BDV benefits for businesses and the public sector, while engaging citizens as prosumers to accelerate acceptance and take-up.

Given the broad range of objectives around focusing on the different aspects of big data value a comprehensive implementation strategy is needed. The BDVA SRIA (BDVA 2015) details an interdisciplinary implementation approach that integrates expertise from the different fields necessary to tackle both the strategic and specific objectives of the BDV cPPP. The strategy contains a number of different types of mechanisms, including cross-organizational and cross-sectorial environments known as i-Spaces, as illustrated in Fig. 16.3, which will allow challenges to be tackled in an interdisciplinary manner while also serving as hubs for research and innovation activities, lighthouse projects which will raise awareness of the opportunities offered by big data and the value of data-driven applications for different sectors, technical projects which will address targeted aspects of the technical priorities, and projects to foster and support efficient cooperation and coordination across all BDV cPPP activities.

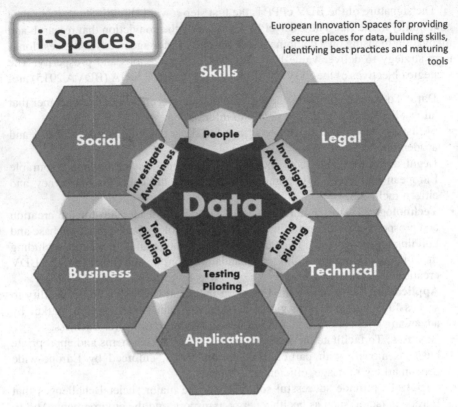

i-Spaces

European Innovation Spaces for providing secure places for data, building skills, identifying best practices and maturing tools

Skills

People

Social

Investigate Awareness

Legal

Investigate Awareness

Data

Testing Piloting

Testing Piloting

Business

Testing Piloting

Technical

Application

Fig. 16.3 Interconnected challenges of the BDV cPPP within i-Spaces [from BDVA (2015)]

16.11   Conclusions

A key objective of the BIG project was to define a European big data roadmap that takes into consideration technical, business, policy, and society aspects. This chapter details the resulting cross-sectorial roadmap and associated action plans.

The second objective of the BIG project was to set up an industrial-led initiative around intelligent information management and big data to contribute to EU competitiveness and position it in Horizon 2020. The Big Data Public Private Forum, as it was initially called, was intended to create the path towards implementation of the roadmaps. The path required two major elements: (1) a mechanism to transform the roadmaps into real agendas supported by the necessary resources (economic investment of both public and private stakeholders) and (2) a community committed to making the investment and collaborating towards the implementation of the agendas. This objective was reached in collaboration with the NESSI technology platform with the launch of the Big Data Value Association (BDVA) and the Big Data Value contractual Public Private Partnership (BDV cPPP) within

Horizon 2020. The BDVA and the BDV cPPP provide the necessary framework that guarantees the industrial leadership, investment, and commitment of both the private and the public side to build a data-driven economy across Europe. The strategic objective of the BDV cPPP is to master the generation of value from big data and create a significant competitive advantage for European industry that will boost economic growth and jobs.

References

BDVA. (2015). N. de Lama, J. Marguerite, K. D. Platte, J. Urban, S. Zillner, E. Curry (eds) European Big Data Value strategic research and innovation agenda. Big Data Value Association.

Becker, T., Jentzsch, A., Palmetshofer, W. (2014). *D2.5 Cross-sectorial roadmap consolidation*. Public deliverable of the EU-project BIG (318062; ICT-2011.4.4).

Zillner, S., Bretschneider, C., Oberkampf, H., Neurerer, S., Munné, R., Lippell, H. et al. (2014). *D2.4.2 Final version of sectors roadmap*. Public deliverable of the EU-project BIG (318062; ICT-2011.4.4).

Index

A
Abstraction, 238, 243–244
Academic impact, 78
Accuracy of analysis, 154
ACID. *See* Atomicity, consistency, isolation, and durability (ACID)
Acquisition pipeline, 220
Actionable information, 213
Adaptive data, 238
Adaptive data analysis, 159
Added value, 158
Advanced Message Queuing Protocol (AMQP), 42, 43
Advertising, 149
Algorithmic validation, 104
AllegroGraph, 124
Amazon, 126, 251
Amazon Kinesis, 207
Amazon Mechanical Turk, 95
Amazon's Simple Storage Service, 127
Amazon Virtual Private Cloud, 229
Amazon Web Services, 229
AMQP. *See* Advanced Message Queuing Protocol (AMQP)
Analysis of industrial needs in the finance and insurance sectors, 213
Analysis of industrial needs in the health sector, 180–182
Analysis of industrial needs in the media and entertainment sectors, 248
Analysis of industrial needs in the public sector, 199
Analysis transparency, 154
Analytic capabilities, 271
Analytical databases, 133, 208, 272

Analytical insights, 175
Analytical processing, 272
Analytics, 172, 174, 175, 199, 238
Analytics knowledge, 235
Annotation, 265
Annotation frameworks, 190
Anonymization, 159, 191, 220, 231, 268, 269
Anonymized data, 268
Apache Cassandra, 66
Apache Flume, 47
Apache Hadoop, 70, 74
Apache UIMA, 109
Apache ZooKeeper, 47
Apple, 251
Application, 9, 290
Approximate reasoning, 68
AstraZeneca, 102
Atomicity, consistency, isolation, and durability (ACID), 123
Attribute-based encryption, 128
Automated decision, 162
Auto-tiering, 128
Available Media and Entertainment Data Resources, 251

B
Barriers, 173
BDV cPPP. *See* Big Data Value contractual Public Private Partnership (BDV cPPP)
BDVA. *See* Big Data Value Association (BDVA)
BDVA SRIA, 291
Behavioural patterns, 236

© The Author(s) 2016
J.M. Cavanillas et al. (eds.), *New Horizons for a Data-Driven Economy*,
DOI 10.1007/978-3-319-21569-3

Printed in the United States
By Bookmasters

Printed in the United States
By Bookmasters